PENGUIN BOOKS

VICTORIA'S HEYDAY

J. B. Priestley, the son of a schoolmaster, was born in Bradford in 1894.
After leaving Belle Vue High School he spent some time as a junior
clerk in a wool office. (A lively account of his life at this period may be
found in his volume of reminiscences, *Margin Released*.) He joined the
army in 1914, and in 1919, on receiving an ex-officer's grant, went to
Trinity Hall, Cambridge. In 1922, after refusing several academic
posts, and having already published one book and contributed critical
articles and essays to various reviews, he went to London. There he
soon made a reputation as an essayist and critic. He began writing
novels, and with his third and fourth novels, *The Good Companions* and
Angel Pavement, he scored a great success and established an international reputation. This was enlarged by the plays he wrote in the
1930s and 1940s, some of these, notably *Dangerous Corner*, *Time and
the Conways* and *An Inspector Calls*, having been translated and
produced all over the world. During the Second World War he was
exceedingly popular as a broadcaster. Since the war his most important
novels have been *Bright Day*, *Festival at Farbridge*, *Lost Empires* and
The Image Men, and his more ambitious literary and social criticism
can be found in *Literature and Western Man*, *Man and Time* and
Journey Down A Rainbow, which he wrote with his wife, Jacquetta
Hawkes, a distinguished archaeologist and a well-established writer
herself. It was in this last book that Priestley coined the term 'Admass',
now in common use. The Priestleys live and work in a charming old
house in Alveston, Warwickshire.

Victoria's Heyday

J. B. Priestley

PENGUIN BOOKS

Penguin Books Ltd, Harmondsworth,
Middlesex, England
Penguin Books Australia Ltd, Ringwood,
Victoria, Australia

First published by William Heinemann 1972
Published in Penguin Books 1974

Designed and produced by
George Rainbird Ltd
Marble Arch House, 44 Edgware Road, London W2
Picture Research: Mary Anne Norbury
Design: Pauline Harrison
Copyright © J. B. Priestley, 1972

Made and printed in Great Britain by
Butler and Tanner Ltd, Frome, Somerset
Set in Monotype Plantin by
Jolly & Barber Ltd., Rugby, Warwickshire

Contents

List of Colour Plates

Acknowledgments

Acknowledgments are made to the owners and photographers of pictures and prints whose names are given on pages 287 to 292. Quotations in the text have been taken from the following copyright works, and acknowledgment is made to: Jonathan Cape Limited and Schocken Books, Inc. for the quotation from *The Pre-Raphaelite Tragedy* by William Gaunt; Constable & Company Limited for the quotation from *Journal of the Siege of Lucknow*, edited by M. Edwardes, and to that Company and McGraw Hill Company for the quotation from *Florence Nightingale* by Cecil Woodham-Smith; Hamish Hamilton Limited for a quotation from *The Stanleys of Alderley*, edited by Nancy Mitford; Sidgwick & Jackson Limited for a quotation from *A Frenchman sees the English in the 'Fifties*, adapted by V. Pirie; and George G. Harrap & Company Limited and Barnes & Noble, Inc. for the quotation from *Nineteenth-Century Gallery* by S. E. Ayling.

Preface

This volume, which examines a decade that comes nicely between the Regency of *The Prince of Pleasure* and the later years of *The Edwardians*, completes a trilogy of informal social histories. As before I have deliberately left some subjects, better seen than described, for the illustrations to do their share of the work. Where I have used quotations of any length, I have tried to indicate their source, and my thanks are due to any authors or publishers whose permission has been necessary.

For some searching of letters and memoirs, especially for the earlier years of the decade, I am grateful to Mrs Nicola Lacey for her assistance. And once again I am deeply indebted to Mary Anne Norbury (Mrs Sanders) still as before responsible for the illustrations. Finally, John Hadfield remains, even after three volumes, my favourite among publishers' editors and still a friend.

J.B.P.

Arrival

VICTORIA'S HEYDAY is no catchpenny title, even though pennies, in decimal totals, may be welcome. The 1850s, the subject of this informal social history, can justly be regarded as her heyday. No other decade of her long reign gave her so much satisfaction, so many hours of happiness. This may seem odd if we remember that these years also belonged to Lord Palmerston, the minister she thoroughly detested, and that they compelled her to face the Crimean War and the Indian Mutiny. But as soon as we glance at other decades of her reign, the sun begins to shine on these 1850s. The 1840s brought her a happy marriage – she married her cousin, Prince Albert of Saxe-Coburg, in 1840 – but it also brought famine in Ireland, distress in Britain, political and social upheavals at home and abroad, and, what was most important to her, a reluctance (notable in the lower sections of the press and the higher ranks of society) to admire her adored Albert and to applaud her beautiful marriage. It was only towards the end of the 1840s that things in general began to improve, and then of course she soon entered the 1850s, a far better time. It was a time too when she could enjoy her house in the Isle of Wight, Osborne, and, what was even more delightful, her remote and romantic estate, Balmoral, in the Highlands of Scotland. Buckingham Palace had been completed to give her an imposing London residence, but she used it rarely. Albert disliked living in London and so she began to dislike it too. Windsor Castle, Osborne, Balmoral, offered them peace and quiet and were better for the children, now arriving steadily.

It was as if unconsciously she was preparing herself for the tragedy of December 1861, when Albert died, plunging her into one of the longest and severest widowhoods in royal history. In blackest weeds, she then moved between Windsor, Osborne, Balmoral, firmly doing her sovereign duty, because that was what Albert would have wished. But she was invisible to most of her subjects, as remote from them as some ancient Chinese Emperor. There was grumbling; there was criticism, in and out of the press; there was talk, even among prominent public men, of abolishing the monarchy in favour of a republic. However, the ten years between the Jubilee of 1887 and the Diamond Jubilee restored her popularity. There was the little old woman, grimly indomitable, among all that imperial pomp, and even the few remaining republicans had to give her a cheer. No doubt she enjoyed herself as the matriarchal

One of the popular exhibits at the Great Exhibition in 1851 was this inlaid walnut chair with a porcelain plaque of Queen Victoria inset in the back.

Victoria's Heyday

(top left) Balmoral Castle, designed by William Smith in 1853

(below left) Osborne House

head of a horde of royal figures, all of them, including an Emperor of Germany and a Prince of Wales, terrified of her. But what did all this amount to when she remembered herself as she was forty years before, still a young wife and mother with the incomparable Albert by her side? Any possible answer takes us back at once to the 1850s, where we can point to what was probably the happiest day of her whole long life – the first of May, 1851, when she opened the Great Exhibition in Hyde Park – really her Albert's exhibition, for it was largely his creation. To this of course I must return in the next chapter but one. Here I am justifying the chosen title – *Victoria's Heyday*.

That capable and scholarly historian, G. M. Young, who devoted most of his attention and energy to this whole epoch, called these particular years 'The Victorian Noon-Time'. Indeed, he declared that if he had to choose a time and place in which to enjoy another life it would be the England of the 1850s. Under the pressure of various prejudices – radical and ethical, social and aesthetic – some of us (I, for one, certainly) would not be able to share his enthusiasm. To which he could have retorted that in the 1850s we would have been at liberty to express those prejudices, as in fact so many good people did. But this, as I hope to show, would be a dangerous over-simplification. However, he has a strong case so long as we accept his own position and point of view. This might be described as the *comfortable* position and point of view, the outlook of the Fellow of All Souls, Oxford tutor, senior civil servant, the historian who knew he could retire to a clean warm study and always find excellent meals waiting for him in the dining-room. Within these narrow but very pleasant limits, safe from the intrusion of discontented persons or the demands that come from imagination, an historian could put up a strong case for these 1850s. We must do justice to it.

This England – and England is our subject, not the United Kingdom – was rich, powerful, and comparatively tranquil. Though it had a smaller population – under twenty-one million for the whole of Great Britain – than the United States, France, the German states, and even Italy, its industrial production and its foreign trade were unrivalled. It could still claim to be the workshop of the world. Its army might be small and shockingly organized (as the Crimean War was to prove), but its navy could not be challenged. It was free at last from that danger of revolution which had loomed from 1815 to 1848. It could regard with amused complacency the various upheavals on the Continent. If frequent pregnancies and lyings-in were ignored, it could be said that Queen Victoria sat firmly on her throne. Thanks to Sir Robert Peel, its cities were policed, the hateful Corn Laws had been repealed, and Free Trade was bringing cheap food into the country. Through the efforts of evangelical Tories like Lord Shaftesbury, Oastler and Sadler – and perhaps because the radical protesters in the Midlands and the North were no longer seen as so many Jacobins – the very worst crimes of industrialism no longer went unchecked. Coal and Cotton did not have to compel young children to work until they dropped from exhaustion. A 10-hour day was long enough for women and children, and then, because in many industries the men could not go on without the women and children, most of them had a 10-hour day too. Defying the whole spirit of *laissez-faire*, the government sent out factory inspectors. And in 1848 there was even a Public Health Act, a very tentative and feeble affair, especially in view of the fact that there was more and more overcrowding in London and the provincial industrial towns, all riddled with consumption and menaced by cholera.

None of this, largely brought about because Tory landowners were suspicious of wealthy Whig manufacturers, was adequate, of course, but it was *something*. A new humanitarianism was on the move, even if only slowly. There were blankets and soup in the country for 'the good poor', who unfortunately were always outnumbered by the bad poor. There were plans for missions and 'ragged schools' in the dark and fetid slums. Many of the harsher realities of the 1830s and '40s were either banished or softened in the 1850s. So Macaulay, cosy among his books in the Albany, leaving work on his *History*, as popular as any novel, to dine out among rational and highly civilized company, felt that Progress could be left to look after itself. His vast memory told him how much filth and brutality had been left behind. If he lived so much in the past, it was because the present time need no longer worry him. Thanks to the Glorious Revolution of 1688, the later Industrial Revolution, the passing of the great Reform Bill of 1832, and English inventiveness, industry, political sense, keeping the country quiet at last and giving it over 5,000 miles of railways *and* the electric telegraph, all was well and would automatically proceed to get better and better. The many thousands who eagerly bought and read his *History* clearly agreed with him. They floated with him along the shining mainstream. A dyspeptic peasant-prophet like Carlyle, an aesthetic crank like Ruskin, a sensational novelist like Dickens, together with some sour and envious radicals and assorted religious maniacs, might disagree with him, might pretend to see rapids and whirlpools further along that clear, straight mainstream, but they could be ignored. They did not represent, as he and his friends did, serious public opinion. This might occasionally be rather smug, a trifle too complacent at times – but look at what had been done, what was now being done, what could be so widely enjoyed at last!

Thomas Babington Macaulay

The term 'compromise' is an early arrival in any study of Victorian England. In any account of the 1850s, the 'Noon-Time', it must be admitted at once. The central dominating society of these years represents a series of compromises. There were of course many protests against this society, but during this decade no really important changes were made: these came later. It was as if people who at one time would never have shared the same roof now settled down fairly comfortably in one hotel. The principle of 'Live and let live' was at work, even if only within certain well-defined limits. So, for example, evangelical thought and practice still existed, but for the most part it had lost its earlier narrowness and fanaticism. It encouraged a decent piety and, failing that, at least an obvious respectability. The upper class and the middle class (especially if it had money) came closer together. They were no longer glaring and bristling like so many cats and dogs. The Reform Bill, dating back to 1832, leaving five men out of six without a vote because they were not £10 householders, was already out of date, but there would not be another Reform Bill, enlarging the franchise, until 1867. The new oligarchy the old Bill had helped to create had settled down and felt quite comfortable. The English system, which avoided revolution or indeed any startling radical changes by opening the Establishment to any new powerful class, appeared to be working well.

In politics and actual government, as distinct from the general tone and style of society, the upper class in the 1850s was still surprisingly dominant. The foreground in the Westminster scene was filled with lords. Room had to be made for a few commoners, notably Disraeli and Gladstone (both well into their forties) who became Chancellors of the

(right) Lord John Russell

(far right) William Ewart Gladstone

Exchequer, but it was the lords who took over most of the chief ministries, no matter how often new cabinets were formed. Most of these men, like Lord Palmerston and Lord John Russell, sat in the House of Commons. But it would be many years before a popular wit like W. S. Gilbert could raise a laugh by saying that the House of Lords did. nothing in particular and did it very well. In the 1850s the House of Lords did a great deal, though not always very well. Quite apart from accepting or rejecting bills already passed by the Commons, this 'other House' still had a considerable influence on the actual composition of the Commons. The old 'rotten boroughs' had been abolished, but in the county elections a local peer, a great landowner who was important both in his economic patronage and his social pull, might easily decide what safe man should represent the constituency. Many men who resented his patronage and pull might not have had any votes, or, if they had, would find it hard to influence other voters. These might know only too well how their bread could be buttered or might act, after listening to their wives, out of downright snobbery. For one result of the upper class and the more affluent middle class coming together, no longer glaring at one another across a barrier, was the rapid spread of social snobbery. After all, Thackeray's *Book of Snobs* was written only a few years away from 1850.

After Peel's death in 1850 the political scene, as we shall see, was dominated by that other great favourite of the people, Lord Palmerston, a dashing and masterful character who could turn foreign affairs into a firework display. But he was born in 1784, had been a minister in quite a different England, and was not, strictly speaking, a man of this age at all. (In one respect, however, he was ahead of it because he knew how to cultivate and make use of public opinion.) Take away Palmerston and his reckless moves and his fireworks and the whole political scene of the 1850s seems curiously dull, monotonous, almost empty. Disraeli

Victoria's Heyday

and Gladstone were already there, in and out of office, but they were not party leaders yet, to add glamour to the Conservatives, fire to the Liberals. Incidentally, it is typical of this odd interim period that there were Whigs remaining Whigs while other members turned up as Liberals, there were progressive Tories known as Peelites, and Conservatives trying to conserve what Peel had already taken away from them. This House of Commons often seems to be filled with shifting factions rather than large strongly-opposed parties. Forming a new government and making a fresh list of cabinet ministers – and this happened very often – began to look like playing an immensely elaborated game of noughts-and-crosses. Step back only a little from this scene, from the letters to and from Queen Victoria, the memoranda that Prince Albert toiled over, all the hasty messages and private little meetings – and you are reminded at once of the wonderful burlesque of it in Chapter XII of *Bleak House*, with Lords Boodle and Coodle, the Duke of Foodle, and all the other indispensable 'Oodles, and then the Right Honourable William Buffy, with Cuffy, Duffy, Guffy, and all the rest.

The paragraph that follows this burlesque is perceptive and worth quoting:

> . . . . It is perfectly clear to the brilliant and distinguished circle, all round, that nobody is in question but Boodle and his retinue, and Buffy and *his* retinue. These are the great actors for whom the stage is reserved. A People there are, no doubt – a certain large number of supernumeraries, who are to be occasionally addressed, and relied upon for shouts and choruses, as on the theatrical stage; but Boodle and Buffy, their followers and families, their heirs, executors, administrators, and assigns, are the born first-actors, managers, and leaders, and no others can appear upon the scene for ever and ever.

Lord Aberdeen

Dickens's radical sarcasm offers a clue to what was wrong with the politics of the 1850s. Prime Ministers like Lord John Russell and Lord Aberdeen were intelligent and honourable men. All the successive governments worked hard at governing: one of them, in 1858, abolished the East India Company and brought its vast territories under the Crown. Parliament could be sensitive to public opinion: it compelled Lord Aberdeen to resign, bringing down his government, because it carried a motion for a critical enquiry into the conduct of the Crimean War. Moreover, Prime Ministers and their Home Secretaries were no longer the instruments of very severe repression, as they had been in Lord Liverpool's time, thirty years before. But even so, the Westminster scene of these 1850s appears dull, narrow, almost futile, a perfect target for Dickens's mockery and irony. This is because its leading politicians were not doing the work they should have been doing. They were not moving forward but marking time. They were trying to ignore that vast crowd of 'supernumeraries', the People.

The Field Lane Refuge, a poor-house in London

The wages, hours and conditions of work, the food and shelter of the common people may have been better than they had been, but that does not mean they were now satisfactory. Some statistics tell their own tale: in 1850 the people born in Britain but now living in the United States numbered 1,364,986 whereas by 1860 the figure had risen to 2,224,743. In the later 1850s it was estimated that about 48,000 mixed British and Irish emigrated every year to Australia and New Zealand, most of them going to the goldfields of New South Wales. There were lands of opportunity awaiting all these people, but even so, emigrating at this time could be a very rough and risky enterprise and there must have been some pressure on a man, especially one with a wife and family, for him to undertake it. Long hours of work could not be the explanation; he might have to work just as long and even harder at the other end. Nor could he have been thinking about food, because the introduction of free trade had cheapened it and enormously increased its variety. (For example, a report in 1854 tells us that 'upwards of 60,000,000 oranges are imported for the use of London alone, accompanied by not less than 15,000,000 lemons'.) The enormous quantity of meat consumed by the upper and middle classes, astonishing all foreign visitors, was not at the disposal of most working men and their families, but they were not without their modest share of the cheaper cuts, were no longer living on bread and potatoes. So what drove so many people away? Higher wages? Possibly, though the cost of living would be higher too. Opportunity, a chance to better themselves, a feeling they would no longer be class-ridden? This would certainly apply to the more enterprising and independent-minded of these emigrants, looking forward to a society far more democratic, not controlled by an oligarchy. But to this must be added something else – a chance at last of sun and air, well away from overcrowded and disease-ridden hovels.

In these respects the 1850s could show no improvement. The housing situation was no better, perhaps even worse, than it had been. There was a constant drift into London and the industrial cities and towns. The slums multiplied like the families who had to live in them. These could be found even in what could be called, by a writer in 1854, an 'outwardly respectable neighbourhood' of central London where there existed –

> . . . a collection of houses . . . chiefly let in single rooms. The houses are mostly dilapidated, and dirty in the extreme . . . . At the back of most of them, after passing through a long passage, are small, badly paved courts . . . . The water stands here and there in deep puddles. In the courts we saw were conveniences, a dust-heap . . . and a water tank. These are all shared amongst the lodgers in the cellars, say eight persons. If only five persons occupy each of the eight rooms in front, and six the two rooms in the back court, this is all the accommodation of water, etc. provided for 54 persons. . . .

We seem to be groping our way through certain dark chapters in *Bleak House*, deep in the realm of King Cholera and Queen Tuberculosis. And we are not even in the East End, a wilderness of such slums, but only a short walk from Mayfair, from Macaulay's chambers in the Albany – and only another ten minutes from Westminster, where Parliament was so busy with its own affairs. Moreover, in many provincial towns conditions on the lowest level, in tramps' lodging houses and the like, were even worse. In filthy small rooms, with excrement everywhere, adults and children were packed to suffocation, lying on rags and shavings. It is a mystery how so many survived at all, or why, having so little to lose, they did not rise in fury and desperation and set fire to these towns. Victorian Noon-Time indeed!

Such dismal regions saw nothing of the 442,000 men and 1,000 women employed in the building industry, according to the census of 1851. Out of a total population, for Britain, of just under 21 million, the two largest groups of wage earners, each of them numbering over $1\frac{1}{2}$ million, belonged to the land and to the textile trades. The land was not doing badly. A French observer said in 1855: 'English agriculture, taken as a whole, is at this day the first in the world: and it is in the way of realizing further progress.' He noted with approval its quite elaborate though standard routine of crops, from the two roots, potato and turnip, to the two spring cereals, barley and oats, on to the winter one, wheat. But he

'The Last of England', by Ford Madox Brown, was painted between 1852 and 1855 to symbolize the great emigration movement that reached its peak in 1855. Brown wrote later: 'I have, in order to present the parting scene in its fullest tragic development, singled out a couple from the middle classes, high enough through education and refinement to appreciate all that they are now giving up . . . The husband broods bitterly over blighted hopes and severance from all that he has been striving for'. The models were the artist and his wife. Brown had bidden goodbye at Gravesend in 1852 to his sculptor friend Woolner, who was going to seek his fortune in the Australian goldfields, and for a time Brown himself thought of emigrating.

added that the English were not great growers nor 'great consumers of fruit and vegetables, and they are right; for both the one and the other with them are very tasteless.' It is true that Mrs Beeton's *Household Management*, 1859–60, gave little space to fresh fruit, salads, or any wide range of cooked vegetables. Wages were lower on the land than they were for anything except casual labour in the towns, but then wages were less important. The men were often given one or two meals a day and allowances of beer, skim milk, firewood. Then they earned harvest money and their women went gleaning. They may not have all looked as healthy, as plump and rosy, as the pair in Holman Hunt's 'The Hireling Shepherd', painted in 1852; but probably only the skilled men in industry were better off in essentials. But if we include variety of work, sunlight and fresh air, and a glimpse of a garden, among essentials, as indeed we ought to do, then the steadily-employed countryman still wins. However, there was little extra money for gowns, bonnets, shawls, so the girls trooped off in their thousands to try domestic service.

Though working hours and general living conditions were far worse than they were in the years just before the First World War – a time I well remember – wages for skilled men often seem surprisingly high in the 1850s, not very much lower than those of sixty years later. Here are three budgets collected in 1855, and a fair sample:

LONDON. A working cutler living in Whitefriars Street: the house, which has one room to each floor, is less insanitary than most, but damp and sunless. Water is laid on in the cellar and 'latrines'. Four children play in street or Temple Gardens. Grandmother helps in house and wife carries husband's work to and from the master's shop in Oxford Street. Spend £1.16.9 a week (rent 7s. 9d., food £1, coal and light 2s. 10d., cleaning 1s., school 10d., clothes 3s. 2d., sundries 1s. 2d.).

Notice the *school* item: no free education yet. And if a doctor were needed, he would have to be paid out of those *sundries*.

SHEFFIELD. A working cutler, five children, one of whom supports self as dressmaker. For 3s. 4d. has small house with parlour, kitchen, two bedrooms, garden where keeps fowls, pigs, pigeons and canaries. Wife sells ginger pop. . . . Spend £1. 2s. 2d. a week – bought food 11s. 4d., coal and candles 1s. 5d., cleaning 6d., school 5d., clothes 3s. 7d., sundries 1s. 7d.

DERBYSHIRE. Foundryman, 4 children, has 27s. 8d. a week and garden. Meals: Breakfast at 7, parents have tea or coffee with milk and sugar, bread and butter and cold meat, children bread and milk. Dinner at 12, meat, bread, potatoes, vegetables, fruit or cheese. Tea at 4, tea, sugar, bread, butter. Supper at 8, remains of dinner. He works 12 hours a day for 355 days a year at 4s. a day for good employer who supports the sick club and the school.

But all the above were skilled, steady family men. If we go well below their level, taking a dip into Henry Mayhew's London of 1851 and

Trysts and lovers' meetings by moonlight were favourite themes for mid-Victorian painters and poets, perhaps as a release from the rigid conventions of polite society. 'The Tryst', painted *c.* 1852 by Frank Stone, father of Marcus Stone, the Dickens illustrator, is more realistic than most of its kind since there is a hint that the intentions of the gentleman in the straw hat are not strictly honourable, and the object of his interest appears to be the housemaid from next door.

'Answering the Emigrant's Letter', 1850, by James Collinson

finding there an unskilled rough labourer, in this instance 'a scavenger and nightman', the picture is much darker. This man had earned 15s. the previous week, but 1s. of this had gone to pay off an advance of 5s. made to him by the keeper of a beershop. He paid 1s. 9d. as weekly rent for an unfurnished room, which probably remained more or less unfurnished. Shaving, twice a week, cost him 1d. His weekly food bill worked out at 3s. 6d. for bread, 2s. 4d. for boiled salt beef, 1¾d. for pickles or onions, 1d. for butter, and cocoa (a pint a day at a coffee shop) 10½d. Then there was 7d. for tobacco, 2s. 4d. for beer, 1s. 2d. for gin, though he seems to have been given some extra beer and gin for his nightwork. Those who feel that this fellow was too fond of beer and gin should imagine themselves, in the London of 1851, spending night after night among garbage, latrines and sewers. There must have been an immense amount of this semi-casual rough labour, based on such meagre budgets, in all the urban areas.

Very different indeed were the clerks, of whom there were about 50,000 throughout the country. They had to be neat, clean, very respectable, and if they were completely reliable and had been with the firm for many years, then they might count on a steady 30s. a week.

What was expected of them may be discovered in a document, dated 1852, and rather grimly entitled *Office Staff Practices*:

1. Godliness, cleanliness and punctuality are the necessities of a good business.
2. This firm has reduced the hours of work, and the clerical staff will now only have to be present between the hours of 7 a.m. and 6 p.m.
3. Daily prayers will be held each morning in the main office. The clerical staff will be present.
4. Clothing must be of a sober nature. The clerical staff will not disport themselves in raiment of bright colour.
5. Overshoes and top coats may not be worn in the office but neck scarves and headwear may be worn in inclement weather.
6. A stove is provided for the benefit of the clerical staff. Coal and wood must be kept in the locker. It is recommended that each member of the clerical staff bring 4 lb. of coal each day during cold weather.
7. No member of the clerical staff may leave the room without permission from Mr Rogers. The calls of nature are permitted and clerical staff may use the garden beyond the second gate. This area must be kept in good order.
8. No talking is allowed during business hours.
9. The craving for tobacco, wines, or spirits is a human weakness and as such is forbidden to all members of the clerical staff.
10. Now that the hours of business have been drastically reduced the partaking of food is allowed between 11.30 a.m. and noon, but work will not on any account cease.
11. Members of the clerical staff will provide their own pens.

There is a final note saying that 'the owners will expect a great rise in the output of work to compensate for these near Utopian conditions.'

(above) The title-page of Part 1 of Mrs Isabella Beeton's *Book of Household Management*, first published in parts 1859–60

(below) Detail of 'The Harvest Cradle', 1859, by John Linnell

(opposite above) 'South-east view of Sheffield', 1854, by William Ibbitt

(opposite below) 'The Forge', 1849–59, by James Sharples after an oil painting by the same

Why are we still being told that Dickens exaggerated and caricatured people? How can anybody exaggerate and caricature these 'owners', who from some lofty height kindly permit 'the calls of Nature', forbid any 'human weakness', and congratulate themselves on the 'near Utopian conditions' they have created? They are like Squeers smacking his lips over the milk he has watered and crying 'Here's richness!'

The chief occupation of growing girls and young women was domestic service. In 1851 there were in Britain over eight million females of ten years of age and upwards – about half a million more than males – and nearly a million of them were domestic servants of one kind and another. Wages were low, ranging from about £6 a year for a new girl to £18 or so for an experienced cook; living conditions were often poor; and the work long and hard. (For example, half a dozen members of a family might want daily baths in houses without bathrooms, so that hot water had to be carried up morning or evening or both, together with scuttles of coal all over the house; and coal fires everywhere would demand a great deal of cleaning.) There were over a hundred thousand 'domestics' in London alone. On the other hand, conditions in alternative employment might be even worse. Thus, work for a manufacturing milliner might entail (and I quote a report) 'unreasonably long hours in rooms that are artificially heated by steam to a very high temperature, independent of a very large number of gas-lights, thus raising the temperature to almost a suffocating point . . . so that most of the young creatures complain almost continually of sore throats, loathing of the stomach, dizziness or vertigo, and headaches etc. . . .' A domestic servant might do better than this, but even so, a great deal was expected of her.

The evidence may be found in *The Servant's Behaviour Book*, belonging to this decade. I will quote only some of the main headings, between which there is a lot of detailed advice that must be omitted:

> Never let your voice be heard by the ladies and gentlemen of the house except when necessary, and then as little as possible . . . .

> Never begin to talk to your mistress, unless it be to deliver a message, or ask a necessary question . . . .

> Never talk to another servant, or person of your own rank, or to a child, in the presence of your mistress, unless from necessity; and then do it as shortly as possible, and in a low voice . . . .

> Never call out from one room to another . . . .

> Always answer when you receive an order or reproof . . . .

> Never speak to a lady or gentleman without saying 'Sir', 'Ma'am', or 'Miss', as the case may be . . . .

> Always stand still and keep your hands before you, or at your sides, when you are speaking or being spoken to . . . .

> Nursemaids are often encouraged to sing in the nursery; but they should leave off immediately on the entrance of a lady or gentleman . . . .

Never take a small thing into the room in your hand . . . any small thing should be handed on a little tray, silver or not, kept for the purpose . . . .

I have seen servants make the mistake of going to walk or sit in the garden, as if it were a part of the house belonging to them, as the kitchen and servants' bedrooms . . . .

Do not ever choose gay patterns or colours. Not only are such dresses unfit for morning work, after they are a little worn, but they can never look becoming for servants. . . .

Clearly the object here was to widen the gulf between employers and their domestic staffs, between 'ladies' and 'gentlemen' and their 'maid-servants'. A deep class difference is being deliberately created. Because girls came from poor families, they had to enter domestic service, and as soon as they had done that, they were cheated out of their warm natural humanity and almost turned into robots. (This tradition lingered on into our own time, and it partly explains why domestic service became so unpopular among English girls.) When it was not necessary to create and then emphasize a class difference, when a social hierarchy was generally accepted, servants in fact lived in a much freer atmosphere. We can appreciate this at once if we remember the servants in the old plays – the pert maids, the opinionated valets, the grumbling old butlers, housekeepers, coachmen, never afraid of raising their voices and speaking their minds. Aristocrats, or at least established landowners, with an accepted social status, the masters and mistresses of these servants had not to worry about keeping them in their place, about low voices, hands at the sides, calling from room to room or singing. Silent and almost impersonal domestic service was not demanded then (so that more than one Regency madcap, like Lady Caroline Lamb, was bluntly told by an old servant she was making a fool of herself). It came, this new style of service, with the Victorian social compromise and the rise of its middle class. Strictly speaking, its roots were economic and had little to do with birth and breeding or the existence of a traditional social hierarchy. A mid-Victorian young couple might 'marry comfortably on £500 a year and expectations . . . anything from £500 to £1,500 is considered a possible, sufficient or comfortable income' (from a letter written in 1850). Then they would be the 'ladies' and 'gentlemen' of *The Servant's Behaviour Book*, keeping maids who must never take a small thing into a room in their hands, only on a little tray, preferably silver. As soon as that young couple had reached, let us say, £1,000 a year, they were members in good standing of the mid-Victorian ruling class.

This was of course the more prosperous middle class. There might be plenty of social snobbery; the aristocracy and the landed gentry might be admired and sometimes imitated; but the prevailing tone and temper of the age came from this solid class in the middle, which controlled most money, had most votes and most influence. Even the

(opposite) Domestic images of the middle class: six photographic portraits by Camille de Silvy

Monarchy cannot be set against it. By 1850 the style of Victoria and Albert, actually more German than English, had much in common with that of the middle class. Their Court was severely respectable. (They had many reasons for disliking Lord Palmerston, as we shall see, but surely one of them must have been that he was a raffish Regency figure and anything but respectable?) The upper class might still provide most of the Queen's ministers, but a great deal of power now belonged to this middle class. And so did economic power. Here in this class were the manufacturers and the merchants, the hard-headed men in the Midlands and the North. If England was the workshop of the world, they ran the workshop. They enforced their own strict rules of conduct. Their prejudices and tastes governed all but the most rebellious artists, writers, publishers, editors, designers, shopkeepers. We cannot understand these 1850s unless we take a close look at the society this triumphant middle class had created. It sits solidly in the centre, dispensing or withholding its patronage, its praise and blame, a strongly conformist society, apparently complacent and sure of itself. The mid-Victorian novelists have described it for us, but they have not told us everything we need to know. Indeed, they have not told us everything *they* knew, if only because at times and in certain respects they were not its interpreters but were among its prisoners.

'Finish of a race at Hoylake', 1851, by John Dalby. Horse-racing remained a recreation of the landed gentry, viewed with mistrust by the rising middle class.

This powerful middle class, dominating the 1850s, was unlike any society that had existed before. Elements coming to it from the past were not entirely ignored and forgotten but were radically modified. It was not Puritanism all over again. It was not a continuation and spreading of the earlier and very narrow Evangelical way of life. So for example it did not regard all enjoyment or any attention to pleasure as a sin, for which an appalling price would be paid in the next world. But it was sharply divided about religion. In one large section of it religion declined into a decent piety, in which not too fervent daily prayers could be heard both at home or, as we have seen, in the office. (At home the servants

28

would benefit, in the office 'the clerical staff'.) Yet in another large section, as much masculine as feminine, a perfervid Christian faith, now being challenged by intellectuals, was being clutched at and then held in a bigoted and highly emotional fashion. Among all these people, whatever their age, there was endless talk about religion, perhaps more than there has ever been before or since the 1850s. (I discuss this in the chapter on 1853.) All this cannot be shrugged away as mere mid-Victorian hypocrisy, even if the social responsibilities we associate with a true Christianity were too often disregarded. Suffering was inevitable, they felt, in this sad bad world, but true belief in Christian redemption, together with heartfelt devotion and constant prayer, could save every soul. Everlasting treasure in Heaven was being accumulated: it was like lending money with a guaranteed interest of at least 10,000%. Now that we believe that all this was humbug, that the world is not a vale of tears but a provider of happiness, to be grabbed before we are extinguished, we may be more enlightened, but it would be hard to prove we are less discontented than those mid-Victorians.

Again, this middle class as a whole did not refuse to recognize the country's aristocratic tradition. No doubt some of its members were aggressively self-made, like Dickens's Mr Bounderby. Others, notably the Quakers and the stubborn dissenters, ignored the social importance of the upper class. But in general this society moved closer to its social superiors. To prove it was climbing, it looked down from a great height on the class – or classes – below it, as we saw after quoting from *The*

'Nameless and Friendless', 1857, by Emily Mary Osborn. Note the stove-pipe hats on the left

Victoria's Heyday

Servant's Behaviour Book. Probably the terms 'gentleman' and 'gentle-manly' were never more freely used than by this middle class. (It is only fair to add that in Dinah Mulock's *John Halifax, Gentleman*, one of the most popular novels of the later 1850s, the hero is first seen as a poor, hard-working orphan.) And all these 'gentlemen' were the husbands and fathers of 'ladies'. It was not the hard-riding tough aristocracy but this middle class that produced so many vaguely invalidish 'ladies' lying half the day on sofas. With them went those other favourite terms – 'delicate' and 'delicacy'. Many a middle-class 'lady' and the women who waited on her seemed hardly to belong to the same species. The mistress of the house might seem almost too delicate for this world. The women who kept that house clean and warm or worked sixty hours a week in the husband's factory were assumed to be as strong as horses. This mid-Victorian middle class raised itself as high as possible above the common people, by one sex being determinedly 'gentlemanly' and the other sex being so refined and 'delicate'.

At one end then we have this deliberately heightened social status, and at the other end the traces that remained of Puritanism and the Evangelical style of life. Between them was the solid core of com-mercialism, the triumphant trading of mid-Victorian England that earned the money. After all, these were the world's workshop men, who in the 1850s, with their narrow dark clothes and black elongated 'stove-pipe' hats, dressed almost to look like steam engines. No matter what fancywork their wives and daughters might be engaged in, these men could not help being deeply influenced by their engineering, their manufacturing, their careful profit-and-loss accounts. Not for them the careless extravagance of the aristocratic types. They had a strongly conscious dislike and fear, almost amounting to horror, of whatever seemed to them ruinously wasteful, distracting businesslike attention, recklessly consuming energy. It was this, rather than the old puritanical hatred of pleasure, that made them so prudish, so suspicious of sex, so determined that this notorious spendthrift of energy should be kept within narrow bounds. (It is significant that all contemporary warnings, applied to everything from voluptuous heterosexual activities to onanism, emphasize the wasteful effects, the appalling debility following indulgence.) Because the all-important money came not from land but from commerce, from manufacturing, from factories roaring with great steam engines, from a mysterious realm governed by the male, this was a society dominated by the masculine principle, entirely patriarchal. Most women are fairly clear-sighted and realistic and tend to deceive themselves only about some close relationship in which they have heavily invested their emotions – 'I know my son loves me and depends upon me.' On the other hand, most men insist upon deceiving themselves, refusing to be clear-sighted and realistic. They are all the more at the mercy of irrational unconscious drives just because they are so proud of their conscious rationality. We cannot be surprised, therefore, if this

'Angels in the House'

(above) Detail of 'Only a Lock of Hair', 1859, by Sir John Everett Millais

(right) Detail of 'Mary Ann, wife of Leonard Collman', c. 1854, by Alfred Stevens

mid-Victorian middle-class society, dominated as it was by the masculine principle, with Papa so great a figure of authority and wisdom, should remain a monument of self-deception.

It was this society – certainly neither the upper class nor the common people – that put the Angel in the House. (For a superbly well-documented, if rather too Freudian, study of this whole trend, see Gordon Rattray Taylor's *The Angel-Makers*.) Now while most women could enjoy a few angelic endearments, their experience did not encourage them to believe they were sexless beings, especially at a time when pregnancies were all too frequent. But this was also the time when they were economically dependent on the dominant male, so many of them accepted the angel-role, delicate, tender, comforting and sexually undemanding, that he offered them. The accepted authority on sex in mid-Victorian England was Dr William Acton, whose study of *The Functions and Disorders of the Re-productive Organs* was published in 1857. He was chiefly concerned with male sexuality, which from boyhood onwards, he believed, was a menace to health and sanity unless severely checked. Marriage offered the safest refuge. He wrote:

> The best mothers, wives, and managers of households, know little or nothing of sexual indulgences. Love of home, children, and domestic duties, are the only passions they feel.
>
> As a general rule, a modest woman seldom desires any sexual gratification for herself. She submits to her husband, but only to please him; and, but for the desire of maternity, would far rather be relieved from his attentions. No nervous or feeble young man need, therefore, be deterred from marriage by any exaggerated notion of the duties required from him. The married woman has no wish to be treated on the footing of a mistress. . . .

But here, we feel, Dr Acton wrote one sentence too many – the last. In this he gives the game away. Woman herself has now been divided into two. There are modest women, the wives of middle-class citizens in good standing, who submit to their husbands while still thinking about those domestic duties: all the household angels. There are also those sexual demons, the mistresses, delighted to waste a man's money, time and energy. So clearly – and here he was right, as we shall see – a man might have two very different relationships with the fair sex, one delicate and the other wildly indelicate. Indeed, though he does not mention this horror, there might be a woman so lost to decency she could play both roles, submitting in her own house and enjoying herself under another roof. But it is a safe guess that if Dr Acton had contemplated such a creature he would have seen her as a maenad from the raffish upper class or one of the common people caring nothing for middle-class virtue, refinement, delicacy.

No doubt the 'ladies' in this society were ready to be severe with their erring sisters. Even so, I think the harsh demands for absolute 'purity' came from the men. Though they always announced that they were

Household gods

(opposite) A lacquered bedstead, *c.* 1850

(top) A sideboard of 1857, designed and executed by G. Robinson

(above) Stove with painted earthenware Minton panels, designed and modelled by Alfred Stevens, shown at the Great Exhibition

protecting their wives and daughters from shock or pollution, I also think the rigid taboo of sex came from them. It was Papa himself, not the family, who prohibited in popular fiction any account of specifically sexual feelings, motives, activities. It was he who wanted the wretched seduced girl, no longer 'pure', to be buried in shame, a stranger now to decent society. (Though even Dr Acton made the startling disclosure that downright prostitutes often made good marriages instead of sinking into the gutter.) It was Papa and not Mama and the girls who compelled men of genius like Dickens and Thackeray to ignore so much, to write too often with one eye closed. Had the feminine principle been in the ascendant (leading eventually to a 'permissive society') the mid-Victorian novel might have been very different. But the masculine principle was firmly in control of this middle class.

However, what is severely repressed by the conscious mind may return in greater force from the unconscious. So determinedly rational and hard-headed men can be overcome by feeling that is almost hysterical. Employers in this commercial society had to be hard, working as they did within an economic theory that was like a steel mantrap. But either they were frequently overcome by repressed emotion or they deliberately wanted to show how much they could feel. For while their women and girls, as the representatives of sensibility, delicacy and responsive feelings, easily gave way to tears, so too, when the occasion arose, did their masterful men. Expansive pathos, now so distasteful to us, unmanned them at once. Hanging judges would sob over the deaths of Little Nell and Paul Dombey. Dickens in his public readings would have whole audiences in tears, just as when he read aloud his Christmas stories he would be surrounded by weeping friends. A male mid-Victorian quarrel might be ended at the club, not only with a hearty handshake but also with some quick shedding of tears. Macaulay, a Whig stalwart and no softy in public life, could not revive any happy memory without his eyes filling. Reading biographies and memoirs of this age, we begin to feel that all those side-whiskers and beards must have been damp with tears.

It cannot be said that this middle-class society had inherited that curious strain of melancholy, with all its churchyard brooding, which was characteristic of the eighteenth century. It still lost too many of its young children, but its death rate was better, not worse. Yet mid-Victorian fiction is filled with wasting diseases, slow-motion dying, funerals and cemeteries. (Even school stories, like Farrar's, could not do without them.) Where we have sex at every turn, they had death. Where we linger with lovers, after watching them strip, they lingered round the deathbed, aware of each ebbing pulse. We would find this – if any young novelist or playwright risked it – as shaming and shocking as they would have found the removal of a petticoat, a glimpse of a girl's thigh. They were afraid of sex: we are afraid of death. It seems there must be *something* that frightens us. No society can be on easy terms with every-

(opposite above) Detail of 'Ophelia', 1851–52, by Sir John Everett Millais. The model for this painting was Elizabeth Siddal.

(opposite below) Detail of 'Chatterton', 1856, by Henry Wallis

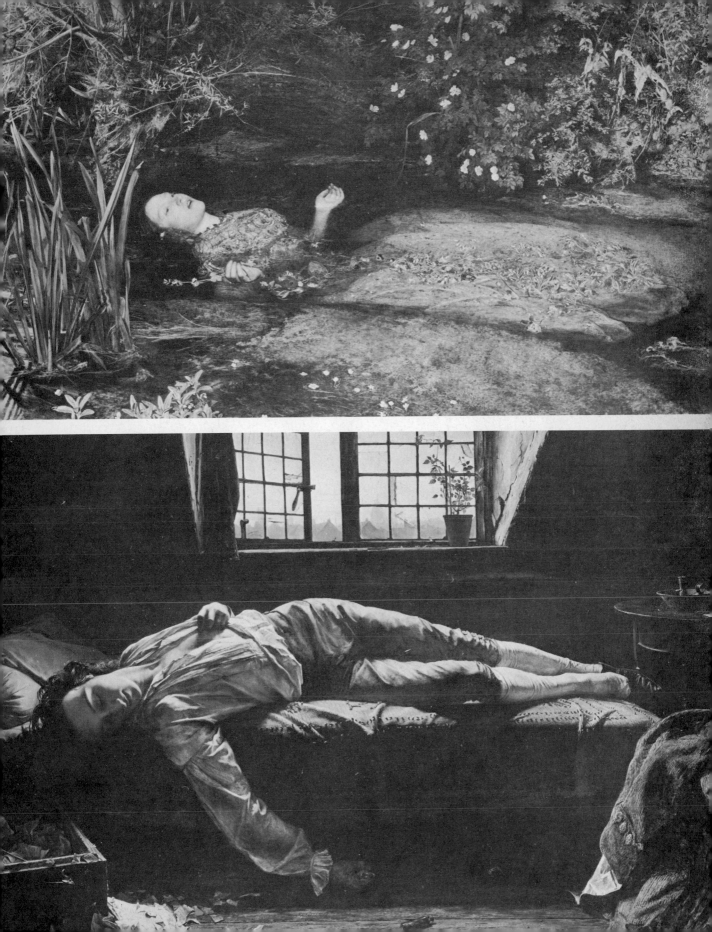

Victoria's Heyday

thing. It is possible – and it has been generally supposed – that the sexual taboo was imposed because popular mid-Victorian fiction was intended for family reading. Dickens, for one, certainly assumed this. We all have a picture of this family, with the older children listening to Papa or Mama reading aloud one of the safer novels, or Macaulay's *History*, or a popular account of astronomy or geology. We feel that this middle-class society was above all *domestic*. The family and the hearth were at its centre. This was probably true of those members of it who lived in the country or one of the new semi-rural suburbs. But it cannot have been altogether true of the middle-class men who lived in London or in one of the growing provincial cities. To begin with, there were more and more clubs, entirely male creations, and there is plenty of evidence that the more prosperous mid-Victorian husband and father was very much a clubman. He cannot have been reading aloud at home or playing Halma or Happy Families if he was also dining and wining his cronies. There was something else that cannot be ignored, something representing the reverse of that shining medal of purity, delicacy, sexual innocence – all that notorious mid-Victorian night life.

'Kit's Writing Lesson' (detail), 1852, by Robert Braithwaite Martineau

The workshop of the world gave way every night in central London to the whoreshop of the world. An hour spent in or around the Haymarket after midnight would have left any member of our own 'permissive society' speechless from shock. Foreign visitors were staggered by it. Once respectability was left behind, they were in a Venusberg. Even Dostoyevsky, no wandering innocent, cried in astonishment at the prostitutes gathering in their thousands. (This was only 1862.) There were mothers, as well as bawds, offering young children. The streets round the Haymarket were crowded with brothels and 'accommodation houses'. Notorious *madames* held nightly festival, to the accompaniment of popping champagne corks, in their own large drawing-rooms of harlotry. The famous courtesans drove down from their villas in St John's Wood for caviare and oysters and more champagne with the nobility and gentry. The taverns and supper rooms might be wide open until 3 or 4 in the morning. Various notorious night haunts mixed chops and baked potatoes with entertainment, often very obscene. In the humbler streets and alleys to the north and east half-naked whores displayed themselves at their windows or even came running out to catch a customer. Not only were hundreds and hundreds of prostitutes and men meeting in the parks every night, there were women waiting to be picked up as far out as the building sites in the new London suburbs, around recently-built suburban railway stations, indeed almost anywhere if there was sufficient light for a pick-up and darkness nearby for some hasty copulation. So long as a man could pay for it, there was no perversion, no sado-masochistic experiment, no degradation of sexuality, that would be denied him. It was as if Aphrodite herself was taking a savage revenge for all that talk of purity, that insistence upon female delicacy, that taboo of sex. Where the modest and merely submissive wives left off, brazen and rapacious whores took over. Eros, as the symbol of natural loving sexuality, was defeated both day and night.

It would be absurd to suggest that most men belonging to this solid middle class spent late nights in or around the Haymarket looking for bawds who would provide them with girls in their 'teens. But, to my mind, it would be equally absurd to believe that this extravagant night life could be maintained without any contribution from the middle class. We read a lot about 'wild young noblemen', on the one hand, and, on the other, about the drunken workmen, sailors and soldiers, ready to spend a shilling or two on a whore. But after all there were not so many young noblemen, and the flash supper rooms, brothels and 'accommodation houses' were well outside the shilling range. This night life must have largely depended upon the patronage of the middle class, which was sufficiently numerous and had the money. However, a fairly large number of its men must have been too timid, perhaps physically too fastidious, probably going in fear of gonorrhea and syphilis (a great scourge during most of the nineteenth century, when so many notable

Evans's Song and Supper Room
(detail), 1859

men were among its victims), to risk adventures with loose women. The result of this was an enormous increase in the publication of pornography, that vast – and very tedious – dreamland of the huge unwearied phallus and its endless procession of delighted sexual objects. There is a useful note on this by Gordon Rattray Taylor:

> By making normal sexual activity more difficult, they increased the amount of auto-erotic, perverted and fantasied sexual behaviour; but since these kinds of behaviour are obsessive in character, individuals who exhibit them have recourse to it more frequently than normal individuals have recourse to normal sexual behaviour.

It cannot be denied that it was this middle class, sitting solidly in the centre and controlling most of the money and the votes, that was responsible for this appalling division in sexual behaviour, as bad for women as it was for men. It was these men, so complacently sure they were right, who created the legend of social hypocrisy so notoriously attached to mid-Victorian England, making other peoples distrust all its opinions and activities.

In the main the upper class – as represented, for example, by Lord Palmerston and his circle – did not share this middle-class view of sex. Nor did most of the lower orders, the working class, the common people, though there were among them some groups that were puritanical or strongly evangelical. By and large mid-Victorian working people still took sex naturally. Their girls were modest until aroused by the appeal of a personal relationship. Some country girls were of course seduced by promise of marriage, and then, after bearing an illegitimate child or having an abortion, fled from their homes and made for London or the nearest city to become prostitutes. But this situation, so familiar in fiction, was not at all the commonest. What drove most girls and women into prostitution or semi-prostitution was poverty, the hard conditions of female labour, and starvation wages. Two points are worth making here. The first is, most of the very people who denounced prostitution and tried to 'rescue fallen women' made no attempt to end poverty, hard conditions, very low wages. The second point is that it was not until much later, in our own time, that the more comfortable members of the working class began to acquire the excessive prudishness of the old Victorian middle class.

The pornography of the mid-Victorian period tells us little or nothing because it is so much fantasy. The best evidence we have so far comes from an extraordinary saga of sexuality, undoubtedly quite genuine, called *My Secret Life*. At this time of writing the full text is not generally available, but longish typical extracts, about as much as most of us want, can be found in 'Walter', *My Secret Life*, recently edited by Drs Eberhard and Phyllis Kronhausen, and *The Other Victorians* by Professor Steven Marcus. Though it is completely frank in its account of a wide range of sexuality, *My Secret Life* is not pornography, no long

'The Outcast', 1851, by Richard Redgrave

(opposite) 'Adopting a Child', 1857, by F. B. Barwell

trip through a priapic dream world, but a completely realistic description of all his sexual adventures by a man unusually obsessed by eroticism. He did not seek out prostitutes, as many men have done, because he hated women and wanted to degrade them. A sexual athlete, he loved having them, all kinds and at all times, and about 1,200 altogether, he calculated. He has left us a loving epic of the English vulva, and no man, English or alien, can ever have doted on it more. With middle age and satiety creeping in, he tries perverse or silly antics, even disgusting himself at times, but throughout most of his chronicle he is genuinely interested in and concerned about his very wide range of sexual partners, and his complete frankness and his attention to details make him a very good witness indeed. Revealing his own Secret Life, he takes the lid off a great many other people's secret lives, male and female, and gives us not merely a transformation scene but a whole hidden panorama of Victorian England with its clothes off. He made use of his money but he was not wholly dependent upon prostitution. His relations with women were far from being completely commercial – more often than not, they enjoyed him because it was so obvious he enjoyed them – and both his sexual and his social evidence are very valuable.

When we leave sex we can find in the letters, memoirs, novels of these 1850s many accounts, hardly enticing, of this dominant middle class amusing itself. Here a notable part is played by its solemn and pretentious dinner parties, with the tables weighed down by massive silver plate and overloaded with food and often graced, snobbery being so rampant, by some titled guest of honour. Ultra-respectability, complacency, stiffness and stuffiness do not help to create a lively or

'Waiting for the Verdict' (detail),
c. 1857, by Abraham Solomon

even easy social life. But one section of this society had broken away almost completely from its general style, manners, prejudices. It was 'Bohemian' (their term, not mine) and largely made up of authors (Dickens prominent among them), journalists, painters, actors, and versatile odd fellows like Albert Smith, the provider of one-man entertainments. Most of them worked hard and were far from being seedy spongers, but when work was done they liked parties, late suppers, planning amateur theatricals, games and singing, and jaunts out of town on Sundays. In the chapter on his early married life, during the 1850s, Edmund Yates in his *Recollections* describes the more respectable Bohemians enjoying themselves:

> As may be readily imagined, I had not very much leisure in the midst of all this employment, but such as I had was always pleasantly passed. Sundays with us were always 'Sundays out' – at Skindles, at that time a delightfully quiet place, with no lawn, no river-rooms, no neighbouring

Guards' Club; at Thames Ditton; at Richmond; at the Swan at Staines; at Laker's Hotel at Redhill – sometimes my wife and I alone, oftener with the Keeleys and Albert [Smith] and a party. On Friday nights, there was always a gathering in Gower Street, at the house of Abraham Solomon, who had just made a hit with his picture 'Waiting for the Verdict', where would be Millais with his 'Huguenot' success upon him, young and handsome, as in the medallion which Alexander Munro had just completed of him; and Frith, putting the finishing touches to his 'Derby Day'. Frank Stone, Augustus Egg, and Sant; Dutton Cook, undecided whether to take to pen or pencil as his means of living; Ernest Hart, whose sister Solomon afterwards married, and William Fenn. A quietly Bohemian evening: a little dancing, a few games of 'tonneau', a capital supper with a speciality of cold fish, then cigars, and singing by Frank Topham or Desanges, and imitations by Dillon Croker, 'and so home'.

(below left) A parian-ware statue of Queen Victoria, c. 1850

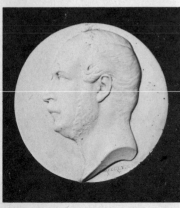

(bottom) A medallion of Prince Albert modelled by Louis Megret and executed in Paris by J. Gille in biscuit porcelain for sale at the Great Exhibition of 1851

(below right) 'Paolo and Francesca', 1852, by Alexander Munro

Victoria's Heyday

But it is time I brought this Introduction to an end. We have to discover what this decade offers us, year by year. Some illustration of its strength and weakness can be found in the quotation from Edmund Yates. It is clear that the 1850s were not all gloomy respectability alternating with a fetid night life, were not all wretched poverty existing below a worship of wealth and rank. A young journalist like Yates, already married and not earning very much, could enjoy himself if he had plenty of friends, could probably enjoy himself rather more than a young journalist would do today. (Those Sunday trips out of town would now be a little hell of noise, heated engines and carbon monoxide.) But while there was a fair amount of modest talent in his circle, it is noticeable that anything like genius was absent from it. However, there were better painters not far away, including the members of the Pre-Raphaelite Brotherhood, which flourished in this decade. English music of any quality did not flourish. Where these years were strongest, a richly rewarding time, was in the very thing not mentioned by Yates, and that of course was literature, whether regarded as entertainment, verbal felicity, confession, social criticism, impassioned protest, or what you will. I have already suggested that the 1850s marked time in their domestic politics. Again, when compared with the 1840s and the 1860s, they lacked those original political ideas that change the world, though just before they ended they gave us Darwin's *Origin of Species* and Mill's *On Liberty*. But they were rich indeed in historical incidents, the clash of personalities, in all the farce, high comedy, tragedy, for which the whole country, not the Theatre, supplied the stage. I cannot help feeling too that of all the Victorian decades this is the *most Victorian*. I cannot prove it: I can only set the years rolling.

This detail from the first of Augustus Egg's sequence of three studies of a faithless wife, entitled 'Past and Present, No. 1', 1858, represents a whole school of story-telling painters who shocked but enthralled members of an un-permissive society highly sensitive to sexual frailty, domestic shame and 'fates worse than death'. The second and third of the series of three paintings are reproduced on page 246.

1850

QUEEN VICTORIA, who had a sharp temper, was now very angry indeed with her Foreign Minister, Lord Palmerston. With Lord John Russell as Prime Minister, Palmerston had been having a high old time at the Foreign Office since 1846. (He had been Foreign Minister before, from 1830 to 1841.) Victoria had lost all patience with him and his high-handed methods, and as good as told him so:

> The Queen sent the day before yesterday the proposed draft to Mr Wyse back to Lord Palmerston enclosing a Memorandum from Lord John Russell, and telling Lord Palmerston 'that she entirely concurred with Lord John, and wished the draft to be altered accordingly'. She has not yet received an answer from Lord Palmerston, but just hears from Lord John, in answer to her enquiry about it, that Lord Palmerston has sent the draft off *unaltered*. The Queen must remark upon this sort of proceeding, of which this is not the first instance, and plainly tell Lord Palmerston this must not happen again. Lord Palmerston has a perfect right to state to the Queen his reasons for disagreeing with her views, and will always have found her ready to listen to his reasons; but she cannot allow a servant of the Crown and her Minister to act contrary to her orders, and this without her knowledge. . . .

Here is merely some of the lava from the volcano boiling below. There were many good reasons why she should have disliked Palmerston so much. It was not only that he acted independently and apparently with great rashness. During the upheavals of 1848 he had thrown the whole weight of England behind the revolutionary or liberal movements, challenging the various reactionary régimes. But the despots he detested were mostly related in one way or another to Victoria and Albert. Her own Foreign Minister was gleefully hurling thunderbolts at uncles and aunts and cousins.

Again – and this was more important – though outwardly polite, decently respectful, Palmerston was contemptuously rejecting the advice and guidance of her beloved Albert and his wise old mentor Baron Stockmar. There was Albert, ready to sit up half the night writing deeply considered memoranda on the state of Europe, and there was Palmerston, ignoring them, taking action, sending a challenge to one capital, an ultimatum to another, before Albert had finished writing the requisite memorandum. She guessed that behind his show

The ideal of the young Victorian woman – beautiful but demure, domestic in her interests but romantic in her environment – is stylishly represented in this portrait of Mary Isabella Grant, *c.* 1850, painted shortly before her death by her father, Sir Francis Grant, President of the Royal Academy.

of respect he regarded Albert and the good Stockmar as a pair of solemn busy-body Germans who would waste his time. Apart from his reckless behaviour at the Foreign Office, she saw him as the leading representative of the more elderly aristocracy who refused to take Albert seriously. And, as she was so ecstatically in love with her husband, all this was infuriating.

Moreover, Palmerston's whole style and private life had a strong Regency flavour. Hers was a respectable Court, and it was common knowledge that Lord Palmerston was not respectable and never had been. Certainly he had married Lady Cowper after her husband's death, but she had been his mistress for years and several of her children were his. And while contriving to be happy with her, both as lover and husband he was so amorous, in that wicked old Regency style, that he had often chased other women. There was one adventure she could neither forgive nor forget, as Greville records in his Diary:

> . . . . And besides this the recollection of his conduct before her [Victoria's] marriage, when in her own palace he made an attempt on the person of one of her ladies, which she very justly resented as an outrage to herself. Palmerston, always enterprising and audacious with women, took a fancy to Mrs Brand (now Lady Dacre) and at Windsor Castle where she was in waiting, and he was a guest, he marched into her room one night. His tender temerity met with an invincible resistance. The lady did not conceal her attempt, and it came to the Queen's ears. Her indignation was somehow pacified by Melbourne, then all-powerful, and who on every account would have abhorred an *esclandre* in which his colleague and brother-in-law would have so discreditably figured. Palmerston got out of the scrape with his usual luck, but the Queen has never forgotten and will never forgive it.

But then Charles Greville had always disliked Palmerston. He was a civil servant (Clerk to the Privy Council), and very few civil servants ever liked Palmerston, who was very much the kind of man to leave any senior civil servant divided between exasperation and terror.

As he was the dominating political figure of the 1850s, we ought to take a closer look at Henry Temple, Viscount Palmerston. He was born and educated in England but was an Irish peer, which meant he could sit in the House of Commons. Well-to-do, handsome as a young man, a charmer who was also ambitious, he became Secretary of War in his middle twenties, remaining in office, a Tory then, from 1809 to 1828. Following Canning, whom he greatly admired, he joined the Whig Ministry in 1830 and, as we have seen, was Foreign Secretary for the next eleven years. When he returned to the Foreign Office in 1846, his experience and prestige were immense, and he had a formidable world reputation. In diplomatic circles he was *ce terrible Palmerston*, apparently ready at any moment, if his warnings should be ignored, to send his dreaded battleships anywhere and everywhere. He had behind him a Britain that was enormously rich and had the most powerful fleet in the world. But at the same time Palmerston was not as recklessly aggressive as he seemed to be. He was an instinctive and intuitive type who knew when a bluff might be called. He was never, strictly speaking, a statesman. He had little more political philosophy than the average man in the street. He toiled for the welfare of Britain abroad and for any Liberal movements that challenged despotic and reactionary governments, while still remaining at home the Tory he had been much earlier, indifferent to reform and largely hostile to any radical appeals. Except on very rare occasions, he was no orator, and was notorious in the House for his undignified, free-and-easy style of speech. Though far from being haughty – or stiffly withdrawn, as Peel was – and almost always approachable and affable, he was not much liked by his fellow members, who tended to mistrust and resent him. But unlike most of them, or most men anywhere, he was not afraid of responsibility but welcomed it up to the highest degree, enjoying as he did superb self-confidence. After all, by 1850 his ministerial experience went back to a time before many of his fellow members had even been born. Moreover, there was something else, even more important. Especially after Peel's death, which belongs to this year, 1850, Palmerston – 'Old Pam' as he was called – was the most popular politician in the country. He was master and had been for years of a tremendous weight and thrust of public opinion.

There were many reasons for this. Palmerston may not have been a great statesman but he was certainly a great 'character', which is what the English relish and admire. Somehow, while being a prodigiously hard-working Foreign Minister, he also contrived to be a sporting country gentleman, hunting and shooting and the rest, as well as being a rather raffish man-about-town, enjoying parties, theatres, and various gallantries. Now reaching his middle sixties and having to dye his whiskers, he was still indefatigable, genial and roguish, still something of the Regency 'buck' he had been in his youth, and not at all a solemn discreet Victorian; and his tall, bulky figure and rather sardonic grin, his offering of two fingers for a hand-shake, were known everywhere. Yet being a born politician he also kept pace with his times. This was the era of John Bull, who would stand no nonsense from anybody, and though nobody looked more unlike John Bull than Palmerston, he was strongly associated in the public mind with triumphant John Bullishness. This is one reason why he was so popular. The other is that he cultivated public opinion by making the fullest possible use of the press. (This is well brought out in Kingsley Martin's *Triumph of Lord Palmerston*, which is a study of English public opinion in the earlier 1850s.) Delane, the famous editor of *The Times*, might disagree with him in print but remained a personal friend. As for the *Morning Post*, Palmerston had it in his pocket, often contributing anonymous articles. He was a favourite with almost all reporters because he would change the times of meetings to suit them or tell them in private what he was about to say. He was the first leading politician continually to appeal beyond his

Henry John Temple, Viscount Palmerston

party to the general public, which was easy for him to do because he was so well reported. By 1850, though nominally a Whig under Lord John Russell, he was in effect a one-man party, able to rely on the support of public opinion. Over and above his political dexterity, this made him very formidable indeed.

That 'usual luck' which Greville referred to was running for Palmerston again, this summer. The only other man of equal stature in the public view now vanished from the scene. On 28 June 1850 the House of Commons heard the voice of Sir Robert Peel, still urging moderation and a peaceful policy, for the last time. The next day, riding a restive horse up Constitution Hill, Peel took a bad fall, and three days later he died, still only in his early sixties. The loss of this great Minister and statesman – for Peel *was* a statesman and not just another politician – was felt throughout Europe. Queen Victoria wrote to her Uncle Leopold, King of Belgium and one of her favourite correspondents: 'Poor dear Peel is to be buried today. The sorrow and grief at his death are most touching, and the country mourns over him as over a father. Every one seems to have lost a personal friend.' This was no exaggeration. The English people had long regarded him as their friend. Through him the monstrous penal laws had been reformed, a police force had been created, the Corn Laws had been repealed, and cheap food had come into the country because he had decided for Free Trade. For the first and last time in our history, the death of a great political figure brought the poor of London weeping into their streets. Years later, another Prime Minister, Lord Rosebery, could write of him:

> Aloof from his party he certainly was. In the Tom, Dick, and Harry business, as it may be called, he was certainly deficient: it is the charge brought against all great ministers. But he had one crowning merit which finds its place in any view of him as a parliamentary leader. He had disciples: he made men: he formed a school. Of no other minister since Pitt can this be said, and even of Pitt only in a lesser degree. What men he shaped! What a creed of honest work he left with them! What a tradition of public duty!

On any Radical view of the politics of the 1850s, this is over-enthusiastic, but it is a fact that the Peelites, as they were called, remained long after their famous leader had vanished. Finally, we ought to remember that Peel was also a collector of pictures and master drawings, and that many of these may be found in the National Gallery.

Peel's death left Palmerston, in terms of public opinion, the only giant the House of Commons could show. This was not the view of the House itself. Tories like the waspish Disraeli were already saying that Old Pam was now too old and ought in decency to retire. (In fact the astonishing man carried on for another fifteen years and was Prime Minister in 1855-8 and 1859–65.) But during this summer there seemed to be a fine chance, even welcomed by some of his colleagues, of bringing him down and finding another and less aggressive Foreign Minister. Palmerston had gone too far, entangling himself and the British Government in a nonsense.

Don Pacifico was a Portuguese Jew who had been born in Gibraltar and was therefore a British subject. A rather shady character, he had brought a claim against the Greek Government because his valuable furniture and other precious possessions, probably imaginary, had been destroyed in a Greek riot. Palmerston, who disliked the Greek Government, had supported this claim, had already sent in his gunboats, and might soon drive Britain into a war with France. Here was the chance to get rid of Palmerston. The Lords passed a vote of censure on the Government's foreign policy. Then the Commons mustered for the final attack, with members of all parties dismissing the Don Pacifico affair as a nonsense, and the Opposition fiercely concentrating on Palmerston and his rash policies. The jaunty and impudent old man appeared to be doomed. But on the second day of the debate, Palmerston rose to defend himself and decided for once to be an orator. He spoke for over four hours, making effective use of every possible device of Parliamentary speech, ridding himself of Don Pacifico but defending the principle that Britain should take care of British subjects, concluding in his peroration:

> As the Roman, in the days of old, held himself free from indignity when he could say *Civis Romanus sum*, so also a British subject, in whatever land he may be, shall feel confident that the watchful eye and strong arm of England will protect him against injustice and wrong.

This one masterly speech destroyed his enemies in the House, rang through the land, and left him more popular and powerful than ever.

Palmerston genuinely disliked being at odds with Victoria and Albert, but somehow it was always happening. So, for example, there was the visit to London this year of Haynau, the Austrian general with the enormous moustache who had ruthlessly stamped out rebellion in Hungary and Italy, where he had achieved notoriety as a great flogger of women. When he went to inspect Barclay and Perkins's brewery, General Haynau and his moustache were recognized at once. The brewery draymen came roaring up, knocked him about a bit, and chased him until he was rescued by the police. The Austrian Government was furious and so were Victoria and Albert. Palmerston was compelled to withdraw his original – and probably rather casual – note of apology to the Austrian Ambassador and put something more fitting in its place. But he wrote to the Queen:

General Julius Jakob Haynau

> The state of public feeling in this country about General Haynau and his proceedings in Italy and Hungary was perfectly well known; and his coming here so soon after those events, without necessity or obligation to do so, was liable to be looked upon as a bravado, and as a challenge to an expression of public opinion.

Baron Koller indeed told Viscount Palmerston that Prince Metternich and Baron Nieumann had at Brussels strongly dissuaded General Haynau from coming on to England; and that he (Baron Koller) had after his arrival earnestly entreated him to cut off those long moustachios which rendered him so liable to be identified. . . .

But Viscount Palmerston can assure your Majesty that those feelings of just and honourable indignation have not been confined to England, for he had good reason to know that General Haynau's ferocious and unmanly treatment of the unfortunate inhabitants of Brescia and of other towns in Italy, his savage proclamations to the people of Pesth, and his barbarous acts in Hungary excited almost as much disgust in Austria as in England, and that the nickname of 'General Hyaena' was given to him at Vienna long before it was applied to him in London. . . .

The tone, as usual, was deeply respectful, but Palmerston, who must have given three cheers in private for the brewery draymen, insisted upon making his points. Victoria and Albert were more anxious than ever to be rid of this Foreign Minister, no matter how popular he was in the country. But they would have to wait until the end of 1851.

Riots at Bankside during General Haynau's visit to London

The year 1850 brought the Victorian Age its poet, Alfred Tennyson. It changed the whole course of his life and work. Until then he had been admired by most of his more important fellow writers, the circle of his old Cambridge friends, and the few readers who cared deeply about poetry, but his work had never reached a wide public. Moreover, the *Quarterly Review* kind of criticism had never stopped sneering and carping, and Tennyson remained neurotically sensitive to such hostility. His life had been a melancholy tale of misfortune. His engagement to Emily Sellwood had been broken off by her family. He had lost his money through speculation, and was so poor that after refusing it

several times he reluctantly accepted, in 1845, a civil list pension of £200 a year, for which he had to suffer further attacks. Trapped in a vicious circle of neurotic depression and bad health, he endured twice the drastic hydropathic treatment accepted then as the best possible cure for mental disorders. He would suddenly appear, a great shaggy figure of despondency and absent-mindedness, among his friends in London, and then would unexpectedly vanish, nobody knowing where he went, until perhaps he reappeared a hundred and fifty miles away. One woman he had known wrote:

> He looked very much like the old man of the sea, as if seaweed might cling to him, unkempt and unbrushed and altogether forlorn as to the outer man. When told he had seen me before he looked hard at me and said 'Now who are you and what are you? Where do you come from?' to which my reply was 'Catherine Anny Franklin, Spinster, Nottingham.' The curtness of the answer appeared to amuse him. . . .

In his most ambitious poem of these years, *The Princess*, there is a curious passage describing an inherited malady of the hero-prince that might have been prompted by his own neurotic experiences:

> Myself too had weird seizures, Heaven knows what:
> On a sudden in the midst of men and day,
> And while I walk'd and talk'd as heretofore,
> I seem'd to move among a world of ghosts,
> And feel myself the shadow of a dream.

(above) Emily Sellwood, Lady Tennyson

(opposite) Alfred, Lord Tennyson

Then 1850 brought a shining transformation scene. In June, at long last, he married Emily Sellwood. They had as yet no home of their own and were compelled to move around, but they were gloriously happy. Emily at that time was far from being the self-effacing invalidish figure that later she often appeared to be. Tennyson's literary friends, not the most lenient judges of womanhood, were delighted with her. And even in his and their looming shadows, she could assert herself. For example, we are told that at the end of one of Carlyle's huge jeremiads, she said firmly, 'That is not sane, Mr Carlyle.' Moreover, it was Emily who suggested the title *In Memoriam*. Ever since the autumn of 1833, when the news came that his close Cambridge friend, Arthur Hallam, was dead, Tennyson had been writing what he called his 'elegies', year by year, in one large ledger. If Hallam had died at the end of a grave illness, the shock would not have been so great. But the news arrived like an appalling thunderbolt out of an unclouded sky. Touring with his father, Arthur Hallam had written Tennyson a lively letter about Vienna, where they were staying. This was on 6 September. Nine days later, Hallam was discovered by his father, who had been out for the afternoon, dead in an armchair in their hotel. It was this cruel stroke of fate, so entirely unexpected, that not only sharpened Tennyson's grief but also compelled him to ask himself what power governed a universe in which such things could happen. So, year after year, in melodious verse after verse, he expressed his sorrow and bewilderment and asked his questions.

In this same fortunate marriage-month, June 1850, Tennyson's publisher, Moxon, brought out *In Memoriam* in a first edition of 5,000 copies. But the circumstances were unusual. The book was anonymous and Tennyson himself had paid the costs of production. (It is doubtful if the anonymity meant very much. Not only Moxon but most of Tennyson's friends knew who had written the poem.) The reviews were favourable, some of them enthusiastic, but it was generally agreed that *In Memoriam* would not reach a wide public. In fact, before the end of the year 60,000 copies had been sold, and very soon *In Memoriam* was considered the finest long poem of the age, even if some religious leaders doubted the soundness of the poet's Christian faith. Its elegiac title heightened its appeal to a society which, as we have already discovered, was haunted and fascinated by the idea of death. It might be meandering and monotonous but it did question the nature of the universe, did suggest the struggle between some belief in science and a simple religious faith, did aim at some metaphysical solution. But what immensely enlarged Tennyson's reputation at this time only left it more vulnerable in a later age. Because he could be disregarded as a great philosophical poet, later critics, forgetting that our literature does not produce great philosophical poets, began to undervalue his poetry itself, denying what their own eyes and ears ought to have told them. Taken simply as a poem, *In Memoriam* is weakest when it is indulging in vague metaphysical speculations – and here we can quote another great Victorian, Disraeli, and say, 'His nonsense suited their nonsense' – and strongest where the superb poet in Tennyson expresses his feelings. If, instead of adding verse after verse, year after year, Tennyson had composed a poem at once out of the dark of his grief, the fury of his resentment, the result would have been a far greater poem than *In Memoriam* was. As it is, this is a work in which what we might call its by-products are more valuable than its totality. But how magnificent these passages are, how sorry we would be to lose them!

There is no room here for ample quotation but a few scattered passages ought to prove my point:

> The seasons bring the flower again,
>   And bring the firstling to the flock;
>   And in the dusk of thee, the clock
> Beats out the little lives of men.

Or the section beginning:

> Dark house, by which once more I stand
>   Here in the long unlovely street,
>   Doors, where my heart was used to beat
> So quickly, waiting for a hand.

Or that other section, opening with:

> To-night the winds begin to rise
> And roar from yonder dropping day:
> The last red leaf is whirl'd away,
> The rooks are blown about the skies.

Or such superb felicities as:

> There twice a day the Severn fills;
> The salt sea-water passes by,
> And hushes half the babbling Wye,
> And makes a silence in the hills.

Or, keeping to sea-water, that verse in which when the mother is praying for her sailor son –

> His heavy-shotted hammock-shroud
> Drops in his vast and wandering grave

where we marvel not at the obvious touch of typical Victorian pathos but at the way in which the poet gives us sheer deadening weight in the first line and then after 'drops' suddenly shows us the wide ocean in 'his vast and wandering grave'. Any contemporary poets and critics who do not consider Tennyson a master of his art are here invited to try to express all that we feel at a burial at sea in a couple of other lines.

It was *In Memoriam*, in this same wonder-working year, that transformed Tennyson into Victoria's Poet Laureate. After Wordsworth's death, Samuel Rogers was approached but he pointed out very sensibly that at eighty-seven he was too old. This left the field open for some months. There were several heavily-backed candidates, with Elizabeth Barrett Browning and Leigh Hunt perhaps heading the list. Tennyson was on it, probably unknown to himself as he was out of London and taking no interest in the proceedings, but his chances were not widely favoured. What improved them enormously was the success of *In Memoriam*, which Prince Albert read and admired. The poet now had Windsor Castle supporting him. The Prime Minister, Lord John Russell, wrote to Rogers to enquire if Tennyson was a respectable and responsible person. Early in November a letter from Windsor Castle asked Tennyson to accept the poet laureateship. Instead of immediately and happily consenting, he took a whole day trying to decide what he should do, and he actually drafted two letters, one accepting, one refusing. It was his friends at dinner that night who pressed him to accept the appointment. There were still a few of his old enemies around, but the news that Alfred Tennyson was now Poet Laureate was on the whole very well received.

This appointment completed what a happy marriage and *In Memoriam* had begun. It turned the giant-gipsy, withdrawn and even dangerously neurotic poet of the 1840s into a public man. Tennyson's hesitation about accepting it is significant. This was a divided man: the Alfred who wrote No, the Tennyson who wrote Yes. And the friends who urged acceptance did the essential poet in him a disservice. This was not because his laureateship, which he took seriously, would from now on compel him to waste time and talent celebrating public occasions, weddings, funerals, idiotic cavalry charges. It was because the shadow of Windsor Castle would fall across his pages. He would soon find himself surrounded and fêted by portentous Establishment figures. He would be accepted as the most graceful spokesman of an age that at heart he detested. The living poet in Tennyson, deeply sensuous, melancholy, often strangely feminine and with a woman's sudden flares of rebelliousness, was far removed from the outlook and values of mid-Victorian England. He would soon have to retreat, with the *Idylls of the King*, into a medieval dream world; but even here his responsibilities as a public man would follow him to check and hinder and then smooth the page. Only in *Maud*, earlier than the first *Idylls* though we shall have to wait five years for it, did the uncrowned Tennyson of the 1840s come striding out again, and even then the violence and frenzy of the poem gave way in the end to blustering nonsense about the Crimean War. But we shall come to it, as its first astonished readers did, in 1855.

This was also to be a great year for another Victorian giant, Charles Dickens. On Saturday, 30 March 1850, there appeared the first number of *Household Words – A Weekly Journal – Conducted By Charles Dickens – Price 2d*. Though certain changes were to be made later, from this time Dickens condemned himself to be responsible for a weekly magazine for the rest of his life. (But he had an invaluable chief assistant in W. H. Wills, ready to keep the editorial office going day and night.) *Household Words* was a popular family magazine, edited on the something-for-everybody principle, and if it was different from and superior to others, that was because it was 'conducted', very ably too, by Dickens. It was not political in the narrower sense, but Dickens, who guessed correctly that there was now a new reading public, was determined to offer it a magazine of strong radical protest. Both as editor and regular contributor, he was moved by a passionate concern for ordinary working people. In his novels he might change his attitude, as indeed he did, towards other classes, but he never weakened in this deep sympathy. He knew there were hundreds of thousands of such people who desired and deserved a better quality of life, and for them he toiled unsparingly. The response was immediate and gratifying. About a hundred thousand copies of the first issue were sold. He was a good editor – cajoling, advising, often trimming and sharpening faulty contributions – and was himself a good if not great journalist, adroit in his choice of subjects, even if only rarely bringing to them a flash of his novelist's genius. We know now that among his contributors were many established writers, like Mrs Gaskell, and some bright youthful journalists, like Sala, Yates, Payn, known as 'Dickens's young men'. Even so, he denied himself others by insisting that contributions should be anonymous. Charles Dickens

This was a bad decision. After all, his own name was there every week.

There can be no doubt that Dickens's chief reason for turning editor was that he wanted a reformist and radical platform of his own. But there were other reasons. The steady income was useful: he took £500 a year as editor, and as part-proprietor he had a half-share in the profits. Then again, he needed a further outlet for his almost demonic energy. He was a man who could play as well as work, but even his play was more demanding and exhausting than most other men's work. What he could not do for long, though he might pretend it was all he wanted, was to keep quiet and take it easy. He rushed into one activity after another like a haunted man trying to escape a spectre.

Furthermore, there was in Dickens a constant desire, not to be satisfied by writing novels, to take command, to organize, to give orders, to impose his will on others. We have read so much about his high spirits at parties – his conjuring tricks, charades, games – that we tend to forget this other side of him, which made him a domestic martinet insisting upon neatness and order, like an officer inspecting a barrack room. (First meeting him, the young Henry James noted his 'military eye'.) One of his greatest admirers and younger friends, Edmund Yates, tells us, 'I have heard Dickens described by those who knew him as aggressive, imperious, and intolerant, and I can comprehend the accusation; but to me his temper was always of the sweetest and kindest.' There then are two very different aspects of his complex personality. One part of him found satisfaction in being the editor and part-proprietor of a successful popular magazine, though it might keep him working half the night. But even while we applaud his reformist zeal, his attempts to rescue the lives of working people from disease, ignorance, ugliness, apathy or despair, we can doubt his wisdom in overloading himself in this fashion.

We can see now that he was beginning to set a course that would bring him, after several years of exhaustion and pain, to his grave before he had reached sixty. True, the public readings would be far more demanding and damaging than this editorship. But we can see it as the first move on a collision course with an early death. He was an extremely conscientious editor, so that even when he took a holiday in France he could not forget his responsibilities, and was in constant communication with Wills and the office. His more important novels, among them some of his best, did not suffer; but he himself did, compelled as he was to exist on overdrafts of energy. He might have lived another ten years – and novelists have done some of their finest work in their sixties – if he had not turned editor and journalist as well as public performer. While he may have done some good to the working people his journalism tried to help, we cannot enjoy and admire his creative genius, which belonged almost entirely to his fiction, without wondering if behind this triumphant first appearance of *Household Words* there was not a dubious and even fatal decision.

Another and more certain triumph came in November this year, when *David Copperfield* was published, after appearing in monthly parts, illustrated by Phiz, in the familiar old fashion. Not only was it well received but very soon both the critics and the public accepted Dickens's own estimate of it as his favourite novel. It became one of the standard classics of the century. It owed its origin and development to a suggestion by John Forster that Dickens might try telling a story in the first person, and to the fact that Dickens had already written several chapters of autobiography. Referring to an early section, Dickens wrote to Forster, 'I really think I have done it ingeniously, and with a very complicated interweaving of truth and fiction.' And so indeed he had, and continued to do until he did some unconvincing plotting in much later sections. Any close student of Dickens can easily be fascinated by the transmutation of truth into fiction, and by the way in which his actual parents never appear as whole distinct characters while various aspects of them, together with his emotional relations with them, can be discovered in widely different characters and episodes. Ordinary readers in search of rich entertainment welcomed then – and can still welcome now – the charm unusual in Dickens, the huge gallery of the book's characters, many of them famous, and the astonishing variety of its scenes and settings.

'Somebody turns up', an illustration by Phiz to Chapter XVII of *David Copperfield* – 'I had begun to wish myself well out of the visit to Uriah and Mrs Heep, when Mr Micawber walked in, exclaiming, "Copperfield! Is it possible."'

To most of us now the magic has faded from the later chapters of *David Copperfield*. Its author's mistakes – for example, the plotting, and the emergence of David, now a dim figure, as a successful novelist (novelists should never write about novelists, not even with downright malice) – are more obvious in these chapters than his creative zest. Strictly speaking, the novel's greatest and lasting triumph, its account of David's childhood, falls outside our decade, belonging as it does to the late 1840s. So we must deal with it briefly. Lecturers in Eng. Lit.

who 'teach' Joyce, Lawrence, Virginia Woolf, or other deeply subjective novelists, are entitled to turn up their noses at Steerforth and Little Em'ly and the machinations of Uriah Heep, but unless they salute Dickens's handling of David Copperfield's childhood they are so many ignoramuses. It is a marvel of subjective narrative, and as far as any childhood is concerned it has not been bettered to this day. The dark and the light of our early life, its sinister shadows and sudden bright hope, its unaccountable twists and turns like those in a fairy tale, all are there, most sensitively and superbly described. Baudelaire said that the ability to recapture childhood at will was the mark of a genius. One part of Dickens never left his childhood. This is the secret of his extraordinary vivifying power: the very furniture comes alive, as it does to children. It is also the secret of his huge comic characters. To say they are mere caricatures is simply stupid. Third-rate fiction is full of caricatures that we forget in a couple of days. Dickens's drollest creations are monsters but somehow credible and memorable because we have all met creatures like them before: they are the more ridiculous friends of our parents, apparently never changing, immortal, that we knew in our childhood.

'I make the acquaintance of Miss Mowcher', an illustration by Phiz to Chapter XXII of *David Copperfield* – 'I never did in my days behold anything like Mowcher as she stood upon the dining-table, rubbing busily at Steerforth's head.'

While we all know that the Great Exhibition belongs to 1851, we must remember that it demanded a great deal of elaborate planning, and this had to be done in 1850. There would never have been a Great Exhibition without the sustained enthusiasm and hard committee-slogging of Henry Cole and Prince Albert. Cole was an unusually energetic and versatile civil servant, who did some painting and engraving and actually designed a very successful tea service. He had already helped to organize some modest exhibitions of 'Art Manufactures'. In 1849 there was a much larger *Exposition* in Paris, though it was not on a grand international scale. Cole was a very active member of the Royal Society of Arts, of which Albert was president. (Whatever his faults,

Albert had a very real interest in education and all cultural affairs.)
Thomas Cubitt, the builder who was then enlarging Osborne for the
Queen, had just had some talk with a friend who had been to Paris, and
he repeated the gist of their talk, in favour of a larger and more international exhibition, to Prince Albert at Osborne. Then a Royal Society
meeting decided that 'particular advantage to British Industry might
be derived from placing it in fair competition with that of other Nations',
a typical mid-Victorian self-confident conclusion. With Albert as
president, a Royal Commission was appointed, going to work with a
will and at a speed that Royal Commissions of today seem to have
mislaid. Its twenty-four members represented all respectable shades
of opinion and types of interest and experience. Guarantors and sub-
scriptions were earnestly invited, but at first there was no eager response.

The truth is that throughout most of 1850 the whole grand project
was not generally taken very seriously, even though the guarantors
finally crept, rather than mounted, up to about five thousand. For
example, *Punch*, still a Radical journal then, came out with:

THE PRINCE'S PETITION

Pity the troubles of a poor young Prince
Whose costly scheme has borne him to your door:
Who's in a fix – the matter not to mince –
Oh help him out, and Commerce swell your store!
The empty hat my awkward case bespeaks,
These blank subscription lists explain my fear;
Days follow days, and weeks succeed to weeks,
But very few contributors appear.

It is much to the credit of Prince Albert – and of the various small
groups who supported him – that he pushed on with the great plan,
ignoring such gibes. There was opposition at home, so that Brougham
in the House of Lords wondered why 'English tradespeople were such
fools as to subscribe their money to provide accommodation for the
traders of all nations to come over and undersell them in their own
market.' Prominent Radicals like Dickens regarded the whole project
with distaste and suspicion. There was some dislike of it abroad. It was
reported from the British Embassy in St Petersburg that passports to
England were being refused to persons of importance and rank but
were easily obtained by artisans and the like: 'The whole affair I believe
to be an attempt of the Russian Government to throw discredit on the
objects of the exhibition.' Southern Europe was no better. Official
Naples shook its head: 'The Exhibition will afford a pretext for the
assembling of all the violent republicans in Europe, and the Neapolitans
by mixing in such society would run great risk of having their minds
tainted with revolutionary doctrines.'

Nevertheless, there was now an executive committee hard at work.
One of its prominent members was Lyon Playfair, a chemist and an
administrator of scientific research. The immediate problem was the

Victoria's Heyday

(far left) Sir Henry Cole

(left) Sir Lyon Playfair

(below) 'The Official Picture of the Royal Commissioners for the Great Exhibition of 1851', by Henry Windham Phillips. The Prince Consort sits facing us. On the right, seated, is Lord Derby and above him to the right Robert Stephenson; next to him stands Sir Robert Peel; the other figure behind Prince Albert is Lord John Russell. Sir Joseph Paxton leans forward towards the Prince with his hand on the table. Seated in front is Mr Cubitt, and Mr Fox stands behind him. Sir Henry Cole is the right-hand figure of the three standing beyond.

classification of the vast amount of material that would be displayed in the Exhibition. After much argument, Playfair's classification was adopted. It divided the exhibits into eight chief categories: A. Metallurgy; B. Chemical Manufactures; C. Vitreous-ceramic Manufactures; D. Textiles; E. Organic Manufactures; F. Engineering and Machinery; G. Architecture, Fine Arts, Music; H. Agriculture, Horticulture. (This does at least give us some notion of the enormous scope of the Great Exhibition.) Manufacturers were divided into twenty-nine groups, each of them then subdivided into sections representing distinct industries. But then of course there were disputes about the exact classification of odd objects – for example, the French Commissioner's walking-stick. This – and it was a test-case – was appearing under a subsection *Machines for the Propagation of Direct Motion*. Challenged, the sensible Playfair put the walking-stick under *Miscellaneous Objects* in a subsection *Objects for Personal Use*. His successful demand for commonsense and simplicity, as against severe logic and pomposity, began to clear the air, and manufacturers who had previously hung back now began to come forward. And it was Playfair who organized the juries, which were half British and half foreign.

But where was the Exhibition hall, obviously very large, to be built? Prince Albert had first suggested Leicester Square, presumably without having seen it for some time. The Building Committee considered other possible sites, but finally returned to Henry Cole's original idea – Hyde Park, and the particular stretch of ground between the Serpentine and the Knightsbridge Barracks. It was agreed that sixteen out of the twenty acres there should be covered by the actual building. But what kind of building? By the middle of March 1850 the Committee was asking the public as well as architects for suggestions and plans, the competition to end by 8 April. There were over two hundred entries and plenty of 'honourable mentions' but no outright winner. So the Committee, perhaps by this time half out of its mind, produced a peculiarly horrible design of its own, which would need nineteen million bricks, would be four times as long as Westminster Abbey, and asked for a cupola even larger than that of St Peter's in Rome. While the Committee was brooding like Frankenstein over his monster, any official appropriation of the Hyde Park site was being denounced by people who said the trees there must be preserved, that riders in the Park would be sadly inconvenienced, that the whole pleasant neighbourhood would suffer annoyance, and so on and so forth. It began to look as if Parliament would not allow Hyde Park to be used. But then Peel died early in July, and as the House knew he would have been the first to support the Hyde Park scheme, its feeling about the appropriation changed, in deference to his memory, and all opposition to it was handsomely defeated. So far, so good; but time was running out – and there was no acceptable plan for the Exhibition building.

Victoria's Heyday

The hour produced the man, as it did more than once in mid-Victorian Britain. And again – for this also happened more than once – the man the hour produced was a complete surprise. Joseph Paxton, the son of a small farmer in Bedfordshire, was apprenticed to a head gardener, tried various jobs to gain experience, and became a foreman for the Horticultural Society. But he was earning only eighteen shillings a week, and in 1826 he was about to emigrate to America. However, the Duke of Devonshire, then President of the Society, had noticed him and had decided that this young man was exceptionally intelligent, with the result that Paxton was made superintendent of the gardens at the Duke's Chatsworth estate. There, between 1836 and 1840, he supervised the building of the largest conservatory in the country, 300 feet long. Ten years later, when there was all this talk of a suitable building for the Exhibition, Paxton had an idea, and it is said that his original sketch of his giant glasshouse was done on a piece of blotting paper, during a committee meeting of the Midland Railway. His elaborated plan met with some opposition in the Building Committee, but he had a very valuable ally in another mid-Victorian original, Brunel the engineer. (Of him, more later.) Working fast, the two of them solved the tree problem by planning to enclose the trees on the site within the vast conservatory. Paxton's scheme had many other advantages. Its chief material, glass, could easily be manufactured in a hurry. In spite of its size, the building would not be difficult to erect and could be taken down with comparative ease. Because its parts were interchange-able, there would be no difficulty in extending or reducing it. So Paxton had his way. By 26 July 1850 the final tender of the contractors, Fox and Henderson, was accepted: it was for £79,800, a sum at which we can only gape enviously. We can be equally envious of their speed: this 'Crystal Palace', as it soon came to be called, was erected in seven months.

Sir Joseph Paxton

The first column was secure on 26 September, and then the work proceeded day and night without a break, at first behind wooden barricades. (These, a temptation to all small boys, provided *Punch* with a few comic drawings. But many of *Punch*'s remarks about the Exhibition were what we should now call snide.) About two thousand men were employed, and as the building went higher and higher they were watched by enormous crowds. These men knew nothing of our modern aids to fast construction, but even so, what were new methods of economizing labour were used in and around the building – for example, machines for producing sashbars and gutters and for laying on paint and glazing. Meanwhile, as the Crystal Palace began to tower above the Park, there was much speculation and worry, in and out of print, about how these hordes of foreigners soon to invade London could be boarded and lodged. It was all very well to have a Great Exhibition, but what if these visitors, of all colours, should bring with them dreadful diseases, plagues from their outer darkness?

(top) The Committee's design for the Great Exhibition

(centre) The original blotting-paper sketch by Sir Joseph Paxton, made at Derby on 11 June 1850

(bottom) A photograph of 1851 by William Henry Fox Talbot showing the east end of the Crystal Palace

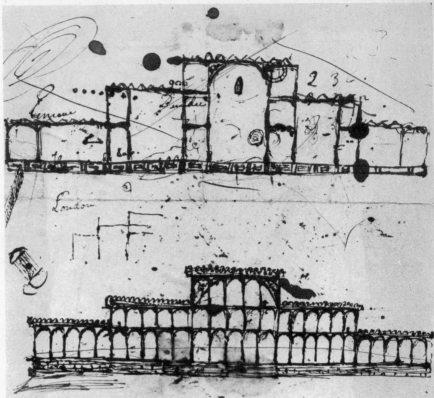

(above) Work in progress on the building of the Crystal Palace

(below) Raising the ribs of the transept roof

There was more worry this year when it was announced that Wiseman, the leading Roman Catholic in the country, was soon to be made a cardinal. This blazed into a fury of popular indignation when the news came later that the Pope was restoring the Catholic hierarchy in England, with bishops here and bishops there, parcelling out the country. It was all very well for Cardinal Wiseman to deliver, in St George's, Southwark, 'Three Lectures on the Catholic Hierarchy', but he was savagely caricatured in the press as the old cry of 'No Popery!' rang through the land. Actually, poor Wiseman, though it was said that Browning based his 'Blougram' on him, was very far from being a scheming, devious and ambitious son of Rome. He was very large and very learned, amiable and ingenuous, and there is an amusing sketch of him in

Cardinal Wiseman

Victoria's Heyday

Lytton Strachey's account of that very different character, Manning. Cardinal Wiseman, Strachey writes,

> . . . devoted much time and attention to the ceremonial details of his princely office. His knowledge of rubric and ritual and of the symbolic significations of vestments has rarely been equalled, and he took a profound delight in the ordering and the performance of elaborate processions. During one of these functions an unexpected difficulty arose: the Master of the Ceremonies suddenly gave the word for a halt, and, on being asked the reason, replied that he had been instructed that moment by special revelation to stop the procession. The Cardinal, however, was not at a loss. 'You may let the procession go on,' he smilingly replied. 'I have just obtained permission, by special revelation, to proceed with it.' His leisure hours he spent in the writing of edifying novels, in the composition of acrostics in Latin verse, and in playing battledore and shuttlecock with his little nieces. There was, indeed, only one point in which he resembled Bishop Blougram – his love of a good table. Some of Newman's disciples were astonished and grieved to find that he sat down to four courses of fish during Lent. 'I am sorry to say,' remarked one of them afterwards, 'that there is a lobster salad side to the Cardinal.'

But by the end of 1850 the Pope (the famous 'Pio Nono') and Wiseman between them seemed to have let ten thousand spitting and clawing cats out of the bag. What – they would divide England between them, would they! When did they propose to set up the Inquisition? A satirical piece in *Punch*, one of many, had more savagery than smiling humour in it. Rome having divided England into Catholic bishoprics, the writer declares, then his readers might soon expect something like this:

> The Hindoo Government has sent over Hoki Poki, to commence his functions as Brahmin of Battersea. Messrs. Laurie, of Oxford Street, have received directions to build without delay a car, with Collinge's patent axles, for the accommodation of Juggernaut.
> The Mizam of Moolrah has sent over Bow Wow to commence his sittings at Marylebone as Mufti of Middlesex, and Rusti Khan goes to Westminster Hall, to take his place in the Court of Chancery as Cadi of Chelsea. We had forgotten to state that the Bow-string is to be introduced at Bow Street, and Kooley Fooley will preside at the burning of a widow, on a pile of weeds collected from all the widows in the Metropolis. . . .

And so on and so forth: crude rough stuff, but hard to endure by members of the Old Catholic Families, as English as the writer, who had never welcomed this new move by Rome. Meanwhile, the indignation of more fervent Protestants was so widespread that the Government had to notice it and take measures to quiet the public. But this would have to wait until 1851, which looked like being a very busy and eventful year.

Queen Victoria's favourite painter was Sir Edwin Landseer, whom she knighted in 1850. The sentimentality and facile repetitiveness of his later work has tended to obscure the fact that in his prime – at the beginning of the 1850s – he was an animal painter of brilliant technique and virtuosity, even if so many of his animals have 'human' eyes. 'The Monarch of the Glen' was painted in 1851.

THE
GREAT EXHIBITION POLKA,
1851,
FOR THE
Piano Forte,
COMPOSED & DEDICATED TO
HIS ROYAL HIGHNESS
PRINCE ALBERT,
BY
FRANK B. TUSSAUD.

ENT. STA. HALL.

Pr. 2/6

LONDON, DUFF & HODGSON, 65, OXFORD ST.

PRINTED IN COLORS BY STANNARD & DIXON, 7 POLAND ST.

1851

BY THE FIRST OF MAY, when Queen Victoria would perform the opening ceremony at the Great Exhibition, everything was ready – if we exclude a few of the foreign exhibits – in Hyde Park. And if there was general excitement – and the Queen herself was sizzling with it – there was plenty to be excited about. It was the building itself, Paxton's astonishing Crystal Palace, that attracted most attention and received most praise: it was indeed, as it well deserved to be, the triumph of the whole project. The clever and versatile Paxton, soon to be Sir Joseph, had produced marvels. Our illustrations can take the place of any description of the building itself, but some figures will give an idea of its size. It finally covered nineteen acres, was three times the size of St Paul's, was six hundred yards long, and offered over eight miles of table space for the exhibitors. It had 2,300 cast-iron girders, 3,300 pillars, 30 miles of rainwater guttering, 202 miles of sashbars, and altogether about 1,000,000 square feet of glass. (Moreover, we must remember that this gigantic structure had been so contrived that it could be taken down and erected elsewhere, as indeed it was, without great difficulty and expense.)

The ingenious Paxton had included all manner of devices for the greater comfort and pleasure of visitors. He had magnifying glasses installed in the side galleries. Canvas over the whole south elevation allowed a current of air between the fabric and the glass roof. There were lengths of trellised boarding on the floor to avoid dust, and mechanically controlled louvres for ventilation, and running on the gutter rails of the roof were little trucks in which painters and glaziers could sit and do their work.

Such details, however, do nothing to make us appreciate the magical effect of this Crystal Palace on London, now mad about glass. 'We shall be disappointed', wrote one humorist, 'if the next generation of London children are not brought up like cucumbers under glass.' Disraeli, with his romantic-auctioneer style, does not help us much, by referring to 'that enchanted pile which the sagacious taste and the prescient philanthropy of an accomplished and enlightened Prince have raised for the glory of England and the delight and instruction of two hemispheres.' (Later he declared that while everybody loved praise, with Royalty it should be laid on with a trowel.) Lord Redesdale in his *Memories* is much better: this Crystal Palace of 1851, he wrote,

A popular art that had its heyday in the eighteen-fifties was that of the colour lithographs which decorated the covers of sheet music. Songs and dance music – polkas, mazurkas, waltzes, quadrilles, lancers – were given titles that were connected, often rather absurdly, with public events, in order that the artists could be given a colourful and popular subject to draw. Frank Tussaud's 'Great Exhibition Polka' was one of many such examples of popular music that celebrated the Great Exhibition. The lithograph is not signed, but was probably the work of John Brandard.

... was so graceful, so delicate, so airy, that its translucent beauty remains graven on my memory as something which must defy all rivalry. When first I saw it glittering in the morning sun, I felt as if Aladdin and the Jin who was the slave of the lamp must have been at work on it – no mere human hands and hammers and builders' tools could have wrought such a miracle. . . . It is idle to talk of this or that exhibit or even of many. There were things beautiful, and things hideous, for art at that moment had sunk very low: but the general effect of beauty and airy grace, together with the delicate framework and brilliancy of the whole structure, was indelible – unlike its more modern successors its size was not so great as to prevent one from gaining a general impression of the whole, and that was a joyous, sensuous revelling in a palace of light. Even those whom I remember scoffing at the idea when it was first mooted were compelled to admit that it was a great conception nobly carried out. . . .

We may smile at faded photographs of our great-grandfathers with their side-whiskers and stove-pipe hats, but we might also ask ourselves if anything bolder and more original has ever been conceived and carried out in London since.

Certainly, magic was in the air at this time. Without it we cannot explain the strange story of the Exhibition sparrows. There were great old trees under this glass roof, and among them innumerable sparrows ready to ruin the exhibits with their droppings. No shotguns could be used because of all the glass; so here was a grave problem. The Queen sent for the old Duke of Wellington, and in his own curt fashion, he said, 'Try sparrow-hawks, ma'am.' To learn what happened then, we must dive into the *Memoirs and Correspondence of Lyon Playfair*:

When the sparrows' scouts informed them that the Duke of Wellington had gone to the Palace, all the sparrows congregated in the tree nearest the

Detail from a drawing of the Crystal Palace seen from the south-east, by George Baxter. George Baxter was the great pioneer in the field of colour wood-block printing.

The Foreign Pavilion at the Great Exhibition

door, and as soon as the advice of sparrow-hawks was communicated they flew in a body out of the door, and the Exhibition was never again troubled with their presence.

In matters more down to earth, foresight and organization were used instead of magic. Months before the opening of the Exhibition its Commissioners asked the Home Office for a thousand extra Metropolitan Police. Special railway excursions were being arranged all over the country. West End shopkeepers were already putting notices in their windows to proclaim that various foreign languages were spoken inside. Advertisements were appearing to announce that their particular goods would be certain to win a prize.

Brave attempts on all social levels were being made to solve the difficult accommodation problem. So there were advertisements for 1851's special Mechanics' Home. It offered astonishingly good value for money, the charge being only one shilling and threepence per night. For this each person was provided with 'a bedstead, good wool mattress, sheets and blankets, soap, towels and every convenience for ablution'. Boots would be cleaned at a penny a pair, and there was a barber on duty. Food could be obtained – soups, pork sausages, bacon, cold meats, potatoes, pickles, salads, fruit pies, eggs for breakfast, tea and coffee. There was a reading-room, and a smoking room that had 'a Band of Music to entertain guests over ale and porter between 8 and 9 p.m.'. There was even a Complaints Book handy in the hall. So visiting mechanics could do themselves proud. It is worth halting a moment to reflect on the way in which mid-Victorian industrial England preferred to call its workmen 'mechanics' and 'operatives'. It is as if they were seen in terms of the great steam engines with which they worked. Now in our day, when they are referred to as parts of 'labour units' and 'work

Victoria's Heyday

forces' and the like, the engines have vanished, some huge abstract plan taking their place. It is against remote and bloodless planners that men today suddenly strike.

But what about the exhibits, now finding their way to Hyde Park from all parts of the world? There were of course difficulties about the amount of space alloted to the countries. So, for example, the Swiss, never a people lacking in self-confidence, grumbled hard about their space, and disliked being told that, after all, theirs was a very small country. At the other extreme, the vast Chinese Empire made no attempt to fill the space it had been given, and wealthy friends of the Exhibition had to lend it valuable Chinese objects from their own collections. (But the Celestial Empire did send some of its tea, as well it might, for the consumption of tea in Britain by this time was over 54,000,000 lb a year.) We are told that there were 13,000 exhibitors, those from Britain and the colonies taking up half the space, with the United States, France and Germany prominent among the countries occupying the other half. I do not need to be told, for I have seen them with my own fearful eyes, that the complete official catalogue runs to three formidable volumes. (Curious readers may now consult re-issues of these at their leisure.) There were of course innumerable examples of handicrafts and so-called (because often quite tasteless) works of art: pictures were forbidden, but sculpture, jewelry, pottery, fancy furniture, were on show everywhere, together with many odd inventions, including a very useful walking-stick for a doctor, so long as he did not do too much walking, for it contained test-tubes and an enema. Two imposing representations could be seen at the very entrance, where Courage took the form of an enormous statue of Richard Coeur de Lion, and Power was to be discovered in a 24-ton block of coal from one of the Duke of Devonshire's mines.

As 1851 had entered the Machine Age it was inevitable that the examples of brand-new machinery should dominate the Exhibition. The man from the *Daily News* might be afraid that this 'most extensive department of the Exhibition' would not be popular, but in fact he was wrong. The machines attracted most attention, and we are told how crowds of farmers – still wearing smocks, so that we are offered a curious picture – hung around examining, admiring, and coveting so many new agricultural implements. There among the American exhibits, which also included – a sinister portent – the Colt revolver, was that ingenious invention, the McCormick reaper, which would soon do much to change the agricultural economy of the world. Indeed, we might say that the first glimpse of the highly mechanized world of today could be obtained in the Great Exhibition of 1851. No doubt some besmocked older farmers, who had not risked the excursion to London, shook their heads as the younger men described these mechanical wonders; and now there may be times when some of us, who have lived to see many of them, shake our heads too.

(below) Wall lamp, by M. Gagneau Brothers (France)

(bottom) Fish knife and fork, by Mappin Brothers

(opposite top right) The McCormick reaper

(opposite centre left) Ornamental scissors, by J. B. Durham

(centre) Patent freezing machine, by Thomas Masters

(centre right) The 'Day dreamer' easy chair in *papier mâché*, designed by H. F. Cook and made by Jennens & Bettridge. 'The chair is decorated at the top with two winged thoughts'.

(bottom left) 'Lady's mechanical escritoire in white wood, constructed in such a manner as to enable the person to write either in a sitting or standing posture.' By M. L. Wettli (Switzerland)

(bottom centre) Jug, by Messrs Charles Meigh & Son

(bottom right) 'The Lion in Love', by G. Geefs (Belgium). The group represents the power of beauty over savage nature. The monarch of the forest, unable to resist the seducing loveliness of a nude female who is seated on his back and fascinating him with her eyes, is quietly submitting to being deprived of his claws.

Victoria's Heyday

However, we must turn to the Grand Opening, that May Day which was also Queen Victoria's heyday, so glorious that it left her ecstatic for days. Thus she could write on the 3rd to King Leopold:

> My Dearest Uncle – I wish you *could* have witnessed the 1st May, 1851, the *greatest* day in our history, the *most beautiful* and *imposing* and *touching* spectacle ever seen, and the triumph of my beloved Albert. Truly it was astonishing, a fair scene. Many cried, and all felt touched and impressed with devotional feelings. It was the *happiest proudest* day in my life, and I can think of nothing else. Albert's dearest name is immortalized with the *great* conception, *his* own, and my *own* dear country *showed* she was *worthy* of it. . . .

And so indeed she did. The people had been given a public holiday, and, wearing their Sunday-best clothes, they packed themselves into the park from dawn onwards. Thousands of others lined the route the Queen would take. Inside the Crystal Palace were 25,000 invited guests and season-ticket holders (Gentlemen 3 guineas, Ladies 2). Macaulay in his diary gives us a fair account of this morning:

> A fine day for the opening of the Exhibition. A little cloudy in the morning, but generally sunny and pleasant. I was struck by the number of foreigners in the streets. All, however, were respectable and decent people. I saw none of the men of action with whom the Socialists were threatening us. I went to the Park and along the Serpentine. There were immense crowds on both sides of the water. I should think there must have been near three hundred thousand people in Hyde Park at once. The sight among the green boughs was delightful. The boats and little frigates, darting across the lake; the flags; the music; the guns – everything was exhilarating, and the temper of the multitude the best possible. . . .
>
> I made my way into the building; a most gorgeous sight; vast; graceful; beyond the dreams of the Arabian romances. I cannot think that the Caesars ever exhibited a more splendid spectacle. I was quite dazzled. . . . I wandered about, and elbowed my way through the crowd which filled the nave, admiring the general effect, but not attending much to details. . . . Home, and finished *Persuasion*. . . .

At 11.40 a.m. precisely, nine carriages left Buckingham Palace, through cheering crowds, for Hyde Park. The Queen, suitably dressed in pink, was in the last carriage, with Albert and her two eldest children. At Hyde Park Corner there were a few drops of rain, just to add a little glitter. To the sound of silver trumpets the royal party walked along the impressive nave of the Crystal Palace towards the wonderful fountain and the blue-and-silver canopied throne, which had a huge elm tree behind it. As the Queen passed them, one organ after another shrilled and thundered. It is all there in her journal: flags of all nations, waving palms, flowers, statues, myriads of people, flourishes of trumpets, together with blessings on her dearest Albert, her dearest country. When the excitement was almost impossible to bear, no doubt Albert calmed it by reading aloud the Report of the Royal Commissioners

'The Greek Slave', 1846, by Hiram Powers. This popular exhibit stood in the middle of the American section under a specially erected canopy and background of red plush.

addressed to the Queen. It ended by a longish 'heartfelt prayer' and those pious sentiments ('bonds of peace and friendship among all nations') heard so often on occasions like this – between wars.

Shortly afterwards, when the Hallelujah Chorus was in full joyful swing and the procession was being formed to tour the building, there arrived from nowhere that Chinese, richly garbed, who moved majestically into the open space before the Queen and there prostrated himself. It was impressive but mysterious. Was he an Imperial Ambassador or some rich mandarin who had found his way from Peking? There was no time now for enquiries to be made, so the Queen, smiling but not too warmly, gave an order that a place should be found for him with the diplomatic corps in the procession. When it had finished its tour of the Exhibition, he vanished. Later it was discovered he was quite bogus, being a certain He Sing (and even that sounds bogus too) who had a Chinese junk anchored in the Thames and every day showed people over it at a shilling a head. So, to describe him as 'The Chinese Commissioner insensibly touched with the solemnity of the scene', as Edward Kater did, was not accurate reporting. But the procession was very impressive, headed as it was by 'the delicate female whose tempered sway is owned by a hundred millions of men (who) pursued her course among the contributions of all the civilized world.' This was the *Gentleman's Magazine* being rather too gentlemanly: Queen Victoria, who was to weather all storms for the next half-century, was no 'delicate female'.

The Great Exhibition was undoubtedly very successful. It remained open – though closed always on Sundays – until the middle of October, in all for 140 days. It had 6,063,986 visitors, though this figure of course includes a great many who went more than once. After the third

Detail of 'Waiting at the Station', 1850, by Lefevre J. Cranstone

(left) The closing of the Great Exhibition

(below) Scene from *Apartments : Visitors to the Exhibition may be Accommodated*, Princess's Theatre, 14 May 1851

(bottom) *Punch's Almanack* for 1852 comments on the purchasing of exhibits after the closure of the Great Exhibition

week, the original admission fee of five shillings was reduced to one shilling on four days in the week. Fridays came down to half-a-crown, and so did Saturdays from August onwards. But it was the shilling days, together with the elaborate railway-excursion arrangements, that guaranteed the popular appeal of the Exhibition. Many thousands of working people – and rural folk who had never travelled in a train before – found their way to it. The daily attendance averaged about 60,000 and finally went up to over 100,000. What was so pleasantly surprising was the orderliness and decent behaviour of these shilling visitors : nothing was broken ; not a flower was picked. Only on one of its last days, 7 October (with the highest attendance of all, 110,000), was there any trouble. That was because the Duke of Wellington, now very shaky, was paying his final visit. He was recognized by the enormous crowd and was cheered and mobbed. The uproar was heard in distant parts of the great building, where people imagined that the glass palace was collapsing, made a rush for the exits and overturned an expensive stand of French china, while the poor old Duke, furious and very shaky indeed now, was carried out by the six policemen who had been shadowing him. But that was the one unfortunate incident in those 140 days, during which, however, no alcoholic drink could be served. (Glasses of filtered water were freely provided.) Soda water, lemonade and ginger beer could be obtained in the refreshment rooms, where Schweppes, who had the catering contract, estimated that they had sold about a million Bath buns, 32,000 quarts of cream, 33 tons of ham and 113 tons of other meats. We are told that the provision of retiring rooms and lavatories was as successful as it was novel, establishing a pattern for any future large-scale functions.

The overall profit of the Great Exhibition came to rather more than £180,000. Prince Albert suggested that this money should be used to buy a considerable acreage of land in Kensington Gore, where various

(above) Jane Welsh Carlyle, by C. Hartmann

(below) The Crystal Palace at Sydenham

Royal Colleges and museums could be built, and where visitors to London may find them to this day. But what could be done with the Crystal Palace itself, for clearly it could not remain in Hyde Park? After much discussion it was taken down and removed to Sydenham, in South-East London, where it was rebuilt, enlarged, and given various fancy courts, and became the home for many years of brass band contests and monster production oratorios. In 1936 I was living in Highgate Village, a vantage point, and I well remember staring across to the opposite hill in the South and seeing the Crystal Palace blazing in the night. It had caught fire, and it was gutted, and that was the end of Paxton's original and astonishing giant glasshouse.

Not everybody, of course, was fascinated by the Great Exhibition itself, even while admiring Paxton's part in it. No doubt Jane Welsh Carlyle was more sharply critical than most women visitors. She wrote on 11 May:

> . . . Such a lot of things of different kinds and of well dressed people – for the tickets were still five shillings – was rather imposing for a few minutes; but when you came to look at the wares in detail there was nothing really worth looking at – at least that one could not have seen *samples* of in the shops. And the fatigue of even the most cursory survey was indescribable, and to tell you the God's truth I would not have given the pleasure of reading a good Fairy Tale for all the pleasure to be got from that 'Fairy Scene!'.

And this must have been what a lot of women secretly thought, after trying to avoid all that machinery.

Victoria's Heyday

Towards the end of this year Queen Victoria enjoyed a second triumph. She was able to write to Uncle Leopold, 'with the greatest pleasure', to tell him that *Lord Palmerston was no longer Foreign Secretary*. She had gained a small victory over Palmerston in October, when Kossuth, the famous Hungarian nationalist leader, arrived in England and was welcomed with enthusiasm. Palmerston, who was one of his admirers, wanted to receive Kossuth at the Foreign Office or, failing that, at his own house. The Queen, alarmed by the Hungarian's 'violent denunciations of two Sovereigns (of Austria and Russia) with whom we are at peace', declared he could not be received by her Foreign Secretary. After a Cabinet meeting Palmerston had to content himself with sending private messages to Kossuth. Victoria had won this little battle, but Palmerston, jaunty as ever, was still lording it in the Foreign Office.

Then, in December, he made a curious bad move. Louis Napoleon, whose long face and short legs had often been seen in London drawing-rooms when he was in exile, now as President of the French Republic carried out his impudent but successful *coup d'état*, based on some wily secret plotting and frequent gifts of beer and sausages to the troops. This took place during the early morning of 2 December. There were immediate arrests of prominent opponents. One decree dissolved the Assembly, introduced universal suffrage, and declared a state of emergency. The other decree demanded a plebiscite that would in fact give Louis Napoleon supreme power. After armed revolts, soon put down, mass arrests and large-scale deportations to Algeria (with Victor Hugo taking refuge in Jersey), on 21 December the plebiscite gave Louis Napoleon and his *coup d'état* an overwhelming majority. A year later he was proclaimed Emperor and Napoleon III. Meanwhile, Palmerston had made his curious bad move. He had told Walewski, the French Ambassador, that he heartily approved of Louis Napoleon's *coup d'état*, and of course Walewski immediately sent the good news to Paris. This was a blunder because it was not in line with British official policy and angered Lord John Russell and the Cabinet as well as the Queen, and also because it alienated Palmerston's Liberal supporters and the radicals. It was a curious move because here was Palmerston, who had been the friend of every democratic movement in Europe, every revolt against despotic government, now welcoming a conspiracy bent on destroying the French Republic and the achievements of 1848. He was acting against his famous Liberal principles. It has been said that he felt that if the *coup* failed there would be anarchy in France, and that if it succeeded then Britain would need Louis Napoleon's friendship, possibly in an alliance against Russia and Austria.

The Prime Minister, Lord John Russell, who had been feeling increasingly exasperated, now asserted himself and dismissed Palmerston. Defending his action in the subsequent Commons debate, Russell took the astonishing step of reading to the House a memorandum that the Queen had sent to Palmerston in 1850, complaining sharply about his

Mrs Amelia Bloomer

(opposite above) William Charles Macready delivering his farewell address at the Theatre Royal, Drury Lane, 26 February 1851

(opposite below) Edward George Earle Bulwer-Lytton, after a painting by Daniel Maclise, painted at Knebworth in 1850

conduct and pointing out that the Foreign Minister was responsible to the Crown. Not expecting this blow below the belt – my term for it, not his – Palmerston made a weak reply to what was an extremely effective speech by Russell, and was left looking helpless, finished ('There *was* a Palmerston', Disraeli sneered.) The most famous Foreign Minister of the century, *ce terrible Palmerston*, had been turned out of office like a footman caught stealing the silver. It was, as Victoria wrote to Uncle Leopold, 'a piece of news which I know will give you as much satisfaction and relief as it does to us, and will do the *whole* of the world.' And indeed, Prince Schwarzenberg gave a ball in Vienna to celebrate the event. But, as we shall see, Palmerston was not the man to remain looking helpless very long; he knew how to make full use, at the right moment, of the great weight of public opinion behind him; and he would soon have his revenge.

Among the large number of American visitors to London this year were Mrs Amelia Bloomer and her entourage of earnest young ladies. Mrs Bloomer was the champion – and hoped to be the deliverer – of down-trodden womanhood. The cause she represented was not silly. Both in England and America women during the 1850s were denied many elementary rights. (For example, in England not only a wife's property but anything she earned belonged to her husband, even if they were separated – see the Caroline Norton affair, later.) There was no reason why Mrs Bloomer should not give lectures in London and elsewhere: she had a strong case. Where she went wrong – at least in London – was in wearing a special outfit she had designed for herself and her girls. It consisted of a broad-brimmed or 'wideawake' straw hat, a coatee or bodice fitting tight around the waist, a short skirt, and then under it, from the knee downwards, pantaloons or 'bloomers' (as they soon came to be called) fastened close round the ankle. It was quite a decorous costume, but far uglier than the prevailing fashion of the time – and the bloomers did suggest a certain masculinity creeping in, an attempt, one might say, to wear the trousers. Alas it was a success only with the comic cartoonists and waggish fellows writing for low periodicals. But if some girls still wear knee-length bloomers in the gymnasium, they might give a thought to the original and brave, if foolish, Amelia, who took London by storm in 1851 but not in the way she hoped to do.

This can take us to the theatre. Two events this year did not encourage playgoers of the 1850s. The first and more important was the retirement of William Charles Macready, the chief tragedian of the time. He gave his farewell performance – as Macbeth, his favourite part – at Drury Lane at the end of February 1851. A public dinner given in his honour had Bulwer-Lytton (a great taker of chairs) as chairman, and Dickens (a close friend) and Thackeray among the speakers. Macready was still not

Victoria's Heyday

sixty – he lived until 1873 – but though he was a fine actor and a conscientious manager, doing much for the theatre, he disliked stage life and
always declared he detested acting. He was a strange man, an odd
mixture of surliness and urbanity, bad temper and charm, better fitted
for romantic performances than for a quiet life off the stage. He was
never popular with the public, but was enormously admired by most
critics and educated playgoers. His departure left a great hole in the
production of tragic drama.

The second event was the marriage, in August 1851, of Helena Faucit
to Theodore Martin, who had been romantically devoted to her for
some years. Martin, an Edinburgh man who settled in London as a
parliamentary solicitor, was as successful in marriage as he was or came
to be in many other things – as a parodist in his earlier days, as an
essayist on the drama, as a translator and adapter of foreign work for the
stage, and as the biographer of the Prince Consort, a heavy labour that
finally brought him a knighthood. Helena Faucit was generally regarded
as the best Shakespearean actress, both in tragedy and comedy, in the
English theatre. It is true she did not retire at once after her marriage.
She played the heroine in Browning's *Colombe's Birthday* at the Haymarket in 1853. Five years later, because she would not accept the chief
part in it, Matthew Arnold gave up the idea of seeing his *Merope* on the
stage. But by this time she no longer wanted to make regular appearances
in London, and though she acted on and off for some years, usually on
special occasions in provincial cities, she more or less vanished from
the sight of the metropolitan audiences. And as yet there was no actress
of equal reputation and wide appeal to take her place.

So the theatre of the 1850s, which largely depended upon great names,
was out of luck. It was deprived of glamour, startling or intensely
moving performances. Restoring Sadler's Wells to respectability,
Samuel Phelps was a kind of one-man Old Vic, producing and acting
in not only the usual Shakespeare repertoire but also offering his
audiences several plays, notably *Antony and Cleopatra*, that had not
been seen for at least a century. Phelps was a good and not a great actor.
Some of Charles Kean's friends, fond of him in private because he was
such a pleasant fellow, held that he was not even a good actor, a tallow
candle compared with the blaze of his father, Edmund Kean. Another
lesser son of his father was Charles James Matthews, without the comic
genius of the elder Charles Matthews, though a graceful light comedian
and a fair mimic, reviving the one-man shows that had made his father
famous. A broader and more popular comedian was J. B. Buckstone,
who also wrote some plays. Equally popular were the odd one-man
mixed entertainments by Albert Smith – *The Overland Mail* and *The
Ascent of Mont Blanc*. Unfortunately short-lived (1816–1860), Smith
was a hard-working zestful man, not without talent, who not only
dramatized several Dickens novels but also, in the 1840s, wrote some
Dickensian picaresque novels of his own that hardly deserve to be

Detail of 'The Opening of the Great
Exhibition in Hyde Park, May 1,
1851', painted between 1851 and
1852 by Henry C. Selous. The
centre group shows the Queen, the
Prince Consort, the Prince of Wales
(in highland dress) and other
members of the Royal Family. On
the left we see some of the British
Commissioners and officials and on
the right the foreign Commissioners
who include the decorative figure of
the Chinaman Hee Sing, who had
no right to be present. The painting
shows the north transept in the
background.

(overleaf) 'Her Majesty the Queen
holding a Drawing Room at St
James's Palace', 1851, by John
Gilbert (detail).

84

forgotten, even though they are flat champagne when compared with the foaming and sparkling wine of his master. But nothing any of these men could do would transform the 1850s into a memorable theatrical decade.

If the acting now never reached greatness, the writing was much worse. No dramatist, as distinct from purveyors of popular entertainment, was in sight. Even plays that were no masterpieces but at least could be revived over and over again, like Bulwer-Lytton's *Richelieu*, *The Lady of Lyons* and *Money*, came earlier, or, like T. W. Robertson's realistic-domestic innovations, arrived in the 1860s. But one success on this level was to come in 1852, Dion Boucicault's *The Corsican Brothers*. An able man of the theatre, producer and actor as well as author, Boucicault wrote scores of plays, nearly always romantic melodramas and often adaptations of novels or French plays. Another prolific writer for the stage was Tom Taylor. The eighteenth-century comedy he wrote with Charles Reade, *Masks and Faces* (1852), has been revived many times, partly because of the attraction of its heroine, the actress Peg Woffington. A later play of Taylor's, *Our American Cousin*, first produced in New York in 1858, had a most unusual history. Among its small parts was that of an affected, be-whiskered, drawling peer, Lord Dundreary, which the comic actor Sothern increasingly enlarged until it dominated the whole play. Charles Reade was essentially a novelist but he had a passion for the theatre, and his version of *The Courier of Lyons* (1854), afterwards known as *The Lyons Mail*, came to have a long life in revivals by Henry Irving and Martin-Harvey. Another frequent contributor to the theatre, dashing off farces and melodramas, was the co-founder and first editor of *Punch*, Mark Lemon, whose stage royalties kept *Punch* going during its first unsuccessful years.

Though it produced so little work of any distinction, the English theatre of the 1850s was prodigiously active. Melodramas, often based on more or less topical themes, a kind of stage journalism, came and went by the score, and short farces, then considered necessary to round off an evening, flashed past by the hundred. Freelance journalists, barristers without briefs, bank clerks, minor civil servants, all wrote hastily for the stage. Outstanding playwrights like Tom Taylor and Mark Lemon were astonishingly energetic and versatile, and must have toiled like demons. Taylor was assistant secretary and then chief secretary to the new Board of Health; he was art critic of *The Times* and *The Graphic*; he wrote several biographies and edited various volumes of memoirs; and all this while writing or collaborating in play after play. Mark Lemon was secretary to Ingram, the publisher of the *Illustrated London News*, and had a hand in its management; he was editor of *Punch*; he contributed to *Household Words* and other periodicals, and even wrote short stories and novels of a sort. Like Dickens, both Mark Lemon and Tom Taylor were enthusiastic and fairly accomplished amateur actors. The usual excuse for these activities was raising money for a charity or for the benefit of some distressed

During the 1850s Shakespeare's plays were performed by every actor and actress of importance, and scenes from his plays were favourite subjects for painters and engravers. The scene from *As You Like It*, of which a detail is reproduced here, was painted in 1854 by Daniel Maclise, who became famous for his frescoes of 'The Death of Nelson' and 'The Meeting of Wellington and Blücher' in the rebuilt House of Commons, but who also spent much of his working life painting scenes from Shakespeare. These were greatly admired by his close friend, Charles Dickens, whose portrait he painted in 1839.

(top left) Samuel Phelps and Isabella Glyn in *Hamlet*, Sadler's Wells, 1850

(top centre) Music front, 'The Ghost Melody', written for Dion Boucicault's *The Corsican Brothers*, Princess's Theatre, 1852

(top right) Scene from *The Courier of Lyons*, afterwards known as *The Lyons Mail*, by Charles Reade, Princess's Theatre, 1854

(above) E. A. Sothern as Lord Dundreary in *Our American Cousin*, by Tom Taylor, first performed in New York in 1858

(right) Helena Faucit, actress and wife of Theodore Martin, the biographer of the Prince Consort

(opposite, below) Photograph of Benjamin Webster as Triplet (standing left) and Mrs Stirling as Peg Woffington (standing right) and other members of the cast of *Masks and Faces*, by Charles Reade, Theatre Royal, Haymarket, 1852

Mark Lemon

(right) George Henry Lewes

(far right) 'George Eliot', Mary Ann Cross (née Evans), by F. W. Burton

fellow-writer. In the more ambitious productions, while the men were all amateurs, it was common practice to engage professional actresses. In his memoirs Edmund Yates describes how he and friends produced a whole pantomime, first performed in March 1855 on a Saturday night at the Olympic Theatre. By Royal command, with the Queen, the Prince Consort and the fourteen-year-old Prince of Wales in the audience, a further performance was given at Drury Lane. And indeed there were amateur theatricals all over the country, especially, then as later, in large country houses. During this happy decade of her reign Victoria herself appears to have enjoyed an evening of playgoing, watching amateurs or professionals. It is typical of the time that Yates, describing the amateur pantomime, is able to quote quite long, detailed, good-natured criticism by the leading critic of *The Times*, John Oxenford, an excellent scholar but too easy and anxious to please in his notices. There was indeed a lack of conscientious serious-minded drama critics. George Henry Lewes could be one, especially in his judgment of acting, but even he did not hesitate to give the stage about ten mediocre plays and farces from 1851 to 1856. Then he kept house with and devoted himself to George Eliot, who may have discouraged any more plays like *A Cozy Couple* or *Give a Dog a Bad Name*.

There is a question to be answered here. The 1850s saw the publication of some of the greatest novels of the century and some of its best miscellaneous writing. Yet their readers, when they turned themselves into playgoers, not only endured but warmly applauded so many plays that were nothing but hasty hack-work, and this at a time when the Continental theatre was making real progress. Why was this? Was it because the middle classes, on which the theatre largely depended, were all too often complacent, thick-skinned philistines? Possibly. But there is another reason, frequently overlooked. Towering above all contemporary plays were Shakespeare's both the comedies and the tragedies of the master dramatist, played constantly by every actor or actress of real importance; and it was the force and splendour of Shakespeare that drained serious interest out of contemporary work. This was a situation in which the English theatre found itself for a great many years. But it was seen at its worst in the 1850s. How could a busy journalist or civil servant, perhaps writing hastily for the Olympic Theatre, hope to be magnificently comic or deeply tragic if *Twelfth Night* was at the Haymarket and *Macbeth* at Drury Lane?

Something must be said about the theatres themselves. Covent Garden, where Macready had made his first appearance and Edmund Kean his last, was now remodelled as an opera house, where Balfe's *Bohemian Girl* and Wallace's *Maritana* were no longer novelties, both belonging to the 1840s. Covent Garden was burnt down in 1856, and the one that delights us now, because of superb acoustics apparently impossible to re-create, was built in 1858. In addition to Drury Lane and the Haymarket, there were in central London the Olympic, the Princess's, the Lyceum, the Adelphi and the Royal Strand Theatres. There were also playhouses of a sort on the Surrey side of the Thames and in the East End, described humorously by Dickens in *Household Words*. How many theatres there were up and down the country it is impossible – at least, for me – to say, but certainly there were a great many, probably three or four times as many as there are today. A great deal of melodramatic or farcical rubbish was served up in these theatres, especially in the smaller towns, but again there was always Shakespeare, with one great speech after another finding its way to the fourpenny galleries and the sixpenny pits.

This same December that saw the dismissal of Palmerston saw the burial, in St Paul's Cathedral, of a far greater Englishman – Joseph Mallord William Turner. Born as long ago as 1775, he was by 1851 an old man, a rather suspicious and eccentric and elusive old man, who for years had disliked 'good society' – though always generous and genial with fellow artists – and enjoyed being 'Captain Booth' or 'Puggy' in merry low company. In our *Dictionary of National Biography*, always severely respectable, his private life is called 'sordid and sensual', and sensual it may have been – after all, he was a great artist, not a monk – but the truth is, he was too continually and deeply pre-occupied with

'Katharina and Petruchio', a scene from *The Taming of the Shrew*, 1852, by Robert Braithwaite Martineau

The Adelphi Theatre

(left) A detail of an engraving of Weston's Music Hall, Holborn, 1857

Watching a Pantomime from the
gallery, *c.* 1860

his art, doing the work of ten men, to bother about respectability and
dining with the right people. He could stay happily in great houses if
the people there really cared about his pictures, and he could 'live
rough' and drink with sailors when it suited him and his work. What he
did in the end, working to satisfy himself, was to paint himself clean
out of his own time. His later pictures both in oil and watercolours (the
latter, to my mind, best of all) offer us the very elements and light
itself. Like the last compositions of Beethoven – and it is not entirely
fanciful to bring them together – they are among the wonders of this
world.

The work of the young painters who called themselves the Pre-
Raphaelite Brotherhood was now beginning to attract attention, for
the most part sharply unfavourable, even though it had John Ruskin for
its warmest admirer. Its three leading members were very different
characters, so that it is not surprising that the Brotherhood did not last
very long. (Unlike its general influence, which, as we shall see, came
to be widely spread throughout Victorian Britain.) These three were
Holman Hunt, John Everett Millais, and Dante Gabriel Rossetti. Hunt

Detail of 'Interior of Turner's Gallery: the artist showing his works', *c.* 1850, by George Jones

(opposite) Detail of 'Work', 1852–65, by Ford Madox Brown

was amazingly industrious and conscientious, solemn and rather puritanical. Millais, who had been a boy prodigy, was an unusually gifted, handsome fellow, too easy-going and worldly at heart to be a member of any Brotherhood very long. Rossetti, the son of an Italian exile, was the most dominating and remarkable of the three, with an almost hypnotic power of persuasion. Technically as a painter he was well behind the other two; but then he was also a poet (and I, for one, prefer his poetry to his painting); and so far as there was a general Pre-Raphaelite influence later, Rossetti was largely responsible for it.

What was central in the Brotherhood was 'Truth to Nature', which meant in effect – for in theory it can be made to mean anything– entirely realistic sharp detail in bright colouring. (They looked everywhere for the right details, and they covered their canvases first with a white ground to heighten their colour.) Along with 'Truth to Nature' went a number of rather vague aspirations – to reject popular Royal Academy subjects, to protest against the materialism of the age, to return in spirit to the Middle Ages, to bring imagination and romantic poetry to their careful details and high colouring. (At the same time, in these early pictures, they used each other and their families and friends as models, somewhat relentlessly.) Millais, the fastest worker, was the most prolific, and by the end of 1851 he had exhibited several ambitious paintings. The one that brought him most abuse – 'revolting' and 'loathsome' from *The Times* and a very silly attack by Dickens in

Victoria's Heyday

Household Words – was his realistic treatment of the Holy Family: the fine painting now called 'Christ in the House of His Parents'. Holman Hunt's 'The Hireling Shepherd' was begun in 1851 while Hunt, a slow worker, was staying in the country, but was not exhibited at the Royal Academy until 1852. It is a splendid picture but it illustrates the ironic weakness of the truth to Nature method, because it never suggests life on an English farm but some strange vivid scene in a dream of rural life. Somehow Ford Madox Brown, though very much an artist with design in mind, escaped this. He was a generous supporter of the Brotherhood and its members, but never joined it himself. Two of his rather rare easel pictures, for he was also a designer of murals and stained glass, namely his 'The Last of England' and 'Work', are among the best-known paintings of the 1850s. As for Rossetti and the general Pre-Raphaelite influence, I shall return to them in the later years of this decade, when they were far more in evidence.

A detail from 'Christ in the House of His Parents' by Sir John Everett Millais. Millais, Dante Gabriel Rossetti and Holman Hunt had formed the Pre-Raphaelite Brotherhood in 1848, and this controversial painting, begun in 1849 and exhibited at the Royal Academy in 1850, typified the sentimental realism at which the Pre-Raphaelites aimed, shocking people like Dickens.

At the end of the last chapter I said that Protestant indignation was so widespread, because the Pope had appointed bishops for English dioceses, that Parliament would have to notice it and take action. But what happened during the following months? Nothing. Then in August 1851 Parliament passed an Ecclesiastical Titles Bill, which prohibited Catholics from calling themselves English bishops in a territorial sense and fined them £100 for attempting it. But what happened then? Again nothing. The statute drifted on, a dead letter, until it was repealed in 1872. After issuing an engaging appeal 'to the reason and good feeling' of the English people, Cardinal Wiseman ruled unchallenged as the head of the Catholic hierarchy in England for another thirteen years, no doubt still enjoying during Lent no fewer than four courses of fish, including lobster salad.

1852

E ARLY THIS YEAR there was an invasion scare. The whole country was wondering what the French might do. This was not entirely absurd. After all, France now had an authoritarian government controlled by another Napoleon. He had under his command a comparatively large and well-equipped army. As a potential invader of England he had now one asset the first Napoleon had never possessed: he had steamships that could land troops anywhere along the southern English coast in one night. So Lord John Russell brought in a Militia Bill, giving local authorities the power to organize their own troops. But Lord John reckoned without the formidable Palmerston, now out of office because he had been recently dismissed as Foreign Minister. Ready for what he afterwards called his 'tit for tat with John Russell', Palmerston demanded in the House an amendment to create a militia on a national basis, carried his amendment and so defeated the Militia Bill, and brought the Whig Government crashing down. After some scratching around, the Tories formed a sketchy government, with Lord Derby leading it and Disraeli as Chancellor of the Exchequer. All this with Old Pam, still out of office and still the most popular politician in the country, sardonically looking on and biding his time.

Detail from 'The Hireling Shepherd' by William Holman Hunt, exhibited at the Royal Academy in 1852. Painted near the River Ewell in Surrey, it was Hunt's first picture with a moral. Doubtless most people interpreted it merely as a rustic couple engaged in love play while the sheep break out into a cornfield. But Hunt wrote that it was intended to be a 'rebuke to the sectarian vanities and vital negligences of the day'. The shepherd, he continued, typified 'the muddle-headed pastors who instead of performing their services to their flock – which is in constant peril – discuss vain questions of no value'. Thomas Carlyle saw the painting during a visit to the artist's studio in 1853 and described it as 'the greatest picture I have seen painted by any modern man'.

Queen Victoria was ready to welcome Lord Derby and his Tories, but she was sorry that Mr Disraeli was to be one of her chief ministers. She had not forgiven Mr Disraeli his bitter attacks, years before, on her 'dear Sir Robert Peel', and anyhow did not take to this over-dressed affected man. This is ironical if we remember that later this same Disraeli became her favourite party leader and Prime Minister. He knew exactly how to flatter and to soothe her. After she had published her Highland reminiscences, with almost sublime impudence he would begin appeals to her with 'We authors, ma'am'. In an England where hardly anybody really likes authors nearly everybody enjoys being regarded as one.

Throughout this year – and it explains Palmerston's high prestige, even though he held no office – there was an uneasy feeling that the national character might be suffering from long years of peace and successful trading. Were the English still the same people who had defied and finally brought down the mighty Napoleon? Or were they now going soft after too much easy living? (Such questions were being asked by journalists, the professional and middle class, certainly not by miners and ironworkers.) But about one man no questions had to be asked. He had himself defied, defeated, and brought down for good and all the mighty Napoleon. He was a living legend of the indomitable British spirit. This was of course the Duke of Wellington, whose hawkish profile was the most famous in Europe. In politics he had opposed every measure of decent reform, a pillar of iron holding up the wrong side. As head of the army he had held on to his belief that it must always be recruited from 'the scum of the earth', to be punished by the lash, that military education was unnecessary, that officers' promotions could be bought and sold. (Soon it would be proved in the Crimea that the army he left behind him had never been properly organized to fight a major campaign.) But all this, and much else, was forgotten when he died, quite unexpectedly, on 14 September 1852. He was a very old man, eighty-three, known to be not as erect and spry as he had been, but he had been around so long, was such a conspicuous and commanding figure in the national scene, that his sudden removal from it seemed a terrible public disaster. Just when so many people were wondering if there was any heroism, any martial spirit, left in English character, the Iron Duke himself had gone. No wonder his death and then his funeral, on a royal scale, were such tremendous events.

Benjamin Disraeli, 1st Earl of Beaconsfield

In a Memorandum written at Balmoral on 17 September Prince Albert commented:

> The death of the Duke of Wellington has deprived the country of her greatest man, the Crown of its most valuable servant and adviser, the Army of its main strength and support. We received the sad news on an expedition from Allt-na-Giuthasach to the Dhu Loch (one of the wildest and loneliest spots of the Highlands) at four o'clock yesterday afternoon. We hurried home to Allt-na-Giuthasach, and today here, where it became important to settle with Lord Derby the mode of providing for the command of the Army, and the filling up of the many posts and places which the Duke had held. . . . Victoria wishes the Army to mourn for the Duke as long as for a member of the Royal Family. . . .

I have before me two successive issues of the *Illustrated London News* for that September, each of them carrying black-bordered Wellington Supplements, and giving – with many illustrations – every possible detail of Wellington's life and triumphant career, sufficient material for a large volume. One surprising figure comes at the end of a feature entitled 'Wellington's Battles At One View'. In a total of sixty-two engagements, from the East Indies to Waterloo, there were about 100,000 casualties – 'of whom about 30,000 were killed, or died of wounds in the hospitals.' *Only 30,000 dead!* How surprised he would have been to learn that after a century, in the First World War, there were English generals who could have over 30,000 men killed trying to advance half a mile! Then, rising above the hundreds of thousands of words in the press, came Tennyson's 'Ode':

Bury the Great Duke
 With an empire's lamentation,
Let us bury the Great Duke
 To the noise of the mourning of a mighty nation . . .

But in fact there were many questions and endless talk about when and where and how the Duke was to be buried. There was to be a gigantic and very elaborate *funeral car*, as it was called, and, as Philip Guedalla tells us,

> Competing Government Departments hung like rival fairies above its cradle. The Lord Chamberlain was gravely exercised; the Board of Works had a word to say; the War Department intervened; and for some occult departmental reason the Board of Trade conceived the matter to be its own sole concern. . . .

While memoranda and minutes were being exchanged the Duke's body remained at Walmer Castle, where he had died, and it was not taken to London until 10 November, nearly two months after his death. There, in the hall of the Royal Military Hospital, hung with black and lit only with wax tapers, the coffin covered with red velvet stood on a platform, on which there was also a table glittering with all the Duke's decorations. Two hundred thousand people solemnly moved past it. The Queen never got so far as the coffin because she burst into tears and had to be led out to her carriage.

The public funeral – certainly the most spectacular event of this whole decade – took place on 18 November, after a night of heavy rain. There were dense but quiet crowds everywhere from Piccadilly to

Wellington's funeral car

Victoria's Heyday

St Paul's. Along with the military bands and muffled drums in the procession, there were three thousand infantrymen, eight squadrons of cavalry and three batteries of guns. High above the troops and the crowds was the immense funeral car, 27 feet long, all in black and gold with elaborate adornments of lions' heads, sabres, laurel wreaths, together with a display of real swords and muskets. Not everyone admired this impressive creation. Carlyle, for one, hated it:

> Of all the objects I ever saw the abominably ugliest, or nearly so. An incoherent huddle of expensive palls, flags, sheets, and gilt emblems and crosspoles, more like one of the street carts that hawk doormats than a bier for a hero . . . this vile *ne plus ultra* of Cockneyism; but poor Wellington lay dead beneath it faring dumb to his long home. . . .

The eye-witness account I prefer to quote here can be found in *The Life of Thomas Cooper: Written by Himself*, published in 1872. Cooper had been a Chartist poet and a fierce radical; so Wellington had been high among his political enemies. But this is what he wrote:

> The funeral of the Great Duke was the most impressively grand spectacle I ever beheld. . . . I witnessed the passing of the entire funeral procession, and the greater part of it twice. First, I got a place on the south side of the Green Park, near the Duke of Sutherland's, and saw the procession come up the Mall, from the Horse Guards. Then I crossed the Park, and got a standing-place opposite the Duke of Cambridge's – the house in which Lord Palmerston afterwards lived – and saw the slow march along Piccadilly. The pomp of the 'Dead March in Saul' was varied by some of the regimental bands playing 'Sicilian Mariners', and others Handel's 'Old Hundred-and-Fourth'. The varied costume of the English regiments mingled with the kilted Highlanders, and Lancers and Life Guards with the Scotch Greys, rendered the vision picturesque as well as stately.
>
> But it was upon the huge funeral car, and the led charger in front of it, that all eyes gazed most wistfully: – above all, it was upon the crimson-velvet covered coffin, *upon* the vast pall – not covered by it, borne aloft, on the car, with the white-plumed cocked hat, and the sword and marshal's baton lying upon the coffin, that all gazed most intently. I watched it – I stretched my neck to get the last sight of the car as it passed along Piccadilly, till it was out of sight; and then I thought the great connecting link of our national life was broken: the great actor in the scenes of the Peninsula and Waterloo – the conqueror of Napoleon – and the chief name in our home political life for many years – had disappeared. I seemed to myself to belong now to another generation of men; for my very childhood was passed amid the noise of Wellington's battles, and his name and existence seemed stamped on every year of our time.

One man who missed the 'grand spectacle' was Thackeray, now sharing the honours of fiction with Dickens. (The rivalry, which could be very sharp, was not so much between the novelists themselves as it was between their respective cliques of admirers.) Thackeray had sailed at the end of October for Boston on his first American lecture tour.

He was to repeat the lectures he had given in London and elsewhere on *The English Humorists of the Eighteenth Century*. These were successful as lectures and still make lively reading, but Thackeray was not another Hazlitt. Though well-acquainted with its literature, he had no naturally close understanding of the eighteenth century; his sensibility was very much of its own time; and his extremely personal prejudices discoloured much of his criticism. Though it meant a separation for some months from his two young daughters, left with their grandmother, Thackeray welcomed this American tour – and for two good reasons. First, he felt he needed the money it would bring him. He had these two girls to bring up, in the style of his upper-middle-class family, and he was also responsible for the care of his insane wife. (We have to remember two things whenever we consider William Makepeace Thackeray: that in his early twenties, through silly investments and gambling, he frittered away the reasonable fortune he had inherited; and that after only four years of a happy marriage his wife, the victim of puerperal fever, went

(above) Jane Brookfield

(right) William Makepeace Thackeray

out of her mind and never recovered her sanity.) So, entirely dependent on his writing, and never sure he could repeat a success, he felt he needed the money he could earn in America.

The second reason why he welcomed an entire change of scene was that he had been feeling deeply unhappy. For some years he had been in love with the wife of his friend, Brookfield, a cleverish attractive man, first a rather fashionable parson and then an inspector of schools. Jane Brookfield was a tall, fair woman, vivacious and notably charming, though she had not escaped the invalidism of so many middle-class wives whose husbands were away too often and when they were at home were too autocratic and demanding. She was genuinely devoted to Brookfield – and any physical relation with Thackeray was out of the question – but the constant and amusing company of the great novelist, whose adoration must have been quite obvious to her, banished her loneliness as well as his, and was altogether delightful. (Perhaps not *altogether* to him, if only because she was extremely desirable, and keeping sexuality in check must have been trying to him. In spite of his slack sedentary bulk – he was six feet four inches tall and heavily built – and in spite of his pretence, even in his forties, that he was already a white-headed old buffer beyond the temptations of Venus, there is at least an oral tradition that he was strongly sexed – and he had neither a wife nor a regular mistress.) Now when he and Jane Brookfield were seeing even more of each other than usual, during the time when the *English Humorists* lectures were being prepared and then delivered, Brookfield, who had been ill, was convalescing at the seaside. He felt neglected, began to be jealous, and finally told his wife she must remember her duty and must stop seeing Thackeray. Rather weakly she agreed, and they began to make plans to spend the winter out of England.

Thackeray wrote her a letter full of angry reproaches, but was persuaded by a friend of them both not to send it. But a letter written to other women friends, while less furiously scornful, shows us what he was feeling.

I wish that I had never loved her. I have been played with by a woman, and flung over at a beck from her lord and master – that's what I feel. I greet her tenderly and like a gentleman: I will fetch, carry, write, stop, what she pleases – but I leave her. I mean I will do what she wishes in decency and moderation – It's death I tell you between us. I was packing away yesterday the letters of years. These didn't make me cry. They made me laugh as I knew they would. It was for this that I gave my heart away. It was 'When are you coming dear Mr Thackeray,' and 'William will be so happy,' and 'I thought after you had gone away how I had forgot, etc.' and at a word from Brookfield afterwards it is 'I reverence and admire him with not merely a dutiful but a genuine love' – Amen. The thought that I have been made a fool of is the bitterest of all, perhaps – and a lucky thing for all it is perhaps that it should be so.

If we remember Thackeray's 'white-headed old buffer' persona, there is something surprisingly *young* about this letter, half-comic, half-pathetic. But his grievous sense of loss was very real, and stayed with him. For a normally reticent man, he was also surprisingly ready to refer to his lost love. His relationship with Jane Brookfield is important if we care about Thackeray's work because all his fiction later than *Vanity Fair* is deeply influenced by his private life. His best biographer, Professor Gordon N. Ray, to whom I am indebted here, has carefully traced the effect of what he calls Thackeray's 'buried life' on the shape, movement and tone of his novels.

In December 1852, in Boston with a newly-arrived copy of *Esmond* in his hand, Thackeray said to Fields the publisher: 'Here is the very *best* I can do.' And for the next forty years or so there were many critics ready to agree with him. For the first twenty years it was appreciated as yet another domestic novel, though one of a strange sort, fascinating but perhaps rather repellent. (The relationship between Lady Ravenswood and Esmond, both as youth and mature man, came in for some severe criticism.) After that, during the R. L. Stevenson era, it was admired enormously as a superbly written historical romance. Since then it has not enjoyed high favour, and now is perhaps as under-rated as it was

'Beatrix knighting Esmond', 1857, by Augustus Egg. Seventeenth-century costume was very popular during the last years of the 1850s and fancy dress balls reflecting this interest were not uncommon.

over-rated earlier. Much of it was written after the enforced separation from Jane Brookfield, and it destroys any notion that Thackeray was too easy-going and indolent. Whatever else it may or may not be, *Esmond* is an astonishing literary *tour de force*. As an attempt to re-create the age of Queen Anne, on a large scale too, it is a brilliant performance. But it leaves me, for one, with the same doubts I feel about the lectures on the eighteenth-century humorists. It is really Queen Victoria who is reigning, not Queen Anne. Thackeray can imitate the early eighteenth century, but his temperament and type of sensibility prevent him from feeling his way right inside it, identifying himself with it. In *Vanity Fair*, *Pendennis* and *The Newcomes* Thackeray is the man we know, the figure we recognize at once. In *Esmond* he is wearing a wig and a satin coat that belonged to somebody else.

An illustration by Thackeray to *Pendennis*

With *Esmond* out and greatly admired by all his friends, Thackeray began to enjoy himself in America, finding more to like and far less to dislike than most previous English authors had done. He was one visitor who put Boston below New York, where a society of wealthy but unaffected men, eager matrons, and pretty, self-confident girls, came as a pleasant surprise. (With one of the prettiest girls, Sally Baxter, aged nineteen, he enjoyed a kind of avuncular flirtation.) His lectures on the whole had large audiences and were well received, though the tour never reached the £4,000 he had been promised, only about £2,500. He was lionized everywhere, even though the press at times was quite savagely abusive – a fact that fails to surprise some of us. After New York, Boston, Providence, he went to friendly Philadelphia, and then down to Washington, which provided rather small audiences but excellent company, and Baltimore, where people were 'stupid beyond all stupidity'. Then he went into the South, spending all March lecturing in Richmond, Charleston and Savannah, but deciding against New Orleans because the journey there and back would take too long. However, he was already among the slave-owners and the slaves. The coloured folk, whom he observed at close quarters, amused him, and he was fond of sketching their impish children, but he certainly did not regard them as potential fellow-citizens. On slavery itself he took a cautious line, believing it to be wrong in principle though rarely detestable in practice, because the actual slaves he saw appeared to be well cared for and reasonably happy, more so than the worst victims of England's grim industrial system. Slavery might occasionally split up families, but then, as the planters argued, so did mid-Victorian industry.

It was probably a fellow novelist who made it hard for Thackeray to dodge the slavery issue. Earlier in 1852 Mrs Harriet Beecher Stowe's *Uncle Tom's Cabin; or Life Among the Lowly* burst upon the world. Originally a serial in a Washington anti-slavery paper, *Uncle Tom's Cabin* had a world success unequalled by any other work of fiction before or since its time. It came to have editions in thirty-seven languages;

and only the Bible, we are told, appeared in more versions. Soon there were Uncle Tom's Cabins, as restaurants, bars, shops and dairies, in streets throughout the world. Its propaganda value can hardly be over-estimated. In America it made the Fugitive Slave Law impossible to carry out properly and so helped to bring about the Civil War. (Lincoln once declared it was the *cause* of the Civil War.) Its popularity lasted so long that the first professional production I myself ever saw, as a small boy, was a dramatization of it. Mrs Stowe herself cannot be considered a great novelist, and nothing else she wrote ever created the same effect. Indeed, she could be downright silly, as in her *Sunny Memories of Foreign Lands*, which Macaulay in his diary for 1854 roundly condemns:

A mighty foolish, impertinent book this of Mrs Stowe. She puts into my mouth a great deal of stuff that I never uttered, particularly about Cathedrals. What blunders she makes! Robert Walpole for Horace Walpole. Shaftesbury, the author of the Habeas Corpus Act, she confounds with Shaftesbury, the author of the *Characteristics*. She cannot even see. Palmerston, whose eyes are sky-blue, she calls dark-eyed. I am glad that I met her so seldom, and sorry I met her at all.

But then poor Mrs Stowe was a long way from home and floundering out of her depth.

Uncle Tom's Cabin is a very different matter from her encounters with the great in *Sunny Memories*. Let us return briefly to Macaulay in October 1852:

I finished *Uncle Tom's Cabin*; a powerful and disagreeable book; too dark and Spagnoletto-like for my taste, when considered as a work of art. But, on the whole, it is the most valuable addition that America has made to English Literature.

An odd conclusion. Questioned by an American girl visitor, Dickens told her that *Uncle Tom's Cabin* was a story of much power but scarcely a work of art, and that while he liked what he saw of the coloured people in the States he thought that Mrs Stowe had made them – and especially Uncle Tom himself – impossibly virtuous. But then from girlhood she had longed to serve a great cause, and she had found it in the anti-slavery or abolitionist movement and become a burning enthusiast. This enthusiasm provided her with a kind of rough genius in assembling the material of her tale and then telling it with such force. It has many familiar ingredients of mid-Victorian sentimental melodrama – desperate escapes, deathbeds, noble self-sacrifice and terrible brutality – but all brought together in a new setting, with slave-owning and slave-freeing glaring at each other.

Oddly enough, Mrs Stowe had seen less of the South than even Thackeray had. She was born (in 1811) and brought up in New England, the daughter of a preacher and teacher, but in 1832 she went with her parents to Cincinnati, where she married another teacher, Calvin

(below) A dramatization of Mrs Harriet Beecher Stowe's book, *Uncle Tom's Cabin*, Olympic Theatre, 1852

(bottom) Mrs Mary E. Webb reading *Uncle Tom's Cabin* in the Hall of Stafford House, London

Stowe, who had poor health, so that she had to earn some extra money by writing. Just across the Ohio River was Kentucky, a slave state, and she was able to visit plantations there and make the acquaintance of Southerners and their slaves. Moreover, runaway slaves kept crossing the river (like her Eliza, desperately jumping from one ice floe to another), and living as she did, both in Cincinnati and then later again in New England, among enthusiastic abolitionists, she knew all about runaway slaves and the attempts both to hide them and to recapture them. So she had ample material at her command, even though she had no first-hand experience of the South itself. She might be unashamedly sentimental-melodramatic and ready at any moment to denounce the institution of slavery, but she tactfully avoided the crudest propaganda. Her Southern planters and slave-owners have their faults but they are presented with some sympathy. The one brute among them, the villain of the piece, Simon Legree, is in fact not a Southerner at all but a New Englander, originally from Vermont. Her chief coloured folk, with poor Uncle Tom at the head of them, might be – as Dickens suggested – altogether too virtuous, too noble, but this was at least a decided change from showing them either as degraded wretches or as small-part comedians. She made the whole world look at them *as people*. After her triumphant (Macaulay notwithstanding) visit to England, where Thackeray found her 'a gentle almost pretty person with a very great sweetness in her eyes and smile', she returned to New England and wrote hard and gave public readings almost to the end of her long life (she died in 1896). She never created another Uncle Tom, but she could tell herself that she had written the most widely-read and perhaps the most influential novel of the nineteenth century. And among her most fervent admirers was another novelist of rather more weight, range and durability – his name was Leo Tolstoy.

Mrs Harriet Beecher Stowe

A term emerged this year that was soon to be a battle cry and after that an explanation of everything. It was 'Evolution'. The word itself had of course been in common use among educated men for a long time. But as a term for a systematic universal development, an unceasing progress towards perfection, it was new and exciting. We associate it with Darwin, but in fact his *Origin of Species* was not published until 1859. The man who introduced the term to the public in 1852 was Herbert Spencer, who was contributing occasional articles to *The Leader*, a radical journal, and it was in the most important of these, the 'Development Hypothesis', that readers discovered Spencer's *evolution*. Long before the end of the century, grinding away at his evolutionary thesis, Spencer was to achieve a world-wide reputation as a philosopher. He became the favourite philosopher, indeed the only philosopher, of millions who, like Spencer himself, never studied the masters of philosophy. In 1852 he was only in his early thirties, and his first book, *Social Statics*, had come out at the beginning of the previous year. It had been very well received, chiefly because it produced a multitude of reasons – as Spencer was apt to do – to justify hard-faced men's prejudices. It was *laissez-faire* taken into the blue yonder. It was individualism pushed to the limit. It argued that the state should maintain an army and navy and a police force and magistracy, and do nothing else except collect a few taxes, and even these a citizen could rightly refuse to pay if he declared he wanted no protection from the state. The state must not control or interfere with anything, from education to sanitation; all government inspectorships must be abolished; people must be left to settle their own affairs. It was an ideal system for about a hundred high-minded persons settled on a South Seas island.

Spencer had not set out to please Lancashire cotton-spinners or owners of East End sweatshops. He wrote in all innocence, blindly following his ponderous but inadequate reasoning. But again, quite innocently, he gave a sinister edge to Darwinism, for it was he, not Darwin, not Wallace, not Huxley, who coined the phrase 'the survival of the fittest', which soon inspired greedy and ruthless imperialists and darkened history. The later nineteenth century would have been happier without Spencer's ingenuous rationalizing. He set whole new nations off on the wrong foot. Even now I could be accused of being frivolous if I said that he seems to me more successful as a giant comic character than as a serious philosopher. Quite early he suffered – and now I quote the *Dictionary of National Biography* – from 'a nervous breakdown from which he never afterwards recovered. The disorder took the form of a peculiar sensation in the head, which came on when he tried to think, as a result of cerebral congestion. . . .' It prevented him too from reading hard or writing systematically. Later he employed industrious researchers, in his quest for masses of facts, and he would dictate for short spells while fishing or playing billiards at his club. Later still, while dining out, he would use ear-plugs to protect himself from talk that might be either too boring or too exciting. He could not even take to playing cards: they also were too exciting. It is not surprising that he never married, nor that the book about him by the two elderly ladies with whom he lodged, *Home Life with Herbert Spencer*, should be almost a classic of unintentional comedy.

However, there were strong rumours in 1852 that Spencer might marry Mary Ann Evans, not then transformed into George Eliot. They were often seen walking by the Thames, near Somerset House, and even at places of amusement together. (Indeed, they actually *sang together*.) He admits this in his autobiography, much of it written many years before it was published, and tells us there were definite reports that he was in love with her, and that they were about to be married. But neither of these reports, he adds firmly, was true. Certainly

Herbert Spencer

his characteristic account of her does not suggest a Romeo describing his Juliet, an Antony his Cleopatra:

> In physique there was, perhaps, a trace of that masculinity characterizing her intellect; for though but of the ordinary feminine height she was strongly built. The head, too, was larger than usual in women. It had, moreover, a peculiarity distinguishing it from most heads, whether feminine or masculine; namely that its contour was very regular. Usually, heads have here and there either flat places or slight hollows; but her head was everywhere convex. Striking by its power when in repose, her face was remarkably transfigured by a smile. The smiles of many are signs of nothing more than amusement; but with her smile there was habitually mingled an expression of sympathy, either for the person smiled at or the person smiled with. . . . Her philosophical powers were remarkable. I have known but few men with whom I could discuss a question in philosophy with more satisfaction. Capacity for abstract thinking is rarely found along with capacity for concrete representation, even in men; and among women, such a union of the two as existed in her, has, I should think, never been paralleled.
>
> In early days she was, I believe, sometimes vivacious; but she was not so when I first knew her, nor afterwards. Probably this was the reason why the wit and the humour which from time to time gave signs of their presence, were not frequently displayed. Calmness was an habitual trait. There was never any indication of mental excitement, still less of mental strain; but the impression constantly produced was that of latent power – the ideas which came from her being manifestly the products of a large intelligence working easily. And yet this large intelligence working easily, of which she must have been conscious, was not marked by any marked self-confidence. Difference of opinion she frequently expressed in a half apologetic manner. . . .

In this account of a woman who was at least for a time a very close friend, it seems to me there can be found almost everything that was wrong with Herbert Spencer: it is ponderous, humourless, too abstract, and never comes to life.

Both foreign and domestic politics were more eventful during the last weeks of 1852. After another carefully stage-managed plebiscite the Louis Napoleon who used to haunt London drawing-rooms was officially proclaimed 'hereditary Emperor of the French' on 2 December. He was now Napoleon III, and the English who crossed the Channel found themselves in the Second Empire, a queer mixture of champagne-gaiety and suppression and censorship. Next year the new emperor would cleverly avoid international complications by marrying away from royalty into the Spanish nobility, his bride being the beautiful and very durable Eugénie de Montijo. (I caught a glimpse of her, a little old woman in a carriage, while route-marching in Surrey in the autumn of 1914.) And not very long after that, by charm, by flattery, by picturesque fuss, Napoleon III would have swept away all Victoria's prejudice against him.

Another future charmer, Disraeli, went down instead of up, later that December. His first budget, increasing taxation, was rejected by the House of Commons and brought down Lord Derby's Tory government. Not himself a Whig but a Peelite, Lord Aberdeen, much liked by the Queen but rather unpopular in the House, consented to scrape together a coalition government. It was impossible to leave Palmerston out – he was far too formidable – but Aberdeen could not see himself going to the Queen to tell her that Palmerston was her Foreign Minister again. Yet something had to be done with him, so he was asked to be Home Secretary. Oddly enough, when we remember that this type of administration was entirely new to him and that he was now an old man, Palmerston proved to be an uncommonly good Home Secretary, working hard to improve conditions, especially in prisons and factories. (But then the greatest social reformer of the age, the noble Lord Shaftesbury, was through the accident of marriage his stepson, probably his constant adviser.) Unlike many Home Secretaries, Old Pam knew how to handle men, and was a great hand at receiving – and dismissing – deputations with a smile and a joke. Disraeli's 'old painted pantaloon with false teeth' was surprising everybody again, and it would not be long before Disraeli would have to eat some of his words, because the old man who was finished would be Prime Minister.

Lord Shaftesbury

1853

THIS IS ONE of those years that seem relatively uneventful, but it might be compared to some quiet field in which seeds of discord and future tragic clashes have been deeply sown. We can discover this first in foreign affairs. When the year opened it was still Napoleon III and the French who were regarded with sharp suspicion. (It was even thought they might capture the Channel Isles.) But then the green limelight, to illuminate villainy, moved to the East, settling upon Tsar Nicholas and his Russian hordes. There had to be an Enemy – the press and the public demanded one – and here it was. But if there was 'a baddy' then there must be 'a goody', the man in the Western who wears a white hat instead of a black. So Turkey, now being hard-pressed by Russia, had to fill the role. Apart from certain strategical considerations – for Russia could not be allowed to control the Dardanelles and the passage from the Black Sea to the Mediterranean – Turkey was an odd choice as an innocent victim, to be enthusiastically supported by Christian chivalry and a democratic people.

If the Russian Empire was a despotism, so was the Turkish Empire – indeed, probably an even worse one. It was a ramshackle affair, and its break-up had been expected for years. But it had some very influential friends in England. The chief of them was Sir Stratford Canning, who had spent many years as Ambassador in Constantinople and believed the decaying Empire could be saved by some projected reforms, which he knew and understood because he enjoyed the confidence of the political group that had planned them. Moreover, he was on the worst of terms with Russia, where he was detested. Given a peerage, now as Lord Stratford he was sent out again to the embassy in Constantinople. If Lord Aberdeen, the premier, and his Foreign Office advisers looked for a peaceful solution of the Russian-Turkish problem, as they undoubtedly did, this was a curiously bad move, in spite of Lord Stratford's expertise. He was notoriously high-handed and quite capable of taking action, on an international level, without any brief from the government he represented. In this mid-Victorian world, when communication was often still slow and difficult, bold spirited ambassadors enjoyed an independence they have entirely lost today, and no other diplomat relished this more than Lord Stratford.

Another friend of Turkey (and of Stratford, who had formerly been his patron) was Henry Layard, the now famous excavator of Nineveh.

'The New Recruit' (detail), c. 1850, by William Powell Frith

Victoria's Heyday

In the late 1840s he had published an account of his first excavations, *Nineveh and its Remains*, that had created a sensation. Now in 1853 he described his second series of excavations, and *Nineveh and Babylon* brought him more wide notice and honours. Meanwhile, being an energetic and ambitious man, he had won a seat in Parliament, and during the earlier months of this year he was Under-Secretary for Foreign Affairs, probably because he was regarded as an expert on the confused politics of the Near East. Then he too was sent out to Constantinople, spent some time roaming around the western shore of the Black Sea, and stayed long enough to see something of the Crimean War and then, later, to give some fierce evidence to the Committee of Inquiry. He had many interests outside archaeology and politics. During these years, when he was a determined radical reformer, he had a far greater reputation as an archaeologist than as a politician. But later opinion considered him to be too rough-and-ready an excavator (he cut up precious tablets of cuneiform inscriptions and gave them away as presents) to be a true archaeologist, and perhaps there is now more to be said for his politics. At the time of the Crimean inquiry, Dickens, who had known Layard for some years, called him 'the most useful man in England' and enlisted all the more radical journalists he knew in a campaign to fight for Layard.

Sir Austen Henry Layard

Russian pressure on Turkey increased, the Tsar insisting that he should be recognized by treaty as the official protector of Christian subjects under Turkish rule: at this time a considerable part of South-Eastern Europe belonged to the Turkish Empire. With Lord Stratford probably at his elbow, the Sultan denounced and utterly rejected the Tsar's demand. France had made a similar demand only the year before, but now Napoleon III swung round behind Turkey, and soon the French fleet was sailing east. Lord Aberdeen was hoping for an alliance with Austria, to avert war, but with the exception of *The Times*, which supported Aberdeen's policy, most of the press believed that the Austrian Empire was in league with the Russian, and was further exasperated by the fact that while France had made a spectacular move Britain had done nothing. Palmerston, who was just the man for this situation, was still caged in the Home Office. Russia invaded and then occupied the Danubian provinces of the Turkish Empire, which, counting on French and English support, declared war. In November, when the English fleet as well as the French was not far away, the Russians engaged and largely destroyed the Turkish fleet at Sinope on the Black Sea. The English and French fleets remained in the Black Sea while the Russian ships took refuge beneath the guns of the fortress of Sebastopol.

Needless to say, this is the very barest outline of events, omitting all the moves and countermoves of a bewildered diplomacy, with Aberdeen and his new Foreign Secretary, Clarendon, still anxious for a peaceful settlement but finding themselves drifting towards war. The Tsar had

Prince Albert

not the least desire to challenge this Franco-British alliance: what he wanted to do now was to save his face. It was the Turks who were increasingly belligerent, thanks not only to Lord Stratford but also to the rising force of public opinion in the West. The Turks were now the heroes of the British press and its readers. A Turkish Empire that had been dismissed with contempt for years was now discovered to be on the point of reforming itself, to be rich in products that Britain needed, to be an ally as valuable as it was gallant. The Tsar was 'a fiend in human shape'. *The Times*, still struggling along with Lord Aberdeen, was a dog returning daily 'to its vomit'. Behind all this, behind the mass meetings of protests against Aberdeen and his government (always excepting Palmerston) was a people tired of a peace that had lasted nearly forty years, and longing for the excitement of a major war. In December Palmerston temporarily resigned from the government, though he rejoined it before the year was out. His motives were mixed and rather mysterious, and it is just possible there was some Royal interference that he resented. Remembering his dismissal in 1851, his enthusiastic admirers, inside and outside the press, were certain he had been the victim of 'courtly distastes and Coburg intrigues'. Such phrases pointed straight at Prince Albert, who now became the most unpopular man in the country.

So the year closed stormily for Queen Victoria, who sent one indignant protest after another to Lord Aberdeen. She deeply resented '*systematic* and *most infamous*' attacks upon her husband. Again: 'A woman *must have* a support and an adviser; and *who can this properly* be but her husband, *whose duty it is to watch over her interests private and public*.' In a further letter to Aberdeen, she went beyond complaint and protest: 'The Queen has been *seriously* meditating *not* to open Parliament in person, as she did not wish, and *could not expose* herself to *some insult*, which she thought might possibly be offered to the Prince and herself on their procession through the streets to the House of Lords.' She did open Parliament, but these attacks on her beloved husband hardened her resolution that the title of 'Prince Consort', already in common use, should be officially bestowed upon him – 'with the highest rank in and out of Parliament, *immediately* after the Queen, before *every other prince* of the Royal Family. . . .' In this she would have her way, but she would have to wait some time.

The most notable event in domestic politics occurred in April, when Gladstone introduced his first budget, considered by some political historians to be his best. History being crammed with ironies, we should not be surprised to learn that this masterpiece of far-sighted finance, designed to cover several years, had to be drastically changed, to cope with the cost of the Crimean War, the very next year. In introducing it, the D.N.B. tells us, 'Gladstone spoke for five hours, and for felicity of phrase, lucidity of arrangement, historical interest, and logical cogency of argument, his statement has never been surpassed.' It repealed the soap tax, lowered the duty on tea, and left a very large number of articles of food entirely free of tax. The duty on advertisements, which had hindered the growth of the press, was reduced by two-thirds. At Gladstone's income-tax plans we can only gape with envy. Income tax would remain at sevenpence in the pound for the next two years; from April 1855 to April 1857 it would be sixpence; then from 1857 to 1860 it would be fivepence; and after that, the millennium having arrived, there would be no income tax at all. In his wonderful five-hour speech Gladstone must have assumed that nothing much could happen, to put a strain on the nation's resources, between 1853 and 1860 – and indeed for ever afterwards; and, as we know, he was quite wrong. But this would not diminish the splendour of his first Budget Day in 1853. Though there have recently been many objections to this annual and very solemn Budget performance, Parliament still insists on its being carried out in all its tedious details. It is – and has been for the last two-and-a-half centuries – Parliament's idea of a work of art.

In October this year Frederick Denison Maurice was dismissed from his professorship at King's College, London. Maurice is largely forgotten now, but he was an important and influential figure in mid-Victorian England. At Cambridge he read law, but soon afterwards he was greatly influenced by Coleridge (though they never seem to have met), became more and more deeply interested in theology, philosophy, political theory, and was active as an intellectual journalist. He took a line of his own, being equally opposed to church-and-state Toryism and to the rationalist and radical outlook of Bentham's disciples. Later, after being ordained into the Church of England at Oxford, he became the leader of the small but influential group of Christian Socialists. Now he was dismissed from London University because in his *Theological Essays*, published in 1853, he had declared that the popular belief in endless future punishment was mere superstition. He realized – what many people have not realized to this day – that eternity must not be confused with an indefinite duration of time, the eternal being outside passing time. For flouting orthodoxy in this fashion Maurice was not even allowed to finish the course of lectures he had been giving: he was *out*. This was a blow even on the lowest level, for Maurice had no private income and had to earn a living. But he had many distinguished friends, among them Tennyson, who addressed a fine poem 'To the Rev. F. D. Maurice':

> For, being of that honest few,
> Who give the Fiend himself his due,
>   Should eighty-thousand college-councils
> Thunder 'Anathema', friend, at you;

> Should all our churchmen foam in spite
> At you, so careful of the right,
>   Yet one lay-hearth would give you welcome
>   (Take it and come) to the Isle of Wight . . . .

proving again that Tennyson was not the complacent Establishment figure he is all too often supposed to be.

This arbitrary dismissal of Maurice, a man who combined unusual modesty and delicacy with a sturdily independent mind, is important because it helps us to appreciate the mental atmosphere of the 1850s.

Arthur Hugh Clough

Ever since Strachey's *Eminent Victorians* the earnest religious debates, the doubts and perplexities, of this age have been good for a giggle. (One of Strachey's chief butts, Clough, was a highly original poet, often writing well ahead of his time.) In this matter Strachey, and even more the 'de-bunkers' of the 1920s, seem to lack imagination. They stand well outside the mid-Victorian age, try to drag out of it a few amusing oddities or shrug their shoulders. After all, it cost Lytton Strachey nothing to be elaborately ironical, whereas it cost Maurice his professorship to make an honest statement; and many other men, whether they moved towards Rome or rationalism, risked even more than he did. There was endless religious discussion and private talk in these 1850s, and most of it carried a highly emotional charge. There was no settling down then to a cool scepticism or (a term not coined by Huxley yet) agnosticism: your immortal soul might be at stake, your whole peace of mind, your spiritual or intellectual integrity, or, for that matter, your professional chair, your college fellowship, your headmaster's study or your vicarage. If we seem so much more tolerant now, this is not because we have achieved tolerance (try us on communism, capitalism, racial questions, abortion and the like) but because we are not always thinking about religion and have not spent weeks, months, years, torn between our faith and our doubts: a battle is still on, but in a different war.

Orthodoxy had stiffened and hardened because it was now being constantly challenged. The great challenge would come at the end of this decade, with Darwin's *Origin of Species*, but the biblical account of the creation of the world, on which orthodox Anglicans and the Nonconformists took their stand, had been under attack, direct or indirect, before the 1850s. For example, Robert Chambers's *Vestiges of Creation*, published anonymously in 1844, combined information in a popular style with evolutionary theory. In it 'Man considered zoologically, and without regard to the distinct character assigned to him by theology, simply takes his place as the type of all types of the animal kingdom'; or again: 'The masses of space are formed by law; law makes them in due time theatres of existence for plants and animals; sensation, disposition, intellect, are all in like manner developed and sustained in action by law.' This was a long way from Genesis, and as one edition of *Vestiges of Creation* followed another – strong disapproval working as hard for a book as any praise – its author was denounced in the press, from the pulpit, in countless drawing rooms and parlours, as a blasphemer and a monstrous atheist.

In 1853 itself Harriet Martineau's translation of Comte's *Philosophie Positive* appeared – a work capable of driving any excitable theologian into a frenzy. George Eliot was busy translating Feuerbach's *Essence of Christianity*, in which our common fears and hopes take the place of divine revelation – not an attitude of mind that could expect a hearty welcome in the 14,000-odd Church of England churches or the 17-18,000 Nonconformist chapels. Liberal Bible criticism and downright rationalism, coming mostly from Germany, was creeping into the country, not only challenging Genesis, like the geologists and biologists, but the Christian Faith itself. For years now – indeed, ever since the Oxford or Tractarian Movement began in the 1830s – theology and doctrinal differences had provided news, together with quarrelsome tracts and angry letters to *The Times*, for educated readers. After Newman's conversion to Rome in 1845, there was a drift towards Catholicism that Pusey, the most learned and energetic of the High Anglicans, could not halt. Twenty years before there had not been a single convent in London, but by the middle 1850s there were nineteen religious houses, two for men and seventeen for nuns. So the Church of England had now to fight a war on two fronts, having to face rationalism on one side and Rome on the other. This would have been bad enough if the Church itself had been strongly unified, one solid fortress ready to repel all besiegers. But it was not, being itself fairly sharply divided into High, Low and Broad, so that even the faithful wore three different faces. The High and Low were equally intolerant. The High – or 'Puseyite' as it was often called – existed on a narrow edge, only a few steps away from Roman Catholicism, and was elaborately ritualistic and

Harriet Martineau

Edward Bouverie Pusey

largely responsible for the new interest in the Middle Ages. The Low was evangelical, passionately devoted to the Bible, sudden conversions, and good works on a rather gloomy level. Both High and Low despised the Broad, which tended to be latitudinarian, very much a vogue term then. Its members were such poor haters, so smilingly easy-minded and tolerant that both High and Low felt they could not be really Christians at all.

The endless religious discussion, taking place on all social levels except the lowest (where people wondered how to get a square meal, a pot of beer, a nip of gin), the wrangling of the intolerant sects, the deep concern, among so many funerals, about the after-life and the destiny of the soul, all this created an atmosphere that was very strange and peculiar to these years. It was intensely charged with emotion. Except on the level of professional theologians and scholars, almost lost to sight in the works of the Early Fathers, it was an atmosphere that encouraged the mawkish and the morbid. Sensible people felt out of place in it, as if they were still taking brisk walks in a plague-stricken city. So thick, so strong, was this atmosphere in the 1850s that it let loose a flood of religious fiction. Bookshops, railway bookstalls, lending libraries were crammed with it. Publishers and printers worked overtime to deliver it. What tales of sex and espionage, detectives and gangsters and cowboys, are to us, the religious novel was to them. And now, like so many characters in these novels, I too have something to confess. While decently dutiful, anxious to help my readers, I could not risk going out of my mind while wading through the religious fiction of the 1850s. Except where well-known writers are concerned, I am indebted for much of what follows to Margaret M. Maison's survey of the Victorian religious novel, called *Search Your Soul, Eustace*, a rather frivolous title for what is a sensible account of a wide range of fiction, mostly bad.

In this decade it was the High Church storytellers who were out in front, as we shall see. But even Low Church writers, even Dissenters, who had previously believed that reading novels was nearly as sinful as going to the theatre, decided that fiction, if it were chiefly concerned with spiritual matters and did not pander to vulgar taste, might do much good. Novelists from each sect wrote strictly and severely from its point of view, avoiding any taint of latitudinarianism. Their heroes might arrive at a spiritual crisis but would be rescued from damnation, often just in time, by some angelic clergyman or by the love of a woman steadfast in her faith. Backsliders and faith-losers became the victims of 'dissipation' and 'profligacy', never described in detail, and inevitably came to a bad end, sometimes being hanged at Newgate. (One was eaten by rats.) These novelists did not cast the first stone, they hurled huge rocks at their sinners. Temptation abounded, provided in High Church novels by Jesuits (artfully villainous everywhere), by vulgar Low Church types, by blasphemous rationalists; and in Low Church novels also by rationalists and by High Church curates, artful slimy creatures whose

'The Vale of Rest', 1858–59, by Sir John Everett Millais

hands were too white, and their voices too seductive. There had to be a continual searching of the conscience, especially by the High Church heroes, modelled on the Tractarian young men at Oxford in the 1830s, when they reproached themselves bitterly for having taken a piece of sponge cake instead of bread and butter.

Allow me to quote Dr Maison here:

> But Guy in his desire to overcome his failings goes further than any previous Tractarian hero in his scrupulous self-examination and self-distrust. He is indeed a genuine self-tormentor, inspecting his tiniest faults and analysing every motive. His 'habit of perverse and morbid intro-spection' frequently produces sudden violent storms of self-accusation: 'Selfish! Selfish! Selfish! oneself the first object. That is the root. . . .'

This is Sir Guy Morville, the hero, doomed to an early death by sheer goodness, of the most popular novel of the whole age, Charlotte Yonge's *Heir of Redclyffe*. Its popularity left Dickens and Thackeray far behind. It was not confined to the usual readers of High Church fiction; it was read eagerly by officers in the Crimea; it was admired by men like Rossetti and William Morris. First published in 1853, it went through edition after edition during the next thirty years, and a missionary schooner was fitted out from its profits. John Keble was Charlotte Yonge's neighbour and spiritual mentor – she was obedience itself – and there was some fear 'that the book might be felt to be too daring.' But though the breadth and force of its appeal may puzzle us now, it was just right for its own age. Where other religious novelists simply brought piety and prejudice to their work, Charlotte Yonge brought some originality and a novelist's imagination.

For once, *The Heir of Redclyffe* took the religious novel out of vestries and vicarages. It might be permeated by Tractarian soul-searching and

Detail of 'Convent Thoughts', 1851,
by Charles Collins

rather neurotic religiosity, but the simple story it told was highly effective. It had a real High Church hero in Sir Guy, a devoted heroine in Amy, at least half a villain in sneering Cousin Philip. It had false accusations, misunderstanding, rehabilitation and noble self-sacrifice, with Guy catching fever after gallantly nursing Philip. It had of course a deathbed scene but one far superior to the routine deathbed of religious fiction. The story could even go beyond the death and the funeral. So, when poor widowed Amy is looking through Guy's papers,

> She was studying not his intellect, but his soul; she did not care whether he would have been a poet, what she looked for was the record of the sufferings and struggles of the sad six months when his character was established, strengthened and settled.
>
> She found it. There was much to which she alone had the clue, too deep, and too obscurely hinted, to be understood at a glance. She met with such evidence of suffering as made her shudder and weep, tokens of the dark thoughts that had gathered round him, of the manful spirit of penitence and patience that had been his stay, and of the gleams that lighted his darkest hours, and showed that he had never been quite forsaken. . . .

Another popular novel of the period, Dinah Mulock's *John Halifax, Gentleman*, already mentioned, was a social and domestic tale, not to be classed as one of the religious novels, yet so strong was the atmosphere of that time that a young husband of a very young pregnant wife talks in this fashion:

> 'I wonder,' he said at last, 'if, when I was born, *my* father was as young as I am: whether he felt as I do now. You cannot think what an awful joy it is to be looking forward to a child; a little soul of God's giving, to be made fit for His eternity. How shall we do it! We that are both so ignorant, so young – she will be only just nineteen when, please God, her baby is born. Sometimes, of an evening, we sit for hours on this bench, she and I, talking of what we ought to do, and how we ought to rear the little thing, until we fall into silence, awed at the blessing that is coming to us.'

But while this is priggish and unduly solemn, it is not downright mawkish. However, there was so much of the mawkish and the morbid that it could find its way, dropping its tears on every page, even into school stories.

I am not thinking now of *Tom Brown's Schooldays*, which arrived during these years, to be reprinted over and over again, for its author, Thomas Hughes, like his friend Charles Kingsley, belonged to the 'muscular' section of the Broad Church. But among my readers there must be some seniors who remember, as I do, reading as a small boy Farrar's *Eric, or Little by Little*. Essentially a Low Church evangelical school story, it is a dreadful affair, but I must admit that for one small boy it had a certain horrible fascination. Though perfectly brought up, Eric could not resist temptation once he was in his 'teens at a public school. He began using rude words and cribbing; this led to lying and stealing; and little by little he went down and down until he was smoking

'Prayer Time', by Charles West Cope, 1854, sums up the Victorian ideal of domesticity, with strong religious undertones. Cope was a genuinely lyrical painter of small domestic cameos, mostly on the mother-and-child theme. Other characteristic examples of his work were 'Beneficence', which shows a girl helping her father up the steps of a church, and 'Palpitation', which shows a young woman waiting for the postman.

cigars and a victim of the 'deadly habit of tippling'. It was not long before a wasted and ruined Eric was lying on his deathbed, which Farrar must have had in his mind all the time:

> They gathered round him, they soothed, and comforted, and prayed for him; but his soul refused comfort, and all his strength appeared to have been broken down at once like a feeble reed. At last a momentary energy returned; his eyes were lifted to the gloaming heaven, where a few stars had already begun to shine, and a bright look illuminated his countenance. They listened deeply – 'Yes, mother,' he murmured, in broken tones, 'forgiven now, for Christ's dear sake. Oh, Thou merciful God! Yes, there they are, and we shall meet again. Verny – oh, happy, happy at last – too happy!'
>
> The sounds died away, and his head fell back; for a transient moment more the smile and the brightness played over his fair features like a lambent flame. It passed away, and Eric was with those he dearliest loved, in the land where there is no more curse.
>
> 'Yes, dearest Eric, forgiven and happy now,' sobbed Mrs Trevor, and her tears fell fast upon the dead boy's face, as she pressed upon it a long, last kiss.

It is honest emotion, sympathy, empathy, being raped. While there were men at the time who realized this, the story was responsible for many conversions, and the edition lent to me at least sixty-five years ago was not an old one and had been quite recently illustrated. And there must have been scores and scores of religious novels in the 1850s as lachrymose and mawkish, morbid and false, as *Eric, or Little by Little*.

However, it was the silly Low Church evangelical novels that by their bad example encouraged George Eliot to write fiction. She had been very severe with them in an article in the *Westminster Review*, from which I take some extracts:

> A more numerous class of silly novels than the oracular (which are generally inspired by some form of High Church, or transcendental Christianity) is what we might call the *white neck-cloth* species, which represent the tone of thought and feeling in the Evangelical party. This species is a kind of genteel tract on a large scale, intended as a medicinal sweetmeat for Low Church young ladies; an Evangelical substitute for the fashionable novel. . . . Thus, for Evangelical young ladies there are Evangelical love stories, in which the vicissitudes of the tender passion are sanctified by saving views of Regeneration and the Atonement. . . . The Orlando of Evangelical literature is the young curate, looked at from the point of view of the middle class, where cambric bands are understood to have as thrilling an effect on the hearts of young ladies as epaulettes have in the classes above and below it. In the ordinary type of these novels, the hero is almost sure to be a young curate, frowned upon, perhaps, by worldly mammas, but carrying captive the hearts of their daughters, who can 'never forget *that* sermon'; tender glances are seized from the pulpit stairs instead of the opera box; *tête-à-têtes* are seasoned with quotations from Scriptures, instead of quotations from the poets; and questions as

'Old Schoolfellows', by Alfred Rankley, was exhibited at the Royal Academy in 1855. The catalogue entry included a quotation from the *Book of Proverbs*: 'A friend loveth at all times, and a brother is born for adversity'. The invalid old school-fellow's embrace, his prosperous friend's handclasp, and the proffered banknote, all testify to an extra-ordinarily un-self-conscious indulgence in simple sentiment.

to the state of the heroine's affections are mingled with anxieties as to the state of her soul. . . .

With very much more to the same deadly effect.

Before Mary Ann Evans had broken away, in more senses than one, to become George Eliot, she had grown up in what was virtually a Low Church and Evangelical community, half-urban, half-rustic. So, challenged by all this religious-novel silliness and unreality, she presented her own version of life in such a community in the three tales of her *Scenes from Clerical Life*. Here not all traces of the more melodramatic religious novel have vanished. She gives us wasting diseases and sudden deaths, dipsomania and wife-beatings, terrible sins and sudden conversions. But at last both realism and humour arrive on the scene. Consider, just as a random example, the attitude of Mr Pilgrim, one of the two Milby doctors, towards his fellow-townsmen. When they were in good health he had a poor opinion of them:

A good inflammation fired his enthusiasm, and a lingering dropsy dissolved him into charity. Doubtless this crescendo of benevolence was partly due to feelings not at all represented by the entries in the day-book; for in Mr Pilgrim's heart, too, there was a latent store of tenderness and pity which flowed forth at the sight of suffering. Gradually, however, as his patients became convalescent, his view of their characters became more dispassionate; when they could relish mutton-chops he began to admit they had foibles, and by the time they had swallowed their last dose of tonic he was alive to their most inexcusable faults. . . .

It is in her creation of Milby, in the last and strongest of the three tales, *Janet's Repentance*, that George Eliot reveals her quality. It is a real town, whereas Dickens's Coketown, to which we shall come in the next chapter, is merely a gloomy stage set. But if there had been no silly Low Church novels, we might never have had Milby.

There were not many Broad Church novelists, but they included Charles Kingsley, who brought out *Hypatia* in 1853 and *Westward Ho!* two years later. He was very much the muscular Christian, the type of parson, continuing throughout the whole Victorian age, who believed that exercising the body brought its own grace and that it was better to get out into the open air than to slump in the study indulging in morbid introspection. Kingsley was a good man with a genuine talent for story-telling, but he was more at home with sea-fights or combats of any sort than he was with theology and the religious temperament, as he was to discover later when he rashly challenged the formidable Newman. *Hypatia* is no masterpiece of historical reconstruction, no earlier *Salammbô*, but it is a dashing impressionistic attempt to bring before us a particularly fascinating time and place, Alexandria in the fifth century. Its extraordinary mixture of bigoted Christians, Jews, philosophers and the last devoted pagans may have appealed to him as a romantic and highly-coloured enlargement of the religious divisions

(above) The Rev. F. W. Farrar

(opposite) Charlotte Mary Yonge

Charles Kingsley

of his own time. It was in more ways than one a bold tale for a vicar to tell in 1853, risking the disapproval of the narrow-minded. For what does he make his hero, Philammon, say after all his adventures are over and he is an abbot?

> Tell my brethren that I pray nightly for two women: both of them young; both of them beautiful; both of them beloved by me more than I love my soul; and tell them, moreover, that one of the two was a harlot, and the other a heathen.

That may or may not have been easy to say in a fifth-century abbey, but it took some courage for a serving clergyman to offer to the London of 1853. As for *Westward Ho!*, it follows the example of many religious novels in making the Jesuits the villains of the piece, but in essence it was what it has long remained – a spirited adventure story for boys of all ages.

What did this flood of religious fiction, the bitter conflicts of the sects, the endless talk of soul-saving, the highly charged atmosphere of religiosity, combine to produce? Did they give religion itself a deeper truer meaning? Did they hurry forward the civilizing of England's social and economic life? Did they halt the drift towards an idiotic war? The answer must be that they did not.

Matthew Arnold, now an inspector of schools, decided at last to publish his *Poems* with his name attached to them. In 1849 he had brought out *The Strayed Reveller, and other Poems, by A*; and in 1852 he had tried again with *Empedocles on Etna, and other Poems, by A*. Though they contained some of his best work – for example, 'The Forsaken Merman', one of his little masterpieces, was in the 1849 volume – they aroused no interest outside his circle of Oxford friends. In the hurly-burly of literary editorship and reviewing, slender volumes *by A* can easily be overlooked. *Poems, by Matthew Arnold*, the 1853 collection, had a better chance of attracting attention, even if it would be many years before Arnold gained a fairly wide and solid reputation as an essayist and critic. (To my mind he is far better as a poet than as a critic. His criticism reacts so strongly against 'provincial' values and judgment, is so determined to be cosmopolitan, that while he allows the Germans to be German, the French to be French, he will not allow the English to be English and so tends to under-rate our native genius.) His 1853 collection included most of the poems in the two earlier volumes but left out 'Empedocles on Etna' and brought in some new work, notably the long narrative 'Sohrab and Rustum', 'The Scholar Gipsy', and the favourite of the anthologies, 'Requiescat'.

What cannot be found in this volume is his magnificent 'Dover Beach', which most readers, I imagine, consider his finest short poem, a triumph of imagery, thought and feeling. It first appeared in his *New Poems* of 1867, but modern authorities on Arnold's poetry and life believe it was written in 1851, when he stayed some days in Dover, and was then

Matthew Arnold

revised in the 1860s. This might explain the famous concluding lines, with their 'Swept with confused alarms of struggle and flight,/Where ignorant armies clash by night', because it is doubtful if such images would occur to a young poet in 1851, still in the long era of peace, whereas by the middle 1860s war had succeeded war and the newspapers had been filled for years with the clash of armies. We ought to notice in this 1853 volume his 'Tristram and Iseult' because when we come to 1859 and the arrival of Tennyson's *Idylls of the King* we shall have to consider the curious spell that the Arthurian legends cast upon the Victorians. Arnold was early, but Tennyson had been earlier still, with his 'Morte d'Arthur', and then and later Tennyson seems far more at home in this legendary kingdom than Arnold. There are some splendid moments in 'Tristram and Iseult', as for example when the dying Tristram, hoping to see his other Iseult, with an abrupt (but, I think, justified) change of rhythm, cries –

> What voices are these on the clear night air?
> What lights in the court? What steps on the stair?

Nevertheless, with all his faults, Tennyson the bard seems to me to create a mythological atmosphere that does not exist in Arnold's poem, which, ironically enough, is too naturalistic. There is a further irony in the rather severe Preface that Arnold contributed to this 1853 volume. In it he condemns us – the English again – for looking for and admiring the 'profoundness of single thoughts', the 'richness of imagery', and 'abundance of illustration', in place of appreciating poems as an artistic whole. But Arnold himself – not unlike his own favourite, Wordsworth – has long given us most delight in single magical passages, often occurring in poems that seem to us faulty, clumsy, indecisive. There may be personal prejudice here, but it does seem to me that he is most a poet, and a very fine poet indeed, when he drops his cool classical pose and speaks out as a late and rather melancholy romantic. Had he been the kind of poet he thought he was, then almost all his poetry would not have belonged to his earlier life, it would have kept pace with his development later as a student and critic of contemporary life and religious belief. Larger and stronger poets express themselves at all ages.

Bleak House had been appearing in monthly parts throughout most of 1852 and '53, selling even more than *David Copperfield* had done, a steady 35,000 each number. This kind of serial publication, not of a completed novel but one being written as it came out in parts, has often been denounced, so now I shall say something in its defence. While it encouraged sprawl and some clumsy devices, there were times when it brought a novelist a brilliant idea. So, for example, when it was obvious that his readers were losing interest in *Martin Chuzzlewit*, Dickens suddenly changed course and sent Martin and Mark Tapley off to America. This may not have rescued the novel as a work of art but it did at least give us some passages of glorious burlesque. But there is another and more important reason why publication in parts, certainly as far as Dickens and Thackeray are concerned, is not entirely indefensible. It compelled them at times, when they were falling behind, to drive themselves as hard as they could go. This might mean some dubious devices and loose writing, but – and of this I am sure – it could also mean that sheer desperate drive, opening the unconscious, gave them some of their finest scenes and passages. The parts made the big novelists unequal, but there were gains as well as losses.

The complete novel of *Bleak House*, running to 380,000 words, came out towards the end of 1853. The sheer creation of such an enormous complex story is probably Dickens's most astonishing feat of writing. He was editing and contributing to *Household Words*; he was performing in amateur theatricals; he was superintending the alterations to Tavistock House, which was to be his last address in London; he was busy with Miss Coutts on a housing scheme; he was wining and dining and making speeches all over the place; he was dashing about from London to the seaside or over to France; and no wonder he was feeling exhausted – and indeed he ran into kidney trouble – before the novel was finished. If *Bleak House* had been one of his old rambling improvisations, its creation would not have been such a feat; but, as we know, it is a most elaborately organized novel, offering us interdependent groups on an unusual variety of social levels, with backgrounds ranging from stately Chesney Wold to the slum horror of Tom-all-Alone's. It is a huge panorama of early-Victorian England that gradually shrinks, tightening its action until it is almost like a detective story.

(below left) The title-page of *Bleak House*

(below right) 'Tom-all-Alone's', an illustration by Phiz to *Bleak House*

Victoria's Heyday

Good as it is, it would have been a better novel if it had never suggested a detective story. But Dickens wanted to give his readers everything he had, and he could not resist offering them a complicated plot, forcing his broad rich story into it. Once he began to plan, he had to plot, often to the disadvantage of what he had really set out to do. He could have shown us the interdependence of his social groups without all that contriving. Lady Dedlock and much that directly concerns her seem false, belonging to some other and much worse novel. (Sir Leicester Dedlock, however, is surprisingly well done.) Then there is Esther Summerson, a more convincing figure than his earlier heroines; but she should not have been allowed to tell half the story herself. When at first she is very much herself, she makes us feel frustrated and irritated because the sweep and force of the novel have been held up and damped down. Then later we begin to feel that Dickens has half-forgotten he must see people and events through Esther's eyes and mind, so that we lose confidence in her as a narrator. This faulty use of Esther and the artificial stagey plot are serious defects if *Bleak House* is strictly considered as a novel. But like most of Dickens's fiction, it is really something else, for which we have no handy accepted name. It is closer in essence to a huge, grotesque, comic-pathetic-dramatic *prose poem*. It is perhaps best regarded as a terrible accusing *vision* of Victorian England – and the whole of it, not simply its monstrous legal practices. The indictment in *Bleak House* is far wider and deeper than any satire of the legal system, going down to the rotten roots of society and its civilization, which Dickens, when fiercely creative and beyond the grasp of conscious opinion, was beginning to reject.

We can appreciate the variety and richness of mid-Victorian fiction if we remember that Mrs Gaskell's *Cranford* appeared only a few months before *Bleak House*. Dickens had made a friend of this beautiful and altogether delightful woman before he began editing *Household Words*, and, apart from Dickens himself, she was perhaps its most important early contributor. Out of the sketches of a tiny country town which she wrote anonymously she created *Cranford*, soon to be a little classic of feminine observation and humour, less faulty and more satisfying than any of her more ambitious long novels, with the possible exception of *Wives and Daughters*.

Elizabeth Gaskell was the mid-Victorian middle-class woman raised to a higher power by talent and temperament. She was the daughter of one Unitarian minister and the happy wife of another; she had seven children; she lived a full life and knew a great deal – but all in an intensely feminine mid-Victorian fashion. She was not a second Jane Austen; she had talent and charm but not genius. She is our prose poet of both urban and rural domesticity. While the contemporary male novelists went ranging and roaring about in all kinds of society, she poured tea in the drawing-room; but what happened there, down to the smallest flick of character, never escaped her. She was bad on men, those 'huge,

Mrs Elizabeth Gaskell

clumsy, hairy creatures, incapable of understanding those aspects of life which most interested her', to quote David Cecil's perceptive account of her in his *Early Victorian Novelists*. But she understood and could create delightful convincing girls, the creatures that the male novelists always saw through a haze. She could magically transform apparently dull and dreary spinsters into fascinating characters. Her life seems to have had the charm of her best fiction; she was a woman of considerable culture; she had an exceptionally wide circle of friends, many of them from abroad, including a surprising (for that time) number of Americans. A more attractive person in the literary and social life of the 1850s would be hard to find. She died (1865) while only in her middle fifties. Mid-Victorian England seemed to hurry so many of its leading writers to the funeral service and the graveyard. As well as Mrs Gaskell, Dickens, Thackeray, Macaulay, Kingsley, and Elizabeth Barrett Browning failed to reach their sixties.

A dip into the Stanley letter-bag (see *The Stanleys of Alderley*, edited by Nancy Mitford) brings 1853 very close to us, for there were strikes then too. So, Lord Stanley to his wife, 29 July 1853:

> The great event since you have been gone has been the Strike of the Cabs, as on Wednesday morning London awoke to find she was cabless, & the country arrived by the railway to find they must walk to their destination & carry their luggage or sit upon it till porters and donkeys could be discovered. It is expected that the strike will not last long as it is expensive to keep horses doing nothing, & carriages are being hired for the day & doing the work of cabs at the railways, in the meantime however London is all the pleasanter as you can walk about without being in danger of your life. Before the strike took place Fitzroy had agreed to relax the act so far as to allow 1s. a mile beyond 4 miles & to let them charge 6d. for a 4th person in the cab as well as 6d. for the 3rd. They do not mean to give way on any other point so the battle must be fought out between cabs & public. . . .

However, the strike only lasted three days, the public discovering that they could walk or hire unlicensed vehicles and the cab drivers being faced with a loss of £2,000 a day. So the cabs came out again, and, as Lord Stanley dryly added, 'neither less extortionate, nor more civil nor more clean'.

There was far more excitement and talk in London a few weeks later. The end of summer, a county court, and the columns of *The Times* were all enlivened by another quarrel in public between Caroline Norton and the husband from whom she had been separated for many years. Mrs Norton deserves more than a brief note. She was one of three dazzling sisters, the granddaughters of Sheridan, whose flashing dark eyes and wit she seems to have inherited. Like many another brilliant

Designed & Etched by George Cruikshank

girl, she made a stupid marriage, her husband, the Hon. George Chapple Norton, being an incompetent barrister and a coarse vindictive fellow. Back in the early 1830s he had brought a case against Lord Melbourne for being too friendly with his wife, already estranged, but it came to nothing. (The talk was that he had been encouraged by the political opponents of Melbourne.) Caroline now kept herself and her three children by writing, chiefly verse for the *Annuals* and *Keepsakes* popular at the time. All accounts agree that she was a fascinating creature, but she was a versifier rather than a poet. If Byron wrote his poetry on brandy and soda-water, she might be said to have written her verses on Byron and soda-water. Later she tried other forms, going from lyrical to narrative verse and even writing some novels. Without great talent, she was as brave and self-reliant as she was beautiful, and it was her misfortune to live at a time when a wife (with three sons to keep) separated from a vindictive husband was in a desperate situation.

'Passing Events of 1853', by George Cruikshank

Victoria's Heyday

This became obvious again, with the whole mess of the marriage open to public view, in August 1853. Norton was not only paying her no allowance but was now claiming her literary earnings, which the common law as it stood fully entitled him to claim. (A wife had no rights except through some cautious marriage settlement, which is why rich men insisted upon such settlements, after keeping young men without means well away from their daughters. The law really encouraged and favoured matrimonial adventurers.) Caroline now blazed away at this impudent brute of a husband, then brought out a pamphlet, *English Laws for Women in the Nineteenth Century*, and followed it up with other eloquent protests against the legal status of wives and mothers. She probably did as much as any woman to further the feminist cause and to bring about some necessary reform. Even so, we gather that the beautiful and tempestuous Mrs Norton was not widely popular among the other women – the earnest Harriet Martineau was the type – who were devoting themselves to the feminist cause: perhaps Caroline was too feminine. (There is more than a suggestion of her character and career in Meredith's *Diana of the Crossways*.) Born in 1808, Caroline Norton really belonged to the romantic 1830s and not the sedate 1850s, and we can see her among the lawyers of this time like a bird of paradise flashing before the unwinking stare of owls.

'The Doubt: "Can these dry bones live?"' A problem picture directed at three of the preoccupations of the mid-Victorians – religion, death and the idealized young woman. It was painted by a little-known artist, Henry Alexander Bowler, who was evidently under the Pre-Raphaelite influence, though not a member of the circle. He exhibited this picture at the Royal Academy in 1856. Clearly it voiced the same doubts about immortality as were raised by Tennyson in *In Memoriam*:

I stretch lame hands of faith and grope
And gather dust and chaff, and call
To what I feel is Lord of all
And faintly trust the larger hope.

The germinating chestnuts on the grave slab inscribed with the word *Resurgam* suggest the answer to the question in the title of the picture.

(overleaf) 'Ramsgate Sands', by William Powell Frith. This, the first of Frith's panoramas of contemporary life, was begun three years before it was exhibited at the Royal Academy in 1854. It was an instant success, and was immediately bought by a dealer who sold it to Queen Victoria for a thousand guineas. Its reception was such as to encourage the artist to produce his second and most famous panoramic painting, 'The Derby Day'.

Sacred
to the
MEMORY
of
John Faithful
Born 17.. Died 179..
"I am the Resurrection
and the Life."

1854

O N 28 FEBRUARY 1854 Queen Victoria wrote from Buckingham Palace to her Uncle Leopold:

The last battalion of the Guards (Scots Fusiliers) embarked today. They passed through the courtyard here at seven o'clock this morning. We stood on the balcony to see them – the morning fine, the sun rising over the towers of old Westminster Abbey – and an immense crowd collected to see these fine men, and cheering them immensely as they with difficulty marched along. They formed line, presented arms, and then cheered us *very heartily*, and went off cheering. It was a touching and beautiful sight; many sorrowing friends were there, and one saw the shake of many a hand. My best wishes and prayers will be with them all. . . .

And those 'fine men' were going to need those best wishes and prayers. They were about to take part in one of the most foolish wars in British history. There was not one substantial reason why it should ever have happened. As John Bright, still leading a small peace party, pointed out some months later, Britain was fighting for a country, Turkey, that had refused our mediation against a country, Russia, that had actually accepted our terms. Lord Aberdeen and most of his cabinet were not really in favour of going to war. They were driven to inventing various excuses for it: Gladstone, for example, had no brief for 'heroic Turkey' but said that the power of Russia must be checked. Delane, editor of *The Times*, while allowing his paper to strike a belligerent note, confessed in private that he thought the war unnecessary, which indeed it was. But Delane, like most of the politicians, simply could not withstand the sheer pressure of public opinion.

The people, of all classes except the Quakers and a small group of Liberal pacifists, wanted a war. They demanded glory, excitement, wonderful news, blood-stirring events. There had been close upon forty years of peace, and they had had enough of it. The nation must be tested again and must triumph again. War was not evil but good, sweeping away mere profit-seeking or idleness, triviality and love of comfort, insisting upon self-sacrifice, challenging the nation's manhood. Tennyson, who ought to have had more sense, was infected, and chimed in with:

> For the peace, that I deem'd no peace, is over and done,
> And now by the side of the Black and the Baltic deep,

'The Orphans', painted by Faed in 1854, the year of Charles Dickens's *Hard Times*, bathes in a rosy glow of sentiment the harsh realities of the life of the poor. Thomas Faed was a Scotsman who followed in the footsteps of Wilkie. His work has a marked Scottish character, and, as in 'The Mitherless Bairn', which made his name when exhibited at the Royal Academy in 1855, he always brought a warm sympathy to his scenes of poverty and cottage life.

> And deathful-grinning mouths of the fortress, flames
> The blood-red blossom of war with a heart of fire –

rhetoric that avoids any mention of dysentery and cholera, which would soon be felling men in their thousands. Tennyson's friend Carlyle resisted the infection, and grumbled in his diary:

> Russian war: soldiers marching off, etc. Never such enthusiasm among the population. Cold, I, as a very stone to all that: seems to me privately have hardly seen a madder business. . . . It is the idle population of editors, etc., that have done all this to England. One perceives clearly the Ministers go forward in it against their will. . . .

But an overheated atmosphere had now been created in which anybody who came up with a rational objection to this warmongering was immediately denounced as a coward and a traitor. Men like Bright and Cobden were viciously attacked in the press, and howling mobs burnt their effigies. John Bull was now hysterical.

Once war had been declared, the hysteria, defying commonsense, took two different but equally foolish forms. The first was a kind of boys'-magazine attitude towards the conflict. Any of our brave fellows could lick half-a-dozen of those wretches. You had only to see them marching away and cheering to know that. They were the same sort of

'Parade of the Scots Fusileer Guards at Buckingham Palace on the morning of their departure for the Seat of War', an engraving by E. Walker after G. H. Thomas

Queen Victoria and Prince Albert, 1854. A photograph by Roger Fenton

men who had beaten the great Napoleon and all his fancy Marshals, so Tsar Nicholas and his Cossacks didn't stand a chance. If the lower classes adopted this boys'-magazine attitude, the upper classes welcomed the war as a glorified large-scale picnic in some remote and romantic place. It was almost as if the Black Sea had been opened to tourism. Wealthy officers like Lord Cardigan decided to take their yachts. Some commanders' wives insisted upon going along, accompanied by their personal maids. Various civilians cancelled their holidays elsewhere to follow the army and see the sport. And what men they would be following! – the stern-looking infantry and the cavalry in their brilliant uniforms! But even *The Times* had to point out that uniforms like those of Lord Cardigan's notorious 11th Hussars, with their very short jackets and ridiculously tight plum-coloured pants, were clearly unfit for war service and were better suited to female hussars in a ballet.

It ought to have occurred to somebody on *The Times* that day, late in April 1854, that perhaps the whole British Army was unfit for war service. Indeed it was, as events amply proved. It was brave enough, almost manned by heroes: what it lacked was a few clever cowards, ready to use their brains. The truth was, it had been living for years and years in a dream of old Peninsular War victories. Decade after decade had gone by, under Wellington's stern eye, without any real attempt to bring the army up-to-date. To begin with, it was not big enough to fight a European war, as against a mere punitive expedition. There were no adequate reserves for the 27,000 men who finally reached the Crimea, with the result that the loss of regular troops had to be made up with raw recruits. It had nothing like enough artillery. Its supplies might have been the work of Dickens's Circumlocution Office, they were so appallingly inadequate. It was as if nobody had given any thought whatever to all that an expeditionary force, at the other end of Europe, would need. Its staff work was sketchy and amateurish. Officers still bought their commissions, so that this was an army without any body of highly-trained professional soldiers. The officers who were more or less professional soldiers, and had seen active service, came from the Indian Army and were despised by commanding officers at home entirely for social and not military reasons. Finally, the man appointed to command this army in the Crimea, Lord Raglan, was well into his sixties.

Fitzroy James Henry Somerset, now Lord Raglan, was the younger son of the Duke of Beaufort, and had been A.D.C. and military secretary to Wellington in the Peninsular War and at Waterloo, where he lost an arm. He had continued to serve Wellington through most of the long years of peace. His fine personal qualities were universally admired, but his experience and temperament made him the wrong man for independent command (his first) in the field. A younger and tougher man might have done much better. Raglan was not personally responsible for the breakdown in transport and supplies – the home authorities were at fault there – but a less patient and sensitive man might have protested more vigorously from the first. He was brave enough, and, like Wellington, cool and impassive under fire, but he could not help spending most of his time at his desk, as if he were still a military secretary and not a commander-in-chief. Moreover, he was old for his age – we are told he kept referring to the Russians as 'the French', forgetting that the old enemy was now an ally in the field – and far from robust, dying in 1855. Finally, he had to fight alongside a French army always better-equipped and soon much larger than his own.

Two things saved this small, odd, rather absurd British Army, challenging so far from home a gigantic empire, from immediate defeat and then total disaster. First, the Russians, with more men in the field and immense potential reserves, were even bigger muddlers than their invaders, and seemed to move in a vague dream of battle. Secondly, and not for the first or the last time, the British owed almost everything to the courage, obstinacy, and superb discipline of the regular infantry-man. The cavalry might catch the eye and get the applause, but it was the stolidly trudging infantry that won the battles. Recruited from rather desperate youths, wretchedly paid, badly fed and even worse housed, ferociously disciplined still by the lash, asking for nothing but some hours off the parade ground and plenty of drink, these men, under their long-term non-commissioned officers, became soldiers magnificent in war. Only disease at its worst – and until our century the British Army was a notable victim of diseases – could subdue their spirit and make them fall out. Their 'thin red line', standing firm against almost any

Lord Raglan, photographed by Roger Fenton

William Howard Russell, photographed by Roger Fenton

odds, justly became famous. And even if I were not an old infantryman myself, I think I would still cry 'Bravo – the British Infantry!'

Readers who want military history, details of advances and retreats, must now look elsewhere. Fortunately they have been well catered for. It is one of the odd features of this odd war that it was so thoroughly reported and described. The journals and letters of wives who went out with their officer-husbands are not easy to find now (Mrs Henry Duberly, whose husband was in the 8th Hussars, is a good example of them, and deserves to be remembered just for writing 'Neither the commanding officers afloat or ashore appear to have the least idea of what they are about'). But a sensibly-edited version of Russell's *Despatches* was published recently, and is highly informative and lively. William Howard Russell, a born war correspondent, was the leading representative of *The Times* at the Crimea. The High Command thoroughly disliked his presence there – and well they might, because he raised the whole country against them – but they dared not send him home. On the other hand, there was still no military censorship, as there was during later campaigns, so he could write what he pleased – and did. Again, gathering dust on many shelves there is A. W. Kinglake's monumental *Invasion of the Crimea* in eight large volumes, the last two not appearing until 1887, by which time nobody cared. Admirers of his *Eothen*, one of the liveliest travel books of the nineteenth century, will consider, as I do, this over-conscientious history a waste of a good writer, demanding as it did almost all Kinglake's time and energy. But there it is, with almost every skirmish, up to the death of Kinglake's friend, Lord Raglan, set down in carefully polished prose.

So off they went, many regiments being accompanied by forty of their wives, who would serve as more respectable *vivandières*. An advance force sailed as early as 23 February to Gallipoli, to support the Turks, if necessary. But war was not actually declared by Britain and France until 28 March. By the end of May about 25,000 British troops, together with about 30,000 French, were encamped at the Bulgarian port of Varna on the Black Sea. Their presence there was unnecessary because the Turks had already driven the Russians out of that region. And the British Army was already in poor shape. The voyages in packed transports had been long and trying; the fine horses of the cavalry, which the French had sensibly left at home, had suffered terribly; and now dysentery and cholera, the lightning executioner, were spreading among the men. At Scutari, on the outskirts of Constantinople, the Turks had lent the British enormous empty barracks to be used as a base hospital. Even if all the arrangements had been adequate – and they were soon found to be appallingly inadequate – the Scutari barracks would have been unsuitable for a hospital. Its sanitary facilities would have closed a cattle market. Disaster was on its way, and soon Scutari would be a name of horror.

The expeditionary forces – now 27,000 British, 30,000 French,

Victoria's Heyday

7,000 Turks – landed in the Crimea, without any opposition, in the middle of September. They were many weeks later than they had originally intended to be, so that Prince Menshikov, commanding the Russian Army, had been able to occupy the Alma heights barring the approach to Sebastopol, only about thirty-five miles to the South. Here it must be stressed that the sole object of this invasion was to seize and then destroy this powerfully fortified naval base, Sebastopol. Once this was done, the war would really be over. And though it seems incredible, it is a fact that if the Allies had had one first-class general in command Sebastopol could have been captured within a few weeks, instead of holding out, as it did, until September 1855. However, in September 1854 the Russians on the heights barring the way to Sebastopol would have to be fought, so on the morning of the 20th there began the Battle of the Alma.

So far as it was a victory, it was a victory of the regular British Infantry. The men were weak from sickness; they had spent nights without shelter under heavy rain; they had to march up steep slopes facing a withering fire; and they captured the heights not once but, owing to a wrong order to retire, *twice*. Apart from this display of discipline and fortitude, the battle was a huge nonsense, a masterpiece of the inept. Marshal St Arnaud was already a sick man (he died shortly afterwards) and he and dreamy Lord Raglan hardly seemed to understand one another but contrived to miscalculate where the bulk of the Russian force would be. It turned out that they were massed against the British on the Allied left, and not, as it was thought, against the French on the right. No proper reconnaissance was carried out by Raglan, who also, for some extraordinary reason, never divulged his general plan, if he had one, to his commanding officers. He was in fact so dreamy that at one point in the battle he occupied an observation post actually behind the Russian front line. Then there was that wrong order for the infantry to retire, so that they had to start all over again. When finally the Russians were in retreat, Raglan failed to pursue them with his cavalry, which he seemed to regard as being too precious to be risked in battle. However, the Allies were now on the heights, though short of water and further away from their supplies. They could not stay there – so what next?

Meanwhile, Prince Menshikov, another master of ineptitude, had decided not to take his army into Sebastopol, though it had wide and formidable defences, but to continue his retreat away from it. There is little doubt that if at this point the Allies had flung everything they had into the attack, Sebastopol would have fallen. (Indeed, it was believed for a time at home that Sebastopol *had* fallen.) Knowing nothing – for if there was any military intelligence at work in this war, there are no signs of it – Raglan and poor sick St Arnaud decided to do it the hard way. They needed a port to land supplies, felt they would have to make do with the tiny harbour of Balaclava, well on the other side of

(opposite above) 'Sevastopol', by John Brandard from a drawing by W. Telbin

(opposite below) 'The Battle of Alma, from the Sea', by William Simpson from a sketch by Captain Gordon

(below) Marshal St Arnaud

Victoria's Heyday

Sebastopol, and began a flank march, through difficult country, hilly and thickly wooded, all round the fortress. Such was the muddle that they actually crossed the rearguard of the retreating Russians, and there were a few skirmishes. The Allies having conveniently removed themselves, the Russian army came back, and then, with the invaluable help of a brilliant siege engineer, Todleben, began at once to enlarge and strengthen the Sebastopol defences.

The Allies, with the French now commanded by General Canrobert, dug themselves in at a reasonable distance from the Russian lines. The British, on the right, were six to eight miles from their base, and the task of taking all the heavy guns, which had come round by sea, up the hills was murderous. A glimpse of one of Russell's despatches to *The Times* is illuminating:

> We heard strange things from the deserters who began to join us. They said that thirty Russian ladies went out of Sebastopol to see the battle of the Alma, as though they were going to a play or a picnic. They were quite assured of the success of the Russian troops and great was their alarm and dismay when they found themselves obliged to leave the telegraph house on the hill, and to fly for their lives in their carriages. . . .

But now he sounds an ominous note:

> During the first three weeks of our stay in the Crimea we lost as many of cholera as perished on the Alma. [About 2,000 British.] The town [Balaclava] was in a filthy revolting state. Lord Raglan ordered it to be cleansed, but there was no one to obey the order, and consequently no one attended to it.

This happened to too many of Raglan's orders, and already Russell, while admitting Raglan's personal qualities, had suggested he was not fit for high command. The French Army was altogether better equipped than the British, both in its supplies and its handling of the wounded, and it was commanded with more psychological insight. Russell points this out now:

> The silence and gloom of our camp, as compared with the activity and bustle of that of the French, were very striking. No drum, no bugle-call, no music of any kind, was ever heard within our precincts, while our neighbours close by kept up incessant rolls, fanfaronnades, and flourishes, relieved every evening by the fine performances of their military bands. The fact was many of our instruments had been placed in store and the regimental bands were broken up and disorganized, the men being devoted to the performance of the duties for which the ambulance corps had been formed. I think, judging from one's own feelings, and from the expression of those around, that the want of music in camp was productive of graver consequences than appeared at first blush from such a cause. . . .

It is a sensible complaint, but a trifle when compared with the furious despatches that Russell and his fellow journalists would soon be sending home.

The Battle of Balaclava, on 25 October, was initiated by the Russians who came out of their Sebastopol defences to attack the supply base of the Allies at Balaclava. The approach to it was covered by the Turkish contingent, in redoubts; and in support of them, directly defending the town, Sir Colin Campbell's Highlanders and the Light and Heavy Cavalry brigades, both considerably below strength. The Russian forces were far more numerous and included their finest cavalry, a great weight of horsemen. They routed the Turks and captured their guns, which Raglan deeply resented because this loss of guns would suggest a notable Russian victory. However, the Russians were now swarming towards Balaclava and its scanty defences, and there now occurred three events that made this battle famous.

The first was the stand of Campbell's Highlanders, formed only in two lines – 'I did not think it worth while to form them even four deep', Campbell said afterwards – who coolly faced and then broke up a massive thundering cavalry charge, a triumph of cold courage and musketry skill. This was the origin of 'the thin red line', a phrase used so often later; though Russell in his despatch called it 'that thin red streak tipped with a line of steel'. Equally gallant and equally valuable was the second event, the charge of the Heavy Brigade, under Brigadier-General Scarlett, against double or treble its number of *élite* Russian cavalry. Let Russell, at his most eloquent, take up the story:

As lightning flashed through cloud, the Greys and Enniskilleners pierced through the dark masses of Russians. The shock was but for a moment. There was a clash of steel and a light play of sword-blades in the air, and then the Greys and the redcoats disappeared in the midst of the shaken

'The Town and Harbour of Balaklava, from the camp of the 93rd Highlanders', by O'Reilly, after Lieutenant Montagu: (left to right) an old Genoese tower and castle, seamen's camp and Kadi Koi

and quivering columns. In another moment we saw them emerging with diminished numbers and in broken order, charging against the second line. It was a terrible moment. The first line of Russians, which had been utterly smashed by our charge, and had fled off at one flank and towards the centre, were coming back to swallow up our handful of men. By sheer steel and sheer courage Enniskillener and Scot were winning their desperate way right through the enemy's squadrons, and already grey horses and red coats had appeared right at the rear of the second mass, when, with irresistible force, like one bolt from a bow, the 4th Dragoon Guards, riding straight at the right flank of the Russians, and the 5th Dragoon Guards, following close after the Enniskilleners, rushed at the remnants of the first line of the enemy, went through it as though it were made of pasteboard and put them to utter rout. . . .

Lord Lucan

And though it reads like a story in a boys' paper, it was true enough: the whole body of Russian cavalry retreated in haste and confusion.

Now for the third episode, the most famous of all, equally gallant but, unlike the other two, completely futile and daft: it was of course the Charge of the Light Brigade. To say, as Tennyson did originally in his poem on the subject, 'Someone had blundered' was to understate the case: there were blunders all round, a chain of ambiguity and mis-understanding. Lord Raglan passed down a message to the cavalry to advance rapidly and try to prevent the enemy from carrying away the captured guns. (It was probably the thought of those guns that made Raglan be so imprecise.) A dashing Captain Nolan took the message to Lord Lucan, in command of the cavalry division. Lucan was not clear where he had to go, and Captain Nolan could only point a finger and say something to the effect that there were the enemy and there were the guns. Nobody knew exactly what he said because he was killed in the action that followed. Lord Lucan passed on the order, and Nolan galloped down to the valley below where the Light Brigade, kept in reserve, had been drawn up, not knowing what was happening.

The Light Brigade was commanded by the same Lord Cardigan whose fancy uniforms for his hussars have already been mentioned. He was Lord Lucan's brother-in-law, and they had long heartily detested each other. Unlike Lucan, the better soldier, who shared his men's discomforts, Cardigan, haughty, very rich (£40,000 a year), selfish and stupid, retired at the end of each day to dine and sleep on his yacht. If he had had any sense he would have realized that Raglan did not want him to advance here in this valley, with the Russians in force, bristling with cannon, only just over a mile away. He had only his 700 men and no support whatever. However, he would obey the order he had received, and, lacking sense not courage, he went to the front of his brigade, setting it trotting along the plain and then charging the battery of thirty cannon that awaited it. Russell wrote:

We could scarcely believe the evidence of our senses. Surely that handful of men were not going to charge an army in position? Alas! it was but too true – their desperate valour knew no bounds, and far indeed was it removed from its so-called better part – discretion. . . . At the distance of 1,200 yards the whole line of the enemy belched forth, from thirty iron mouths, a flood of smoke and flame. . . . The first line was broken – it was joined by the second, they never halted or checked their speed an instant . . . they flew into the smoke of the batteries; but ere they were lost from view, the plain was strewed with their bodies and with the carcasses of horses. They were exposed to an oblique fire from the batteries on the hills on both sides, as well as to a direct fire of musketry. . . .

It is remarkable that rather more than a quarter of the brigade found their way back. '*C'est magnifique, mais ce n'est pas la guerre,*' said Marshal Bosquet, unknowingly claiming an entry into all dictionaries of quotations. Lord Raglan, for once, was really angry: he had just lost his Light Brigade.

Here we must hold up the war itself to say something more about Lord Cardigan. He may have been a hero but he proved himself to be a bad commander of a brigade. He had received a lance wound in the leg, but it was only slight; yet instead of staying to rally his men he rode away, presumably in the direction of his yacht. He had never been much liked by his fellow officers, and many of them were indignant when, after Cardigan returned to England in January 1855, he was regarded as a national hero. The press was full of him, his portraits were to be seen everywhere, and he was the honoured guest at a Mansion House banquet in February, when he made a speech not noticeable for modesty. Graciously accepting the many honours that came his way – and by this time Lord Raglan had died in the Crimea – Cardigan insisted for years on playing the part of a national hero, and brought an action for criminal libel, which he lost, against Raglan's nephew and A.D.C. for writing that after the charge at Balaclava, 'unfortunately Lord Cardigan was not present when most required.' He had now married his mistress, a notorious *equestrienne* with the stunningly appropriate name of Adeline Horsey de Horsey, who, after her husband died from a fall from a horse in 1868, lived to a very ripe old age, rich in gossip and ancient scandal. Lord Cardigan deserves this much notice because he is the best example of what was wrong with the British Army. His aristocratic background and his wealth enabled him to secure rapid promotion; he spent £10,000 a year to make his 11th Hussars the very smartest-looking regiment in the country; he was harsh with his men and intolerably autocratic with his officers; and he never acquired the genuine knowledge and sense of responsibility needed to command a squadron, let alone a regiment and a brigade. When after the Crimean War there was some reform of the army at last, perhaps the reformers had Lord Cardigan in mind.

On 5 November there came the oddest battle of the war. This was Inkerman, often called 'the soldiers' battle' because it began with a surprise attack by 40,000 Russians on the British line, through early

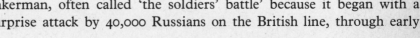

Victoria's Heyday

morning fog and drizzle, and largely consisted of desperate hand-to-hand engagements. Later in the battle, which lasted six hours altogether, mostly in confusion, the French brought reinforcements, but it was the British infantry that had most of the grim work to do. The attack cost Menshikov, who had to withdraw, over 12,000 men. The Allied losses, mostly British, were about 3,300, among them an unusually large proportion of senior officers, rushing into the action and then being picked off by the Russians. After describing a grisly tour of the battlefield, two days later, Russell ends with this:

> If it is considered that the soldiers who met these furious columns of the Czar were the remnants of three British divisions, which scarcely numbered 8,500 men; that they were hungry and wet, and half-famished; that they were men belonging to a force which was generally 'out of bed' four nights out of seven; which had been enfeebled by sickness, by severe toil, sometimes for twenty-four hours at a time without relief of any kind; that among them were men who had within a short time previously lain out for forty-eight hours in the trenches at a stretch – it will be readily admitted that never was a more extraordinary contest maintained by our army since it acquired a reputation in the world's history.

The paragraph above deserves to be quoted not because it is an eloquent tribute, though of course it is, but because phrase after phrase in it begins to look ominous. This is an army already in appalling straits, mismanaged by the War Department at home and incom-

(left) 'Adeline Horsey de Horsey', 1862, by A. F. Prades

(right) 'The 7th Earl of Cardigan relating the story of the Charge of Balaclava, to the Prince Consort and the Royal children', 1854, by James Sant

'The Field of Inkerman from the Three-gun battery showing the ground on which the principal struggle on November 5 took place. Where Zouaves, guards and other infantry fought and fell mell with the Russian columns', by E. Walker from a sketch by Captain M. A. Biddulph

petently handled at the front. Here it was, wasting away – with three divisions only able to muster 8,500 combatants – shivering in trenches, pretending to besiege a great fortress wide open for reinforcements on the other side and strengthening its defences every day. Winter would soon arrive; the whole British position was badly chosen; the landing facilities at Balaclava were poor; the only good road out of it was now controlled by the Russians; and the famished and exhausted transport animals had to stumble up mere tracks, eight miles of them, deep in mud, to bring any available supplies. And worse was to come, as if incompetence and folly bent bad luck towards them. On 14 November a storm so exceptionally severe that it has been described as a hurricane wrecked nearly thirty supply ships, so that urgent and invaluable stores of food, forage, winter clothing and medical supplies were lost.

In *A Voice from the Ranks: A Personal Narrative of the Crimean Campaign by a Sergeant of the Royal Fusiliers* we are shown the plight the British Army was in now:

... The Commissariat had completely broken down. All that was wanting was someone with a head on to put things straight – all was higgledy-piggledy and confusion. The cavalry horses, that had cost an enormous amount, sank up to their knees in mud at every step, until they dropped exhausted; and all the way from the camp to Balaclava were to be seen dead horses, mules, and bullocks, in every stage of decomposition. And our poor fellows – who had fought so well at the Alma, Balaclava, and the two Inkermans – were now dying by hundreds daily.

The army was put upon half rations – half a pound of mouldy biscuit and half a pound of salt junk (beef or pork); coffee was served out, but in its raw green state, with no means of roasting it. No wood or firing was to be had, except a few roots that were dug up. Men would come staggering into the camp from the trenches soaked to the skin and ravenously hungry, when a half-pound of mouldy biscuit would be issued, with the same quantity of salt junk, so hard that one almost wanted a good hatchet to break it. The scenes were heart-rending.

Victoria's Heyday

The whole camp was one vast sheet of mud, the trenches in many places knee deep; men died at their posts from sheer exhaustion or starvation rather than complain, for if they reported themselves sick the medical chests were empty. And amidst all these privations the enemy kept peppering away at them. . . .

The winter when it came was an unusually hard one. But even before the very worst weather arrived, the indomitable Mrs Duberly in Balaclava confided to her Journal: 'Auctions of deceased officers' effects occupied almost everyone today. The prices were fabulous. An old forage cap fetched £51. 5. 0; an old pair of warm gloves £11. 7. 0; a couple of cotton nightcaps £11. 1. 0.' And a little later, on the icy hills above, such things, offering at least a little warmth, would have fetched more still. The misery of the men up there was now complete.

Increasingly indignant press reports and letters from the front alarmed and then infuriated people at home. One cultivated elderly woman, writing to a friend abroad, tells us what persons of her class were feeling (*Correspondence of Sarah Spencer, Lady Lyttelton, 1787–1870*), in a letter dated 2 December 1854:

> You can imagine how entirely unreserved are the accounts from the Crimea, which are daily read by every reader in England. The descriptions of the sufferings, and losses, and sickness, and reduced state of the army, of its discouraging failure as to the progress of the siege, of the dying off of the reinforcements, of the insufficiency of everything sent over to help the troops, are written with immense power by Mr Russell and universally

The cooking house of the 8th Hussars, 'Queen's Royal Irish'. A photograph taken by Roger Fenton

believed. I assure you the gloom and weight on one's spirits are dreadful; it appears to me that war never before was so horrible. . . .

It was all the more galling that the French, being properly looked after, were now in such an obviously superior position. Early in the New Year General Canrobert, with 78,000 under him, had to take over a large and very important section of the line from the British, now reduced to no more than 12,000 fit for duty. The seriously sick and the badly wounded among the British had from the first to be packed into ships, many of them too small and too slow, for the voyage of three hundred miles across the Black Sea to the large base hospital at Scutari, now a name of ill omen indeed.

This brings us inevitably to that extraordinary woman, Florence Nightingale. So much has been written about her, from earlier gush about 'The Lady with the Lamp' to Lytton Strachey's dry sketch-portrait and Mrs Woodham-Smith's full and splendid biography, that a few essential facts must suffice here. Born in 1820, she was a girl of the upper class who was resolutely determined not to lead the kind of life offered to such girls. Two passions were at work in her: one for the actual business of nursing, for which she had herself thoroughly trained; the other for organization and the acquisition and right use of power. An energetic and strong-willed woman, knowing exactly what she wants, is probably more than a match for most men, but even so it is doubtful if Florence Nightingale would have succeeded, against masculine prejudice and bureaucratic opposition, if she had come from

A quiet day in the mortar battery. A photograph taken by Roger Fenton

Victoria's Heyday

a lower social level. But she knew some men in the right places, the most important of them, a close friend, Sidney Herbert, Secretary of War. Already Scutari was a scandal; there was to be an official inquiry; and money was pouring into a special patriotic fund. On the very day she wrote to Sidney Herbert, offering her services, he wrote to her, asking her 'to go out and supervise the whole thing', pledging, rather optimistically, 'the fullest assistance and co-operation of the medical staff'. With a staff of thirty-eight nurses, she arrived at Scutari on 4 November, just in time to cope with the wounded from Balaclava and then six hundred more from Inkerman.

What she found in Scutari is best described by Mrs Woodham-Smith in her remarkable biography, *Florence Nightingale*:

> Day after day the sick poured in until the enormous building was entirely filled. The wards were full, the corridors were lined with men lying on the bare boards because the supply of bags stuffed with straw had given out. Chaos reigned. The doctors were unable even to examine each man. Mr Sabin, the head Chaplain, was told that men were a fortnight in the Barrack Hospital without seeing a surgeon. Yet the doctors, especially the older men, worked 'like lions' and were frequently on their feet for twenty-four hours at a time. . . .
>
> The filth became indescribable. The men in the corridors lay on un-washed rotten floors crawling with vermin. As the Rev. Sidney Godolphin Osborne knelt to take down dying messages his paper became covered thickly with lice. There were no pillows, no blankets, the men lay, with their heads on their boots, wrapped in the blanket or greatcoat stiff with blood and filth which had been their sole covering perhaps for more than a week. There were no screens or operating tables. Amputations had to be performed in the wards in full sight of the patients. . . .

The frontispiece and title-page of *A Shilling Cookery for the People*, by Alexis Soyer, published in 1855

There were more than a thousand men suffering from acute diarrhoea, and proper sanitary arrangements had ceased to exist even before the Turks handed over the place. The wretched men had to use huge wooden tubs in the wards and corridors that might be left unemptied for twenty-four hours. The men's food might be lying on floors thick with filth. The stench from the hospital was so strong it could be smelled outside the walls. 'We have Erysipelas, fever and gangrene,' Miss Nightingale wrote. 'The dysentery cases have died at the rate of one in two . . . the mortality of the operations is frightful. . . . This is only the beginning of things.' We might remember here that these men had been sent out to fight by the richest nation in the world. And those social historians of ours who would rather have lived in the 1850s than at any other time were certainly assuming they would not have been drafted to the Crimea.

That there was any improvement – and gradually there was con-siderable improvement – was chiefly due to the almost superhuman efforts of Florence Nightingale. She superintended all the nursing, did some herself, and went round the wards at night (actually carrying a

A

HILLING COOKERY

FOR

THE PEOPLE:

EMBRACING

AN ENTIRELY NEW SYSTEM OF PLAIN COOKERY
AND DOMESTIC ECONOMY.

BY

ALEXIS SOYER,

AUTHOR OF "THE MODERN HOUSEWIFE,"
ETC. ETC.

Eightieth Thousand.

LONDON:
GEO. ROUTLEDGE & CO., FARRINGDON STREET.
NEW YORK: 18, BEEKMAN STREET.
1855.
The Author of this work reserves the right of translating it.

lamp) offering a comforting word or two here and there. This would have been more than enough for most women, but at the same time she was battling, angry and fearless, with the military and the bureaucrats – especially the wretched commissariat – furiously slashing at their red-tape. Even though she could count on the support of Sidney Herbert in London, most of the credit for bringing order out of chaos, creating some reasonable sanitation, steadily improving hospital conditions, dramatically reducing the death-rate month by month, must be given to this astonishing woman. When it was all over, in September 1856, she visited Queen Victoria at Balmoral and explained her plans for the complete reform of the military medical service. 'Such a head!' the Queen cried afterwards. 'I wish we had her at the War Office.' And certainly Florence Nightingale had a good head; but what made her great was a peculiarly feminine mixture of compassion and practicality, blazing energy and an indomitable will.

A very different figure arrived in the theatre of war not long after Miss Nightingale. This was Alexis Soyer – master chef. Though still very young when he left Paris for London in 1830, Soyer had already had a thorough training as a chef. After working in several great houses he was appointed master of the kitchen at the Reform Club, where his banquets soon became famous – club cuisine clearly being very different from what it is now – and where he delighted in inventing extravagant new dishes and giving them romantic or brightly topical names. He was a flamboyant fellow, who loved showing off and publicity, but he had a genuine desire to improve English cookery, publishing several books on various culinary levels, including *A Shilling Cookery for the People* that sold at least 250,000 copies. But though always wildly energetic and ingenious, he was not always successful. In 1851, when he realized that in the Great Exhibition there would be nothing worth eating and drinking, he transformed with all manner of fantastification Gore House, across the road, into a 'Gastronomic Symposium of all Nations'. But it was all too expensive and fantastic for sober middle-class London, and it failed disastrously, ruining poor Soyer. However, he bounced up again.

Then came the Crimean War and reports from the front that the soldiers' food, all too often raw and cold, was a scandal. Soyer offered to go out, even paying his own expenses, to see if he could teach the military to attempt some decent cookery. What he saw at Scutari and in the Crimea convinced him at once that even the worst reports hardly did justice to the dreadful situation. He worked harder than he had ever done before in his life. But, as he afterwards declared, he 'felt more proud to work for the soldiers' than ever he did 'working for the greatest epicures and the first lords of England.' He designed and constructed bakeries and cooking stoves, and actually invited the Allied high command to a dinner – and a very successful one too – that he had created simply out of army rations. He showed army cooks, who knew nothing, how to turn their half-raw meat and dreary stews into tasty dishes, and the troops loved him. By the time he had done with the Crimea army it was eating well. Dying so soon afterwards, as early as 1858, did Alexis Soyer create for the British Army a tradition of tenderly-cooked meat and exquisite sauce, delicious bread and biscuits? Alas! he did not, as so many of us can testify.

The Crimean War clearly demonstrated the increasing power of the press, which helped to create public opinion and then lent it a powerful voice. Shortly, as we shall see, Lord Aberdeen's government, which had made such a muddle of the war, was brought down, and probably no two men did more to bring it down than William Howard Russell, *The Times* man at the front, and his editor Delane. Newspaper men at the front, with the electric telegraph at their disposal, changed the whole attitude of the press. Wellington's greatest victories, settling the fate of Europe, had been belatedly and briefly announced in the press, without big headlines, and there had been no eye-witness accounts of his campaigns, for which, in spite of his victories, he must have been deeply thankful. But now Russell and his colleagues and their editors were in a particularly favourable position; the war correspondents were on the spot, though never made welcome, and as yet there was not the military censorship that was bound to come. The telegraph had arrived, but not the blue pencil. It was a good time for a born newspaper man like Delane.

We have not yet taken a look at the newspapers and periodicals of the 1850s. The year 1854 is important, not only because the Crimean War was reported so fully, but also because it was the last full year in which the so-called tax on knowledge was imposed. This was the stamp duty, imposed by repressive governments not for additional revenue but to prevent the spread of cheap newspapers that would inevitably attack them. By 1815 the stamp duty had risen to fourpence a copy, with the result that there was a lively 'black market' in cheap radical papers, and there were endless prosecutions. Thanks chiefly to Bulwer-Lytton in the House of Commons, the stamp duty in 1836 was reduced to a penny a copy, and in 1855 it was abolished. Both advertisements and paper itself had been severely taxed, making really large circulations impossible, but these came to be modified, with the result that the later 1850s saw the arrival of a number of serious and important provincial newspapers, some of which, notably the *Manchester Guardian*, the *Yorkshire Post*, and the *Birmingham Post*, have survived to this day.

In the middle 1850s there were six morning papers in London. *The Times, Morning Advertiser, Daily News, Morning Herald, Morning Post, Morning Chronicle.* The order here is in terms of circulation, with *The Times*, now about 59,000 daily, far ahead of its rivals. Indeed, their circulation was minute, mostly well under 10,000. It is sad to see the old *Morning Chronicle* at the bottom of the list, for it went back to the eighteenth century and had had a wonderful list of contributors,

Throughout the 1850s John Leech was one of the mainstays of *Punch*. (opposite above) 'A substitute for the Sea Side, or the Serpentine as it might be'

(opposite below) 'A Pic-nic in the Drawing Room – a capital thing for a Wet Day'. Picnics were very fashionable and were apt to proceed despite poor weather conditions.

including Sheridan, Lamb, Hazlitt, Tom Moore, Byron, Thackeray and John Stuart Mill; and Dickens in his youth had been its star reporter. But the life was ebbing out of it, and in 1862 it vanished. The London evening papers were the *Globe, Sun* and *Standard,* all with tiny circulations.

I have in front of me a list of over twenty weekly newspapers and periodicals published in London at this time, their prices ranging from ninepence (for the old-established *Spectator*) to threepence, but with the majority at sixpence. As we have already noticed Dickens's *Household Words,* we can omit it here. The most successful of the general periodicals was the *Illustrated London News,* which sold over 130,000 each week. In 1855 the *Saturday Review* came to rival the *Spectator,* bringing with it a sharp sardonic style of comment. *Punch* kept going, but this was not one of its richer decades. It had lost Thackeray, and in 1850 because of its strong anti-Catholic bias it had lost 'Dicky' Doyle and his unique combination of drollery and charm in illustration. Its mainstay throughout this decade was the amiable and industrious John Leech, whose work seems to some of us to have been over-rated.

The heavy quarterlies, so famous in the Regency, still existed but had lost much of their influence; it was the newer and rationalistic *Westminster Review* that carried the bigger guns. Half-crown monthly magazines like *Blackwood's* and *Fraser's* and *Bentley's Miscellany*, which men of letters found hospitable, still survived, but the serious monthly magazines at a shilling, led by Thackeray's *Cornhill*, first came out in the 1860s. There were, however, in the 1850s any number of religious-cum-domestic periodicals and magazines. It was in 1852 that Samuel Beeton, a very enterprising publisher, blazed a trail familiar enough to us now, bringing out a monthly *Englishwoman's Domestic Magazine*, costing only twopence. As it announced, it was dedicated to 'the improvement of the intellect, the cultivation of the morals and the cherishing of domestic virtues', with special emphasis on the latter, offering articles and notes on fashion, cooking, gardening, care of pets and also, in 'Cupid's Letter Bag', advice to the lovelorn. It was this Mr Beeton who was the husband of our famous Mrs Beeton: Isabella, who had trained as a pianist, who was young, handsome, delicate (she died young) and altogether very far removed from our image of the stout Victorian matron commanding us to take two dozen eggs and a quart of cream.

Neither the false image nor the pathetic reality of Mrs Beeton must tempt us to overlook the foremost journalist of the time. This was the man who had sent William Howard Russell to report the Crimean War and could not be bullied into calling him back: John Thaddeus Delane, editor of *The Times* and, like Russell, Irish by birth. Delane was born in 1817, took his degree at Oxford in 1839, began writing for *The Times*, of which his father was financial manager, and at the astoundingly early age of twenty-three became editor (he was the youngest member of the staff). Delane edited *The Times* for thirty-six years. Unlike editors before or since, he wrote very little for it himself but he was completely responsible for its policy and its organization as a great newspaper. He supported no political party for its own sake, took an independent line whatever government was in power, and only on very few occasions – the situation out of which the Crimean War came being one of them – allowed the sheer pressure of public opinion to change the policy of *The Times*. He was not always wise – and his position highlighted any unwisdom – but almost always he was sensible, fairly liberal-minded and undoubtedly courageous. Above all, he was a great journalist, having had a passionate devotion to the idea of journalism from early youth. Continually and often with much ingenuity he improved the collection and communication of news, to the benefit of fellow editors everywhere. His power was enormous, making governments tremble, but he tried to use it soberly and conscientiously; he takes a secure place among the great editors of the nineteenth century.

Victoria's Heyday

Thackeray's *The Newcomes* was not published in volume form until 1855, but throughout 1854 it was appearing in monthly parts, so we may reasonably consider it here. He had been still uncertain what to do next, in the summer of 1853, when the publishers, Bradbury and Evans, offered him £3,600 for a new novel, to come out first in twenty-four monthly parts; and there would also be £500 from Harpers and Tauchnitz. 'It's coining money, isn't it?' he wrote to his mother. It was money he needed badly, and he welcomed it, but he gave many a weary shrug at the idea of committing himself to a long novel, which this would have to be. He did not warm to the work at all at first. But he had been moving in high society, and this may have offered him a theme. He must have remembered too his advice to his young friend, Sally Baxter, in New York, when he warned her against 'the heartlessness' of London society. He was still feeling restless, chiefly because there was no chance of seeing Jane Brookfield on the easy old terms. Moreover, his two motherless daughters were no longer little girls; they were growing up; and if he felt like travelling abroad, they ought to be given a chance of going with him.

Thackeray's indolence is always being mentioned, but when he found himself in a situation that demanded some hard close work he faced it manfully. So, for example, during two months in Rome, when he had his daughters on his hands and some sickness to cope with, he was able to finish Number 6 of *The Newcomes*, and write the whole of Numbers 7 and 8 and part of 9. And he was not telling some dramatic tale that wrote itself; he was having to carry forward a whole family and a thickly populated section of London society. However, he had adopted one device, making his former hero, Pendennis, his narrator, that made things easier for him and avoided his usual constant interruptions in his own person, as author. (But rather tactlessly he drops the Pendennis mask at the very end of the novel.) Finally, *The Newcomes* takes its place with *Vanity Fair* and *Esmond* among the more ambitious of Thackeray's novels, and Professor Ray, his tireless biographer, tells us it is 'in some respects the richest, not only of Thackeray's books but of all Victorian fictions.'

This is a bold claim, and the reputation of *The Newcomes* today does little to support it. True, Thackeray himself is undeservedly out of fashion. (It might be said of him that he is always a better writer than you think he is going to be.) Dip into *The Newcomes* and scene after scene comes to life. Yet as a whole it is somehow unsatisfactory, falling well below *Vanity Fair*. I have always liked the story of the little girl whose teacher lent her a book on penguins and afterwards asked her what she thought of it. The little girl replied, 'This book tells me more about penguins than I want to know.' And somehow Thackeray's novel tells us more about the Newcomes than we want to know. Or we can put it another way and declare that it goes on too long on the particular level that Thackeray had chosen, even though it has a wide variety of backgrounds. We could also say that while Clive and Ethel are convincing rounded figures, Colonel Newcome is too good and Barnes Newcome and Mrs Mackenzie are too bad, which would not matter in a rather melodramatic tale but remains a serious defect in an elaborate novel of social comment. Though Trollope acknowledged Thackeray to be his master, at his best he would have told this tale better than Thackeray did. On the other hand, if we take *The Newcomes* as an indictment of a society, then I feel that the later Dickens, notwithstanding his lack of easy realism, his theatricality and grotesque exaggeration, would have hit that society much harder. And somehow *The Newcomes* is long and thick but not *rich*, even though it offers us some pretty writing, some persons and scenes that come to life, and an astonishingly detailed Victorian social panorama.

(left) Initial letter, 'In which we hear a soprano and a contralto', to Thackeray's *The Newcomes*, by Richard ('Dicky') Doyle

(centre) Initial letter, 'Returns from Rome to Pall Mall', to Thackeray's *The Newcomes*, by Richard Doyle

(right) Initial letter, 'The Old Ladies', to Thackeray's *The Newcomes*, by Richard Doyle

However, *The Newcomes* is better Thackeray than *Hard Times* is Dickens, who attempted with it an experiment – and failed. Because the circulation and profits of *Household Words* were dwindling dangerously, Dickens allowed himself to be persuaded by his partners and publishers, Bradbury and Evans, to write a novel that could appear as a weekly serial. The result was *Hard Times*, which arrived with the first April issue, ran right through the summer, and put an end to any immediate worry about circulation and profits. It came out in volume form later in 1854, but did not repeat, then or afterwards, the success it had had as a weekly serial. But it has had its special admirers, particularly among those who see Dickens as a propagandist for their own political-economic ideology. We are told that one Cambridge pundit, a few years ago, declared that the only Dickens novel worth reading was *Hard Times* – surely one of the most foolish statements of this age. It would be far more sensible to reverse this judgment, to say that of all the novels of Dickens's maturity *Hard Times* is the least worth reading. It is muddled in its direct political-social criticism. As a novel it falls far below the standard set by Dickens himself from *Dombey and Son* onwards. Here for once it is almost as if we are seeing Dickens through the eyes of his hostile critics, for in *Hard Times* there really *are* reckless and theatrical over-statements, there really *are* characters that are nothing but caricatures, there really *is* melodramatic muddled emotionalism. On the other hand, only in a few odd places is there any evidence of Dickens's unique grotesque-poetic genius, so obvious in *Bleak House*. We may join him in condemning an industrialized commercial society, its values, its economics, its education, its withering relationships, but this does not mean we have to pretend an unsatisfactory novel is a masterpiece, just because it favours our side.

There is almost every possible excuse for Dickens's comparative failure here. He was rushed into writing a novel, without having had time to brood over it. Weekly serialization and the shorter length imposed upon him he found constricting, irritating, frustrating. Within such limits, promising characters like Louisa Bounderby and Stephen Blackpool, no mere caricatures, could not be properly developed. There was no room for that expansion – with imagination in full flight – which has given us some of the finest passages in his late long novels. *Hard Times*, we feel, was very much a conscious effort. It was a task to its author and remains something of a task to us, his readers. We may agree with its social criticism, its disgust and despair, yet still find it unconvincing and unattractive as a novel.

The truth is, Dickens did not know enough about industrial England. He had given a public reading in Birmingham, which provided him with some horrifying glimpses of the grim Midlands. Because there was a big strike in Preston, he paid it a visit, but he found no drama there. He came away deeply sympathizing with the men but feeling doubtful about trade union organizers. He was not on any ground familiar to him. So his Coketown is merely a horrible appearance, and in order to offer us a sharp contrast to Gradgrind and Bounderby, their outlook and style of life, he sketches a travelling circus to represent arts, skills, warm personal relationships. But he could have found all these, together with many odd attractive characters, in Coketown, if he had really known it and not simply looked at it from a railway train. As it is, Coketown belongs to propaganda and not to creative imagination.

'The Allied Powers', one of the many Staffordshire pottery ornaments and figures made to satisfy the vast popular interest in the personalities and events of the Crimean War. In this group, made in 1854, Victoria is standing between Napoleon III (on her right) and the King of Sardinia.

(overleaf) 'Florence Nightingale receiving the wounded at Scutari, 1856', by Jerry Barrett (c. 1814–1906). This is the original sketch for a group entitled 'The Mission of Mercy'. Florence Nightingale is left of centre, standing behind the kneeling man with the stretcher. Next but one to Miss Nightingale, on her right, is Alexis Soyer.

THE ALLIED POWERS

1855

EARLY THIS YEAR there were more dramatic events in and around Westminster than there were among the frozen hills of the Crimea. Press and public alike were now crying for a change of government, and for the most part were demanding that Palmerston should leave the Home Office and take charge of the war. Before Parliament reassembled in January, John Arthur Roebuck had given notice that he would introduce a motion for an Inquiry into the conduct of the war. This sounds mild enough, but everybody in the House knew it was a big gun that Roebuck had been busy loading. Member now for Sheffield, where he was enormously popular, Roebuck had been in Parliament for many years and was an effective old hand. He was not really a party man, and he tended to be radical at home and somewhat reactionary abroad. He was, as the D.N.B. says, 'short in stature, vehement in speech, bold in opinion', and his power of invective was notorious and dreaded. Even before Roebuck could bring in his motion Lord John Russell resigned from the government, declaring that it was impossible for him to defend the conduct of the war. On 29 January Roebuck's motion was carried – and the government heavily defeated – by 305 against 148, and Lord Aberdeen immediately resigned.

Both Russell and Lord Derby were asked to form an administration and failed, and the Queen most reluctantly – 'I had no choice,' she wrote to Uncle Leopold – sent for Palmerston, who would now be her Prime Minister for many a year. He had been stoutly in favour of the war – indeed, he had suggested at the outset that Sebastopol was not enough, that the Allies should take the whole of the Crimea and then invade Georgia in the Caucasus – but as Home Secretary he had played no part in the disastrous conduct of the campaign. After some hesitant weeks, his old unique combination of decision, drive and bonhomie, in the House or Downing Street, began to succeed again. He gave the military departments an energy they badly needed; he compelled the Admiralty to organize a special transport branch; he gave orders to improve the Crimean commissariat; and sent out a sanitary commission to bring some sense and order at once into the hospitals and camps. Meanwhile, on 2 March the formidable Tsar Nicholas I had died and was succeeded by the milder Alexander II. During the spring months the British, though still in their trenches in front of Sebastopol, were no longer in the appalling situation in which they had been throughout the winter.

Detail of 'The Cavalry Charge at Balaklava, October 25, 1854', by Ed. Morin, lithographed by Day & Son, and published by Paul and Dominic Colnaghi, 28 November 1854; from *Russian War Series of Views*, 1854–55

Victoria's Heyday

Good roads and even a railway had been constructed; supplies arrived regularly; and the death-rate dwindled to an astonishingly low figure. Reinforcements brought the divisions up to strength, though now most of the tough and well-disciplined regulars had vanished and the new drafts consisted largely of almost raw recruits: this was not the army of Alma and Inkerman. It would be enough now if Sebastopol could be taken. Palmerston no longer had dreams of occupying all the Crimea and then invading the Caucasus.

There were changes in both High Commands. At odds with his Emperor, Canrobert resigned as commander-in-chief but gallantly insisted upon still serving in the field. His place was filled by General Pélissier, a more aggressive and resolute soldier. The Allies, including a large number of Turks, were now joined by 15,000 Sardinian troops. A bold joint move at the end of May cut the supply line to Sebastopol, which was now completely besieged. The Russians working to restore defences under the fire of the Allies' heavy guns suffered considerable losses every day, but the great fortress was still immensely strong, and two Allied assaults in June were repulsed, with many casualties on both sides. That nice man in the wrong place, Lord Raglan, ailing and deeply disappointed by the British failure to hold the ground it had gained, died on 28 June. His successor was General Simpson, who did not want the command himself and was wanted by nobody else except those in London who appointed him.

The general atmosphere, ability and morale of the British Army, with so many new young soldiers in its ranks, can be discovered in a letter from Johnnie Stanley to his mother, Lady Stanley, dated 18 July 1855:

> We got into what the *Illustrated London News* calls the Valley of Death. The road is good, it is covered with great big shot and along it there were some dead bodies which have been covered with lime to prevent the smell but it at the same time quite preserves the features only looking very white. The coat is opened in order to put the lime over the body, the stomach generally sinks in very soon & as they cross the hands over it, it has a very peculiar appearance of a man lying down with his hands inside his body. . . . About 12 p.m. the Russians somehow made a sortie or at least came into collision with the French & there was very heavy musketry fire for ½ an hour. There were plenty killed but it led to nothing, some of our young soldiers thinking they ought to do something & seeing some men firing immediately opened fire. It was a French advance, we very soon put a stop to it. [*Presumably the firing, not the advance.*] The Scots Guards were not so lucky, they fired at what they thought were Russians & wounded 3 men of the Welch fusiliers. I am sorry to say 2 of our men were in great fright, they would not look over the parapet I had a good mind to kick one, he was trembling so that you heard his haversack rattle. . . .

General Simpson

In August the Russians in great force made a last desperate attempt to break the siege, and failed, with heavy losses. Two key fortresses, the

174

enormous Malakoff and the Redan, remained to dominate the situation. On 8 September, after two days of constant shelling, the Allies advanced to take the forts by storm. Pélissier set 36,000 French troops swarming into the attack, determined to capture the Malakoff, while General Simpson, perhaps determined to outdo Raglan in futility, sent forward just under 1,400 men to take the Redan, keeping most of his army in reserve, for some reason best known to himself. The result was that this last great action in the Crimean War was an inglorious day for British arms; for the French, after some hard fighting, took the great Malakoff, but the British penetrated but could not hold the Redan. 'There was a feeling of deep depression in camp all night,' Russell wrote. 'We were painfully aware that our attack had failed . . . and sad stories ran from mouth to mouth respecting the losses of the officers and the behaviour of the men.' But then next day he could hear the Russians blowing up the remaining forts; he saw flames and then rows of mansions burning away; the Russians were destroying everything they could destroy before abandoning the town: Sebastopol had fallen at last.

The Russians had had enough. (There was no railway as yet to the Crimea, and the long, long roads there were not good.) Indeed, apart perhaps from General Pélissier and his more fiery officers, everybody had had enough. The Sultan of Turkey was spending the money he had been lent not on the war but on himself. Napoleon III was now more interested in his financiers than in his generals, and, backed by Austria, wanted peace at a price Palmerston was not ready to pay: Palmerston in fact was sufficiently unrealistic for a time to want to carry the war into a third year. All the people in England who had once shouted for war had had enough too. Sebastopol had fallen, and that would do. There was rejoicing throughout the country, even as far as the Highlands, where Queen Victoria, happy anyhow at Balmoral, wrote in her Journal on 10 September:

General Pélissier

All were in constant expectation of more telegraphic despatches. At half-past ten o'clock two arrived – one for me, and one for Lord Granville. I began reading mine, which was from Lord Clarendon, with more details from Marshal Pélissier of the further destruction of the Russian ships; and Lord Granville said, 'I have still better news;' on which he read, 'From General Simpson – *Sebastopol is in the hands of the Allies.*' God be praised for it! Our Delight was great; but we could hardly believe the good news, and from having so long, so anxiously expected it, one could not realize the actual fact.

Albert said they should go at once and light the bonfire which had been prepared when the false report of the fall of the town arrived last year, and had remained ever since, waiting to be lit. . . . In a few minutes, Albert and all the gentlemen, in every species of attire, sallied forth, followed by all the population of the village – keepers, gillies, workmen – up to the top of the cairn. We waited, and saw them light it; accompanied by general cheering. . . . About three-quarters of an hour after, Albert came down and said the scene had been wild and exciting beyond everything.

Victoria's Heyday

The people had been drinking healths in whisky, and were in great ecstacy. The whole house seemed in a wonderful state of excitement. The boys were with difficulty awakened, and when at last this was the case, they begged leave to go up to the top of the cairn.

We remained till a quarter to twelve; and, just as I was undressing, all the people came down under the windows, the pipes playing, the people singing, firing off guns, and cheering – first for me, then for Albert, the Emperor of the French, and the 'downfall of *Sebastopol*'.

This summer, Victoria, accompanied by her husband, her eldest daughter, Vicky, and the young Prince of Wales, had paid a state visit to Napoleon III. So we find her writing to Uncle Leopold, from St Cloud, on 23 August 1855:

I am *delighted, enchanted, amused,* and *interested,* and I think I never saw anything more *beautiful* and gay than Paris – or more splendid than all the Palaces. Our reception is *most* gratifying – for it is enthusiastic and really kind in the highest degree. . . . Our entrance into Paris . . . quite over-powering – splendidly – illuminated – immensely crowded. . . . The Emperor has done wonders for Paris, and the Bois de Boulogne. . . . We have been to the Exposition, to Versailles – which is most splendid and magnificent – to the Grand Opéra, where the reception and the way in which 'God save the Queen' was sung were *most* magnificent. Yesterday we went to the Tuileries; in the evening *Théâtre ici*; tonight an immense ball at the Hotel de Ville. They have asked to call a new street, which we opened, *after me*!

'Entry of Queen Victoria into Paris, August 18, 1855', by E. Guérard

'Their Majesties at the Opera, Paris, August 21, 1855', by Eugène Lami

And if she was delighted and enchanted, so was her thirteen-year-old son, the small fair Prince of Wales (in Highland costume too) who was endlessly cheered by the Paris crowd. It was all so wonderfully different from his restricted and colourless life at home that when it was time to return there he begged the Empress Eugénie to let him stay on. This was not possible, but ever afterwards, both as Prince of Wales and then as King Edward VII, the enchantment lingered on, so that he never fell out of love with France.

At the end of March 1855 Charlotte Brontë died. She was of course married now, to Arthur Nicholls, her father's curate, whose original proposal had been dismissed with furious scorn by the tyrannical old man. Charlotte at first had felt nothing but compassion for poor Nicholls, but when at last she was able to marry him she began to love even his rather possessive and dictatorial manner. When she had published *Villette*, early in 1853, it had been warmly welcomed by everybody except her friend, Harriet Martineau, who complained, both in private and in the *Daily News*, that Charlotte's female characters were altogether too much concerned about being loved. 'It is not thus in real life,' Miss Martineau declared. Her real life was not Charlotte's real life, which flowered wonderfully as soon as she was married. But

177

the trials of early pregnancy and a cold she could not shake off laid Charlotte low, and the tuberculosis lying in wait for her took hold of yet another Brontë. Mrs Gaskell gives us the last scene of all:

> . . . Long days and longer nights went by; still the same relentless nausea and faintness, and still borne in patient trust. About the third week in March there was a change; a low wandering delirium came on; and in it she begged constantly for food and even for stimulants. She swallowed eagerly now; but it was too late. Wakening for an instant from this stupor of intelligence, she saw her husband's woe-worn face, and caught some murmured words of prayer that God would spare her. 'Oh!' she whispered forth, 'I am not going to die, am I? He will not separate us, we have been so happy.'

So the last of those four eager and imaginative youngsters, once so happily engaged in their chronicles of Angria and sagas of Gondal, left that doomed house in Haworth. Our lives are a mystery, following patterns invisible even to Harriet Martineau.

Charlotte Brontë

It was in 1855 that John Ruskin began publishing his *Notes on the Royal Academy*, which he repeated annually until the end of this decade. The D.N.B., which contains a very full account of Ruskin, tells us:

> The notes were very popular with the public, but less so with the artists. Ruskin hoped that certain criticisms passed by him on a friend's picture would 'make no difference in their friendship.' 'Dear Ruskin,' replied the artist, 'next time I meet you, I shall knock you down; but I hope it will make no difference in our friendship.' 'Damn the fellow!' said another young artist who enjoyed the critic's acquaintance; 'why doesn't he back his friends?'

Detail of the portrait of John Ruskin, 1854, by Sir John Everett Millais

Ruskin's pained surprise at this natural reaction is part of that curious naïveté which he combined with so much insight and genuine wisdom. But these Royal Academy Notes were merely a tiny part of his huge multifarious activities. He could suggest them, partly to amuse her, in a letter to Jane Carlyle in October of this year:

> I have written since May a good six hundred pages. Also I have prepared about thirty drawings for engravers this year, retouched the engravings (generally the worst part of the business), and etched some on steel myself. In the course of the six hundred pages I have had to make various remarks on German metaphysics, on poetry, on political economy, cookery, music, geology, dress, agriculture, horticulture, and navigation, all of which subjects I have had to read up accordingly, and this takes time. . . .

The irony here is that already it was beginning to be thought – and this would be felt more strongly afterwards – that Ruskin ought to be minding his own business, the criticism of the visual arts, and ought to stop trying to write about everything. What did he know about political economy, work and wages, the condition of the people? But now we see that while he was often wrong in his art criticism he was more often than not quite originally and blazingly right when he took his criticism outside museums and art galleries. He was content to sit at the feet of his famous prophet, Thomas Carlyle, but most of us would agree now that, some crankiness apart, he brought more perception and real wisdom to social questions than Carlyle ever did. It was Ruskin who responded best to the desire of the more thoughtful members of the Victorian working-class to educate themselves, a desire that has so sadly dwindled in our own time. We could do with a splendid revival of John Ruskin – not the art critic but the sage, the man who saw that the real test of a society is not the wealth it produces but the kind of people it creates.

We never think of the 1850s in terms of Tax Commissioners, but they existed then, often summoning taxpayers to appear before them. In November 1855 they had served notice on a certain Thomas Carlyle of Cheyne Row, Chelsea, but, being a difficult and selfish husband, he had sent his wife, Jane Welsh Carlyle, to go in his place. I have taken her spirited account of this ordeal from the selection of her letters edited by Trudy Bliss, and it seems to me well worth the space it will take up. So, on 21 November:

> It was with feeling like the ghost of a dead dog, that I rose and dressed and drank my coffee, and then started for Kensington. Mr C. said 'the voice of honour *seemed* to call on him to go himself.' But either it did not call loud enough, or he would not listen to that charmer. I went in a cab, to save all my breath for *appealing*. Set down at 30 Hornton Street, I found a dirty private-like house, only with Tax Office painted on the door. A dirty woman-servant opened the door and told me the Commissioners would not be there for half an hour, but I might walk up. There were already some half-score of *men* assembled in the waiting-room, among whom I

Detail of 'Study of gneiss rock', 1853, by John Ruskin

saw the man who cleans our clocks, and a young apothecary of Cheyne Walk. All the others, to look at them, could not have been suspected for an instant, I should have said, of *making* a hundred a year. Feeling in a false position, I stood by myself at a window and 'thought shame' (as children say). Men trooped in by twos and threes, till the small room was pretty well filled; at last a woman showed herself. 'O *my*!' did I ever know the full value of any sort of woman – as *woman* – before! By this time some benches had been brought in, and I was sitting nearest the door. . . .

'*First-come* lady,' called the clerk, opening a small side-door, and I stept forward into a grand *peut-être*. There was an instant of darkness while the one door was shut behind and the other opened in front; and there I stood in a dim room where three men sat round a large table spread with papers. One held a pen ready over an open ledger; another was taking snuff, and had *taken* still worse in his time, to judge by his shaky, clayed appearance. The third, who was plainly the cock of that dungheap, was *sitting for Rhadamanthus* – a Rhadamanthus *without the justice*. 'Name,' said the horned-owl-looking individual holding the pen. 'Carlyle.' 'What?' 'Carlyle.' Seeing he still looked dubious, I spelt it for him. 'Ha!' cried Rhadamanthus, a big, bloodless-faced, insolent-looking fellow. 'What is this? why is Mr Carlyle not come himself? Didn't he get a letter ordering him to appear? Mr Carlyle wrote some nonsense about being exempted from coming, and I desired an answer to be sent that he must come, must do as other people.' 'Then, sir,' I said, 'your desire has been neglected, it would seem, my husband having received no such letter; and I was told by one of your fellow Commissioners that Mr Carlyle's personal appearance was not indispensable.' '*Huffgh! Huffgh!* what does Mr Carlyle mean by saying he had no income from his writings, when he himself fixed it in the beginning at a hundred and fifty?' 'It means, sir, that, in ceasing to write, one ceases to be paid for writing, and Mr Carlyle has published nothing for several years.' '*Huffgh! Huffgh!* I understand nothing about that.' 'I do,' whispered the snuff-taking Commissioner at my ear. 'I *quite* understand a literary man does not always make money. I *would take it all off*, for *my* share, but (sinking his voice still lower) I am only one voice here, and not the most important.' 'There,' said I, handing to Rhadamanthus Chapman and Hall's account, 'that will prove Mr Carlyle's statement.' 'What am I to make of that? *Huffgh!* we should have Mr Carlyle here to swear to this before we believe it.' 'If a gentleman's word of honour written at the bottom of that paper is not enough, you can put me on my oath! I am ready to swear to it!' '*You*! you, indeed! No, no! we can do nothing with *your* oath!' 'But, sir, I understand my husband's affairs fully, better than he does himself.' 'That I can *well* believe; but we can make nothing of this,' flinging my document contemptuously on the table. The horned owl picked it up, glanced over it while Rhadamanthus was tossing papers about, and grumbling about 'people that wouldn't conform to rules;' then handed it back to him saying deprecatingly: 'But, sir, this is a very plain statement.' 'Then what has Mr Carlyle to live upon? You don't mean to tell me that he lives on that?' pointing to the document. 'Heaven forbid, sir! but I am not here to explain what Mr Carlyle has *to live on*, only to declare his income from Literature during the last three years.' 'True! true!' mumbled the not-most-important voice at my elbow,

'A Chelsea Interior' – Mr and Mrs
Thomas Carlyle at home, 1858, by
Robert Tait

'Mr Carlyle, I believe, has landed income.' 'Of which,' said I haughtily,
for my spirit was up, 'I have fortunately no account to render in this
kingdom and to this board.' 'Take off fifty pounds, say a hundred – take
off a hundred pounds,' said Rhadamanthus to the horned owl. 'If we
write Mr Carlyle down a *hundred and fifty* he has no reason to complain,
I think. There, you may go. Mr Carlyle has no reason to complain.'

Second-come woman was already introduced, and I was motioned to the
door; but I could not depart without saying that 'at all events there was
no use in complaining, since they had the power to enforce their decision.'
On stepping out, my first thought was, what a mercy Carlyle didn't come
himself! For the rest, though it might have gone better, I was thankful
that it had not gone worse. When one has been threatened with a great
injustice, one accepts a smaller as a favour.

Went back to spend the evening with Geraldine when Mr C. set forth
for Bath House. Her ladyship in town for two days.

Victoria's Heyday

The bitter flavour of that last little paragraph is easily explained. 'Her ladyship' was the fashionable and wealthy Lady Ashburton, who liked to see the glowering Scots prophet in attendance upon her at Bath House. There was no sex in this curious relationship; nevertheless, Mrs Carlyle, a woman of spirit, so often left at home, could not help feeling angry and bitterly jealous. And who can blame her?

In July a new volume of poems by the Carlyles' friend, Alfred Tennyson, had come out. It contained some pieces already well-known through press publication – and one long poem, which Tennyson described later as 'a monodrama', *Maud*. It had been written during the last six months of 1854. Tennyson had now settled into Farringford, a house not far from the sea in the west of the Isle of Wight. It is a little region combining extremes: early spring flowers, budding copses, high summers of roses, with great downs and cliffs and screaming south-western gales. All of this went into *Maud*, which in turn combined perfervid and highly subjective narrative with exquisite brief lyrics that linger in the memory. The poet's opinion of it can be discovered in Charles Tennyson's life of his grandfather:

> Alfred had thrown the whole passion of his being into *Maud*, which remained through life his favourite poem. . . . He had never written with more fire or originality, or given his genius freer rein, and he had high hopes of its reception. Unfortunately, these hopes were doomed to bitter disappointment. The public were frankly bewildered, and indeed nothing could be imagined more different from the poem which had won him his high position with the English people, *In Memoriam*.

Most reviewers and contemporary critics disliked the poem too. Yet Tennyson, usually so wincingly sensitive to hostile criticism, for once disregarded it. *Maud* was still his favourite poem, and for many years it was the one he insisted upon reading aloud, making full use of his magnificent deep voice: the ghost of it can still be caught in some very early gramophone recordings, heard more than once on radio. And even in old age he never lost all trace of the broad Lincolnshire vowel sounds of his youth. Yet many of his friends could not disguise their revulsion from the poem; some sections of the press were almost hysterically abusive; and so many nasty letters from the public came to Farringford that Emily Tennyson began reading them first and burnt the worst of them to spare her husband. Only his fellow poets were its enthusiatic admirers. Browning read and re-read it; his wife, after listening to it, declared how 'wonderful, tender and beautiful' it was; and Rossetti, hearing it read, was spell-bound and 'the softer passages and the songs' made him weep.

Maud can be taken in many different ways, none of them without literary and social significance. It can be seen as an attempt, rather belated, to restore to the long poem the dramatic impact and popularity it had enjoyed during the earlier Romantic Age. Here it failed because it

In this detail from Ford Madox Brown's 'Work', a vast semi-allegorical painting begun in 1852 (see also page 99) the artist included portraits of Thomas Carlyle, with beard and moustache, and the Reverend Frederick Denison Maurice representing the 'brain-workers', who, 'seeming to be idle, work, and are the cause of well-ordained work in others'.

bewildered the ordinary reader. The story is drowned in the narrator's intense subjectivity. Its blood-and-thunder events, more than enough to furnish any popular romance, flash by like incidents in a wild but fading dream. It has no characters that come alive, even though one of them may be seen in a sudden glare:

> . . . that dandy-despot, he,
> That jewell'd mass of millinery,
> That oil'd and curl'd Assyrian Bull
> Smelling of musk and of insolence,
> Her brother. . . .

(Surely a magnificent evocation of an 1850s man of fashion.) Though we spend so much time with her, often in heart-breaking moments, Maud herself, the only person named in the poem, never becomes a character, a girl we might have known, but remains – in Jungian terms – an *anima* figure, magically illuminated by the man's unconscious. With characters that are mere outlines, glimpses of events in a thick haze, the whole action obscure and puzzling, Tennyson could not hope to create a dramatic poem that would attract readers now lost to prose fiction. And if that was his intention, then he asked for failure and disappointment.

But was it his intention? He was soon to prove, in his *Idylls*, that he could tell a story that would hold and please his readers. In *Maud* he was trying to do something else – or, indeed, to do several things at the same time. One of them was the expression, using various forms of verse, of a young man's unbalanced mind, from the first obviously neurotic and then later psychotic:

> But up and down and to and fro,
> Ever about me the dead men go;
> And then to hear a dead man chatter
> Is enough to drive one mad.

And here we must remember that he had taken the 'hydropathic treatment' twice, when he must have kept company with some deranged minds. Again, as the friend of Charles Kingsley and F. D. Maurice, he was fiercely condemning the whole age, its blatant commercialism, the darkness and greed of its industry and the dreadful plight of its workers. He resumes this attack at every opportunity. So, for example, we have:

> This new-made lord, whose splendour plucks
> The slavish hat from the villager's head?
> Whose old grandfather has lately died,
> Gone to a blacker pit, for whom
> Grimy nakedness dragging his trucks
> And laying his trams in a poison'd gloom
> Wrought, till he crept from a gutted mine
> Master of half a servile shire,
> And left his coal all turn'd into gold
> To a grandson, first of his noble line. . . .

Arthur Hughes was not actually a member of the Pre-Raphaelite Brotherhood but an ardent disciple of it. 'April Love', 1856, originated as a painting of a girl in period costume, but Hughes wisely decided that the intensity of feeling he wanted to express demanded a figure in contemporary dress.

But behind these radical assaults there was unradical old-family Toryism. There was also, lending the poem its poorest verses, some foolish praise of war as the regenerator both of his hero and of the nation. All this was largely responsible for his hostile press. If he didn't like Manchester, then Manchester didn't like him – or his *Maud*.

However, it is hard to believe that no personal experience, no hidden chapter of his own life, plays any part in this poem. There is on the whole a marked difference in quality between the invented melodramatic stuff and whatever relates directly to Maud, the sixteen-year-old girl who is also the ancient magical *anima* figure. It is only his memory of such an involvement that will explain both his own feeling about the poem and its own triumphant moments. These range from lines of verbal magnificence – *The shining daffodil dead, and Orion low in his grave* or *There has fallen a splendid tear | From the passion-flower at the gate* to the many lyrics at once apparently simple and yet enchanting:

> Go not, happy day,
>   From the shining fields,
> Go not, happy day,
>   Till the maiden yields

until we reach,

> O that 'twere possible
> After long grief and pain
> To find the arms of my true love
> Round me once again!

And we know that this appeared in a periodical as far back as 1837, and that a friend's discovery of it started Tennyson thinking about the idea of writing a long lyrical-cum-dramatic poem. Is this the loss of Arthur Hallam again? To some extent, possibly; but most of the passages expressing the half-mad infatuation with the young girl who is also the fateful *anima* figure, everything that suggests the power and enchantment of the archetype, seem to indicate some buried erotic adventure suddenly brought to light. Obviously unequal, at times absurd and at others splendid or deeply moving, *Maud* is a very strange poem, which asks for close study. Its shifting lights contrive to illuminate both the poet and the age.

Probably the strangest visitor this year was Daniel Dunglas Home, the most astonishing of all spiritualist mediums. He was a Scot, born in 1833, with an odd family background. His father was said to be the illegitimate son of the 10th Earl of Home, and his mother came from a family gifted with second sight. She took Daniel to America in 1841 and when she died, not long afterwards, he was adopted by an aunt. Very soon he was having visions and announced that he was in regular communication with his dead mother. There was nothing startlingly original about this. Beginning with the Fox sisters, Katie and Margaret, from 1848 onwards America produced hundreds of mediums, some of

Daniel Dunglas Home

them children, all of them holding regular séances. In every town there were darkened rooms in which luminous spirit faces appeared, musical instruments played themselves, strange voices were heard prophesying, hands materialized from nowhere, and the faithful shivered in draughts of Arctic air. Spiritualism and its miracles were all the rage. Both the time and place were propitious. New revelations were needed, and the Eastern states of America (like Southern California to this day) were buzzing with strange cults and instant Utopias. Young D. D. Home was only another of these spirit miracle-workers, though it was not long before he became the most impressive of them. We know that Thackeray, arriving in New York in December 1852 for his first lecture tour, was hurried off to a Home séance, was amazed by it, and wrote excited letters to his friends in England. During the next two years, visiting many New England towns and being lionized everywhere, Home went from strength to strength, making furniture float around, materializing spirit hands, and levitating not only tables but himself too. However, the original mass excitement was dying down. Moreover, Home

Victoria's Heyday

was a delicate young man and had been advised by his doctor to try a change of climate. So he sailed at the end of March 1855 for England, first to show London what he could do, and then to appear in one European capital after another.

There had been a certain amount of semi-occult hocus-pocus in London a few years earlier: odd mixtures of phrenology, mesmerism, clairvoyance. So we find Macaulay grumbling in his Journal for May 1852:

> Mahon came, and we went to a house in—Street where a Dr—performs his feats of phrenology and mesmerism. I was half ashamed of going; but Mahon made a point of it. The Bishop of Oxford, and his brother Robert, came soon after us. Never was there such paltry quackery. The fraud was absolutely transparent. I cannot conceive how it would impose upon a child. The man knew nothing about me, and therefore his trickery completely failed him. He made me out to be a painter – a landscape painter or a historical painter. He had made out Hallam to be a musician. I could hardly restrain myself from expressing my contempt and disgust while he was pawing my head, and prying over the rotations and oscillations of his pendulum, and the deviations to different points of the compass. . . .

What was generally called 'table-turning' – that is, making a table move, often quite violently, simply by placing hands on it – had been common enough during the earlier 1850s. Most people did not imagine that the restless table brought them spirit messages. They felt it was all rather uncanny (as indeed it is) but chiefly regarded it as a parlour game. In Lady Longford's *Victoria R. I.* we catch a glimpse of the Queen as a table-turner:

> One spring evening at Osborne in 1853 when the nightingales were singing and all the windows open, she and Prince Albert decided to have a go. The table consented to spin round quite nicely for the royal pair but when Lady Ely applied her hand it fairly rushed along. The gentlemen, however, declined to co-operate. Charles Grey rather irritated Her Majesty by his scepticism. 'Peculiar' was the word she used to describe her own sensations; she felt it was some form of magnetism or electricity, not a trick. . . .

A few years later, Napoleon III had some strange stories about Daniel Home to tell Victoria. Her journal records: 'He told us some certainly extraordinary things'; but for one reason or another she never followed up her curiosity, and her Court, unlike several others, was never represented at any of Home's séances.

However, he could hardly complain. Among his admirers was Bulwer-Lytton, always fascinated by anything occult, and Home stayed at Knebworth with him off and on for the next ten years. There are various accounts of Home's séances, and one by Sir David Brewster is fairly typical. He had announced his scepticism in a letter to the press,

'Visit of the Emperor and Empress of the French, Queen Victoria and Albert to the Crystal Palace, Sydenham'

(opposite) A popular song sheet connected with the visit of Napoleon III and Empress Eugénie in 1855

Have you Seen the EMPEROR
and Empress of the French

To the Tune of "Oh Dear how I long to get Married."

Have you seen how the people did france,
  When thousands of all sorts were mingling,
Have you seen the great emperor of France,
  Come to visit the queen of old england.
Did you hear the band merrily play ?
  Guns fire and village bells ring, sir
Did you see how they travelled so gay,
  From the city of Paris to windsor,
    The emperor and empress so fine.

As through London they travelled along,
  Tens of thousands thro' streets were a flocking
There was coalheavers, dustmen and sweeps,
  And ladies with holes in their stockings,
The lasses their handkerchiefs waved,
  There was such a terrible fuss then,
And a thousand of old women round,
  I wish you'd have me for a wife,
    Such a sight there was near seen before.

And when down to windsor they got,
  The queen and her sweet picaninnies,
Called out for a pint and a pot,
  For the emperor and lovely Eugenie,
The cheers they received I declare
  Caused the old castle walls to be shaken,
And they had for their dinner prepared
  Such a lot of fried liver and bacon,
    And they had a jolly blow out.

To the City to dine they will go,
  The emperor of France and his empress,
They will sit where the closet shall flow
  With the Lord Mayor and his Lady mayoress
They will chorus the Red, White and blue,
  The Guildhall I'm sure near was stronger,
They shall dine upon Irish Stew,
  Until they can tuck in no longer,
    Old women get out of the way.

See how all the world is amazed,
  See how the old ladies are running,
Stand off from my toe if you please
  Can't you see the french gentlemen coming,
From the day I came into the world,
  I never beheld such a tussle—
I say marm, your sweet little girl,
  Has knocked out my eye with her bustle,
    Move on there get out of the way

To Sydenham they went parlevous,
  So grand and in noble condition,

While the music played Red, white and blue,
  As they looked on the great exhibition,
The country women did run,
  Their daughters played such pretty capers,
The nightingale sweetly sung
  While old ladies wolfed hot baked potatoes,
    What wonderful doings was there

The empress the emperor's wife,
  Who at home ne'er neglected her duty
Loves her husband as dear as her life,
  You must own she is really a beauty,
I ne'er saw her equal I'm sure,
  Adorned with such jewells and riches,
She'd a bustle behind and before,
  And a fine pair of callico breeches,
    So handsome, so lovely and grand.

Oh crikey says old mistress Chubb,
  I was never afraid—not of no man,
You make such a great hubbabub,
  Why the lady's no more than a woman,
She has but one head and two eyes,
  I saw her ride into the city,—
But as you seem all to surprised,
  I confess she is wonderful pretty,
    Old women stand out of the way.

J Marks, Printer, 206, Brick Lane, Whitechape
Wholesale Dealers and the Trade Supplied.

'Emperor Napoleon III, Queen Victoria, Empress Eugénie and Prince Albert at the Royal Opera House, Covent Garden, 1855'

but in a private letter to his daughter, not made public for many years, he wrote:

> . . . The most unaccountable rappings were produced in various parts of the table: and the table actually rose from the ground when no hand was upon it. A small hand-bell was then laid down with its mouth on the carpet; and after lying for some time, it actually rang, when nothing could have touched it. The bell was then placed on the other side, still upon the carpet, and it came over to me and placed itself in my hand. It did the same to Lord Brougham. . . . These were the principal experiments: we could give no explanation of them, and could not conjecture how they could be produced by any kind of mechanism. We do not believe that it was the work of spirits. . . .

The séance described by Elizabeth Barrett Browning was more remarkable still. Robert Browning was there too, and clearly he detested Home and all his works as we know from his savage 'Mr Sludge, the "Medium"', which he did not publish until 1864, after his wife's death. She wrote to her sister Henrietta in July 1855:

> At the request of the medium [Home], the spiritual hands took from the table a garland which lay there, and placed it upon my head. The particular hand which did this was of the largest human size, as white as snow, and very beautiful. It was as near to me as this hand I write with, and I saw it as distinctly.
>
> I was perfectly calm! not troubled in any way, and felt convinced in my own mind that *no* spirit belonging to me was present on the occasion. The hands which appeared at a distance from me I put up my glass to look at – proving that it was not a mere mental impression, and that they were subject to the usual laws of vision. These hands seemed to Robert and

me to come from under the table, but Mr Lytton saw them rise out of the *wood of the table* – also he tells me . . . that he saw a spiritual (so-called) arm elongate itself as much as two yards across the table and then float away to the windows, where it disappeared. Robert and I did not touch the hands. Mr Lytton and Sir Edward *both did*. The feel was warm and human – rather warmer in fact than is common with a man's hand. The music was very beautiful. . . .

A fantastic episode that left the Brownings sharply divided.

But whatever Home was, he was no 'Mr Sludge' making use of mediums' familiar tricks. (It is possible that many mediums, found to be fraudulent, did originally produce genuine paranormal phenomena, but then had to resort to trickery to satisfy their clients.) Not only was Home never exposed, though very thoroughly investigated, but as time went on he did more and more extraordinary things. Thus, we know from the Dunraven memoirs that revisiting London in the 'sixties (Home spent much of his later life on the Continent) he produced 'a series of very curious manifestations' – such as jets of flame coming out of his head, the sound of invisible birds flying about and whistling and chirping, the terrifying noise of a great wind rushing through the room – and finally, in broad daylight, elongated himself until he seemed eight feet tall and then appeared to float out of one window of this third-storey room and then float back through another window. This was no fraud, messing about with sympathetic ink and phosphorus. If we reject the spirit hypothesis (as I do), then we must agree that either Home was a para-psychological freak or the greatest illusionist, and possibly hypnotist, the world has ever known. He was a rather negative, delicate, finicky person, just the type that might have acquired, through the shock of his mother's death in his boyhood, a dissociated personality, a secondary self able to draw on mysterious sources of kinetic energy. Certainly Daniel Dunglas Home still offers a challenge to those people who think we know all about ourselves and tell us that the paranormal is nonsense.

(overleaf) '"The Kitchen", Fox-Court, Gray's-Inn-Lane', from Henry Mayhew's *London Labour and the London Poor*, 1851

This summer must have been unusually hot because in July we find Lady Stanley writing to her daughter-in-law: 'I wish one could talk through an *electric tube*, writing is such a fatigue in hot weather.' If Daniel Dunglas Home were still around we might send a message to Lady Stanley, telling her that we now have that electric tube – and very often wish we hadn't.

1856

ON NEW YEAR'S DAY, 1856, Macaulay confided to his journal:

> I am happy in fame, fortune, family affection, – most eminently so. Under these heads I have nothing to ask more; but my health is very indifferent. Yet I have no pain. My faculties are unimpaired. My spirits are very seldom depressed; and I am not without hopes of being set up again. . . . Letters and criticisms still pour in. Praise greatly preponderates, but there is a strong admixture of censure. I can, however, see no sign that these volumes excite less interest than their predecessors. . . .

He is referring here to the third and fourth volumes of his *History of England*, which had been published two weeks before. On 7 January he could add, 'The victory is won. The book has not disappointed the very highly-raised expectations of the public. The first fortnight was the time of peril. Now all is safe.' It was more than that – a triumph. In the first ten weeks 26,500 copies were sold, and this was the big library edition, the floods of various popular editions arriving afterwards. In March the publisher Longman handed Macaulay a cheque for £20,000, an enormous sum in terms of what money could buy in 1856. The *History* was an immediate best-seller in America. Translators were hard at work on it all over Europe – and even in Persia. Foreign honours were showered upon Macaulay. He was the most highly respected, the most widely praised, writer of the age.

In 1841 he had told himself, 'I shall not be satisfied unless I produce something which shall for a few days supersede the last fashionable novel on the tables of young ladies.' He had now succeeded far beyond his original expectations. He had made history – and immensely detailed history too – as easy to read and to enjoy as any popular novel. He had done this after adopting and then perfecting a particular manner and style in his early reviews and essays. It is a manner and style to be found everywhere now in election addresses, bright journalism, and advertising. We might call it 'the picturesque dogmatic.' Macaulay never stopped reading and he had a freakishly capacious memory, which put at his disposal ten thousand odd picturesque details. These he uses with great though not always scrupulous effect. At the same time he is tremendously dogmatic, advancing his Whig history and political philosophy like an armoured column. He is more sure about everything than any honest thoughtful man should be about anything. (Perhaps I ought to add here, if the reader has not noticed it, that his manner is infectious.)

In spite of his excellent personal qualities, Macaulay's unique popularity did more harm than good. He encouraged the complacency of a dangerously large section of the middle class. He bull-dozed, so to speak, the warning intuitions, the growing doubts, of contemporaries who had more imagination and insight than he had. He confirmed wide-spread mid-Victorian prejudices. Though he had a genuine feeling for the broad drama of history and its more picturesque characters, he had none for the arts and little sympathy with anything irrational and intuitive, with men's deeply personal and secret lives. He had a kind of House-of-Commons-and-club-dining-room view of this life of ours. He tended to make the comfortable feel all the more comfortable and to turn them away from the prophets and poets and enthusiastic reformers who made them feel uneasy. Possibly his sheer industry and entertainment value deserved the praise and honours awarded him; but then we must remember that the *status quo* has never been niggardly with its darlings.

We could reasonably begin with Macaulay and his *History* because this was to be a comparatively uneventful year, offering a lull between the follies and miseries of the Crimea and the remote horrors of the Indian Mutiny, due to arrive in 1857. On 1 February an armistice between Russia and the Allies was signed. On the morning of 31 March the Lord Mayor of London, in his Mansion House, read aloud a letter he had just received from the Home Secretary, Sir George Grey, which ran as follows:

> I have the honour to acquaint your lordship that a despatch has been this morning received from the Earl of Clarendon, Her Majesty's Principal Secretary of State for Foreign Affairs, dated Paris, the 30th, announcing that a definite treaty for the restoration of peace, and for the maintenance of the integrity and independence of the Ottoman Empire was yesterday signed at Paris by the Plenipotentiaries of Her Majesty, of the Emperor of the French, of the King of Sardinia, and of the Sultan and also of the Emperor of Austria and of the King of Prussia, on the one part, and of the Emperor of All the Russias on the other.

It was received with loud cheers. The Lord Mayor then proceeded to the Royal Exchange, for another reading and more cheers. Flags flew from all mastheads, and soon the guns in the Tower were thundering away. The war that should never have been begun was now over.

It would be easy, if tedious, to make a list of the promises and guarantees and settlements included in this peace treaty, beginning with Russia's promise not to re-fortify Sebastopol and to keep her warships out of the Black Sea, and going forward to the Sultan's undertaking to confirm the privileges of his Christian subjects; and most solemnly so on and so forth. But it is even easier – and far more to the point – to borrow that quotation from *The Times*, only five years after this peace was signed, which Kingsley Martin notices at the end of his *Triumph of Lord Palmerston*:

> We must frankly own that we feel somewhat more free to act like men and Christians than we could five years ago. That ill-starred war, those half-million of British, French, and Russian men left in the Crimea, those two hundred millions of money wasted in the worst of all ways, have discharged to the last iota all the debt of Christian Europe to Turkey. Never was so great an effort made for so worthless an object. It is with no small reluctance that we admit a gigantic effort and an infinite sacrifice to have been made in vain.

The Times should have been writing in this strain seven years before, but as we have seen it had not been able to resist the huge push of public opinion. Now the people who had been cheering for the war were cheering for the peace, without asking themselves what had been accomplished.

The official celebrations of the peace were delayed until 29 May, which was declared a general holiday. Those of us who have a weakness for fireworks nearly always feel that no display is long enough or big enough. Had we been in London on the night of 29 May 1856 we might have felt satisfied for once. There was not one display, there were four – in Hyde Park, Green Park, Victoria Park and on Primrose Hill – each with identical programmes that lasted over two hours. The night was luminous, we are told, 'with the blaze of suns, stars, comets and streamers, the flight of rockets, shells, and Roman candles, the descent of meteors, parachutes, and showers of pearl, silver and golden rain.' But more – and better – was to come:

> . . . Cascades, fountains and trees and bouquets were represented with wonderful exactness, and – perhaps one of the most beautiful features of the display – the formation in the air of sheaves of yellow corn. But the great triumph of the night was the display which concluded the exhibition. It consisted of five fixed pieces, all of the most ingenious and elaborate construction, the last bearing the words, 'God save the Queen', illuminated in the centre. Simultaneously with this there was a grand discharge of Roman candles, batteries of pearl streamers, tourbillons and rockets in red, blue, green, and yellow, discharged by preconcerted signal from each of the four stations. The effect was magnificent, and, when, in addition to the above, *no fewer than 10,000 rockets* were shot into space, the scene was such as can be witnessed only once in a lifetime.

The italics above are mine and come out of sheer deep envy.

About ten weeks earlier there had been another firework display in central London, much smaller and far more sinister. Covent Garden Theatre, having no opera season at the time, had been sub-let for some weeks to one Anderson, a conjuror and popular entertainer who liked to call himself the 'Wizard of the North'. In an evil hour he had decided to end his engagement with a 'Great Carnival Benefit' which would offer his patrons every possible variety of entertainment, and would begin on Monday morning and conclude with a *bal masqué* on Tuesday night – apparently a mid-Victorian *dolce vita* affair. It was that *bal masqué*, attracting 'the idle and dissipated', which brought down on the place fire, wreck and ruin. Serve it right too, for we learn that at a late hour

> ... the theatre is said to have presented a scene of undisguised indecency, drunkenness and vice, such as the lowest places of resort have rarely witnessed. This abandoned sacrifice to vice was destined to present its crowning offering in the conflagration of the temple. Towards daybreak the debauchees had for the most part slunk wearied or stupefied to their dens; about two hundred of the most debased of the professed debauchery remained, staggering about the area, or snorting in exhausted helplessness among the lobbies and passages. It was now about twenty minutes to five, and Professor Anderson thought it time to close the orgie [*sic*]. He accordingly advanced to the orchestra and directed the musicians to perform *God Save the Queen*, and at the same time ordered the gasman to lower the lights, as signals that the ball was at an end. ...

'The Flight of the Masqueraders during the fire at Covent Garden'

But so – alas! – was the theatre. It was on fire, though accounts vary as to how this was first discovered. What is certain is that there was an immediate rush towards the exits, that several women were trampled on and others were carried out fainting, but that nobody was seriously injured, which must have disappointed our reporters, who could write: 'There was something hideous in this sudden change from mad revelry and shameless debauchery to ghastly fear and painful suffering.' By 7 a.m. the interior of the theatre had gone, and only the exterior walls, including the magnificent front, were left standing. In the afternoon, we are told, the Queen and Prince Albert, together with their two eldest children and 'many of the nobility', visited the smouldering ruins and 'viewed the desolate scene with evident regret'. However, in 1858 a new Opera House arose, and we have it still and must surely cherish it.

Both official and unofficial relations between Britain and America were strained in 1856. So, before the end of this year, we find Victoria writing to her Foreign Minister, Clarendon: 'The mission to Washington will be difficult to fill. Is it necessary to be in a hurry about it? Lord Elgin is sure to perform the duties very well, but is his former position as Governor-General of Canada not too high for him to go to Washington as Minister?' The trouble here was that diplomatic relations had temporarily ceased to exist. Crampton, the British Minister at Washington, had been dismissed, after a strong protest from the American Government against the unlawful enlistment of its citizens as recruits for the British Army. It was not until March 1857 that another British Minister, Lord Napier, was appointed. The unofficial relations almost throughout 1856 seemed to be no better. There was friction between the solemn guardians of London's decorum and American tourists considered to be improperly dressed and so obviously not 'gentlemen'.

(right) Covent Garden rebuilt

But, according to *Punch*, it was the Americans who were chiefly taking offence, for at the end of June it published some rather clumsy verses on 'The American Misunderstanding', from which I extract a few, omitting the clumsiest:

> How can you think, you Yankee fellows,
> That of your progress we are jealous?
> Why, Middlesex as well might worry
> Herself because of thriving Surrey.
>
> We know the spread of your dominion
> Is likewise that of free opinion,
> Which bowie-knife, revolver, rifle,
> And Lynch-law but in small part stifle. . . .
>
> Against us why are you so bitter?
> Because we sometimes grin and titter
> A little at your speech and manners?
> Therefore must ours be hostile banners?
>
> Don't we ourselves laugh at each other?
> Consider, Jonathan, my brother,
> Laugh at our beadles and our flunkeys
> Caparisoned like fools and monkeys?

Victoria's Heyday

> Don't we deride our dolts and asses,
> The snobs of our superior classes;
> And those of an inferior station,
> Our Cockneys by denomination?

And ending with a very mid-Victorian suggestion of conviviality:

> Establish drinks and institutions
> Wherever wholesale revolutions
> Afford a market for the potions
> Inseparable from your notions.
>
> Gin-sling, Enlightenment's resplendence,
> Mint-julep, cocktail, independence,
> We shall consider it a blessing
> Around us to behold progressing.

A final couplet that makes us feel the writer had had more than enough of his subject. And notice *cocktail* in the line above!

If these verses are worth accepting as evidence, then it is difficult not to side with the Americans, for there is about them an unpleasing air of patronage, which is probably what Brother Jonathan disliked. Moreover, while we may laugh at ourselves (though the *Punch* man is not laughing at *himself*), it does not follow that other people three thousand miles away should enjoy our laughing at *them*. Finally, too many *Punch* drawings and jokes seem to suggest that every American dinner was taking place either in a mining camp or in some Bowery basement. Perhaps cultivated Americans, all the way from Concord to Atlanta, Georgia, never saw *Punch*, but if they did, then they had every right to feel indignant.

Rhubarb and spice seller, from Henry Mayhew's *London Labour and the London Poor*, 1851

The balance of criticism was restored to some extent by one Frenchman who visited London in 1856. (I take the quotations that follow from *A Frenchman sees England in the 'Fifties*, adapted from the French of Francis Wey by Valerie Pirie.) For a man who must have known the Paris of the Second Empire, hardly a quiet little town, M. Wey is surprisingly impressed by the crowds, bustle and stir of London:

> I do not know if the English ever rest; but London never sleeps. Yet the day is busy enough. At all hours workshops are full and the resorts of idlers overflow. Although the town has a population of almost three million souls, one cannot account for the numbers of people about. The streets are seething with traffic, entire populations are floating on the Thames, the parks are strewn with loafers, monuments with sightseers, the gardens and pleasances of the neighbourhood are overrun with trippers, and the bustle never decreases during the whole week. . . .

And now – about *eating*:

> They eat at all hours, everywhere and unceasingly. Their cast-iron digestive organs enable them to withstand and even thrive upon an alimentary diet which would more than satisfy the appetite of wolves.

'Buckingham Street, off the Strand, London', 1854, by Edmund John Niemann. At the foot is the York Water Gate. Beyond is part of Hungerford Suspension Bridge, an elegant footbridge designed by Brunel and finished in 1845 though demolished in 1859–60. The chains were then used for the Clifton Suspension Bridge at Bristol. Note the hurdy-gurdy player.

(overleaf) Detail of 'Black Lion Wharf, Wapping', 1859, by James McNeill Whistler

The fare of a delicate, ethereal girl would easily still the inner cravings of two Parisian bargees. . . .

He is of course very severe and satirical about the English dinners to which he was presumably invited. For an honoured guest, he tells us, the fish course would consist of a salmon or a sturgeon (an unlikely choice) with a variety of very strong sauces – 'their flavour as I can best describe it is that of fireworks which have been thoughtfully set alight in readiness for swallowing.' (*Tiens!* My guess here is that instead of a sturgeon with fireworks he merely had herring with mustard sauce – and very nice too!) He is more respectful to the roasts, as well he might be, and merely adds they were 'worthy of Homeric times'. He does not single out any puddings, but mentions 'a sort of cake with sour herbs' and then, going full tilt at the strange English, adds – 'More popular still, the stewed stems of the rhubarb plant whose medicinal properties are well known; yet these prudish people openly advertise the defects of their most private internal economy by their shameless partiality for this

Whistler: 1859.

amazing fare!' As if he found everybody taking hashish, not stewed rhubarb! Then salads and vegetables are quickly dismissed: 'Salad is served on a dish. It mostly consists of a lettuce just cut in two. I have seen it eaten dry with the fingers, and just dipped in salt. Vegetables are simply boiled in water and handed round with the meat.'

Like most visitors from abroad, before or after 1856, he was horrified by Victorian slums:

> Wapping, which stretches from London docks to the tunnel, is a seething mass of misery. One catches glimpses of courtyards full of filth, littered like pig-sties and just as nauseous. Whole families vegetate there – mere skeletons, covered with rags of such incredible dirt that it makes one retch to approach them. Unless you have seen rags in London you can have no conception of the meaning of the word. A man pushes his head through a patchwork of tatters, his arms and legs stick out through the largest holes, and he is clothed. The skin of these wretched creatures is so tanned, so thickened by exposure, so encrusted with grime that it is unrecognizable at first glance. But the most incredible thing is that these scarcely human, half-naked creatures attach the greatest importance to the wearing of a hat, or some portion of one, if only a brim. The women also, however scanty their clothing, always wear some battered, be-draggled, shapeless headdress. If some kind soul gives them a few coppers they rush to the nearest public house and spend it on gin, while their wretched children, naked and crawling over refuse heaps, are reduced to nibbling the parings of vegetable and other offal fit only for swine. This appalling state of things being out of sight in unfrequented districts does not offend the English sense of delicacy. . . .

Even if there is some picturesque exaggeration here, it is a horrifying account of one crowded large region, forming part of what was then the richest capital city in the world. But the suggestion that 'this appalling state of things' went entirely unnoticed is not true. A number of people, including Dickens and Henry Mayhew (*London Labour and the London Poor*), had seen it for themselves. What is true is that if instead of going to war against Russians in the Crimea, England had gone to war against poverty and misery in the East End, London would have been a healthier and happier city.

We left the Brownings in the summer of '55 sharply divided because Elizabeth Barrett Browning was deeply impressed by D. D. Home while Robert Browning thought him a charlatan. They had arrived in London from Italy, each of them bringing an important manuscript. Robert's was a collection of shorter poems, some of them dating back several years, that he had been largely revising; and it was published almost immediately as *Men and Women*. Mrs Browning's was the immensely long narrative poem, *Aurora Leigh*, which still needed more work on it, so that it did not appear until 1857. They had now many friends in London, among them Ruskin, Kingsley, Tennyson, Rossetti, and the Carlyles. (In fact Jane Carlyle, prickly but not a bad judge of character disliked Robert Browning. 'I like him less and less,' she had written in 1852; and, four years later: 'To my mind Browning is as considerable as a "fluff of feathers," in spite of his cleverness, which is undeniable.' Probably his rather loud voice and his extravagant Italian manner, which could include dropping on one knee to do some hand-kissing, prejudiced her against him.) In spite of – or because of – their restlessness, moving between Italy, Paris and London, the Brownings were hard up. However, late in 1856 their kind friend Kenyon, who had been allowing them £100 a year, died after some months of serious illness, and in his will he left Robert Browning £6,500 and Elizabeth £4,500, a total of £11,000 that amounted to a small fortune in the 1850s.

(left) A drawing of Robert Browning, 1859, by R. Lehmann

Elizabeth Barrett Browning, engraved by T. O. Barlow from a photograph by Macaire Havre, 1858

This legacy made a great difference to Browning himself, who now had a small son as well as a rather delicate wife, whose obstinate thick-headed father still refused to recognize her marriage or have anything to do with her. Robert was well-known and much admired in literary circles but had not as yet reached a wide public, and indeed had had some difficulty in getting his *Men and Women* published at all. Nor did its publication bring about any dramatic change in his reputation and readership, and this is ironical when we remember that almost all Browning's poems that were best-known afterwards originally found their way into this particular volume. (In later editions of his work they were differently distributed.) It was not in fact until the later '60s and then in the 1870s that Browning was widely read, with Browning Societies and long courses of lectures on his work to come on afterwards. In the 1850s his wife's reputation was far more impressive than his. And indeed it can be argued that at her very best, suddenly reaching a peak, she seems to many of us now the better poet. But then Robert Browning is one of those poets – and men as different as Swinburne and Whitman seem to me in the same category – who nourish us day and night throughout one season of our lives, usually in youth, and then, with the juice sucked dry, afterwards appeal to us hardly at all.

Elizabeth Barrett Browning's *Aurora Leigh*, which we can consider here even though it did not appear until next year, was a brave attempt, far more ambitious than Tennyson's *Maud* (though to my mind less fascinating), to write a novel in blank verse. And with the mid-Victorian public it certainly succeeded, for edition after edition was demanded. As poetry it is unequal even for E.B.B., some of it being very fine, some of it very bad. It is undoubtedly much too long, Mrs Browning being much too fluent; there is too much weeping, too many warm tears; when it offers us poetry and the poets, ideals, the soul, it is apt to be gushing and when it has to deal with social life and contemporary ideas it sometimes reads like awkward journalism. Even so, just as when she describes Aurora's father watching a procession of Italian girls and *A face flashed like a cymbal on his face*, she flashes on us unexpected splendid imagery and passages in which sharp perception, often coming out of an angry feminism, glitters with wit. It is an impressive performance coming from – in Nathaniel Hawthorne's phrase – 'a pale small person scarcely embodied at all'.

If 1856 had had a 'Novel of the Year' it would certainly have been Charles Reade's *It is Never Too Late to Mend*. Some reviewers denounced its melodramatic exaggeration of prison brutalities, but the general reading public took to it at once and it was enormously popular for many years. From the point of view of the ordinary reader its double plot – with the thief transported to New South Wales and the young farmer who goes to the Australian goldfields to earn the £1,000 demanded by his sweetheart's father – was cunningly contrived. There had been a public scandal about the brutal treatment of prisoners in Birmingham Gaol. There was a continuing interest in the Australian goldfields, where so many young men had gone. Reade was able to describe them and the life of the miners in the most convincing detail, although in fact he had never been near Australia. He had, however, already written a five-act melodrama, *Gold*, on this subject, produced early in 1853 at Drury Lane. (In 1854 he had been mainly responsible for no fewer than five plays for the London stage.) But for this big novel he had collected a huge mass of information – piling up notebooks and newspaper cuttings – both on prisons at home and life on the Australian diggings. He must be regarded as the first of the notebook-and-document novelists, well ahead of Zola. It enabled him to be convincing about all manner of backgrounds (often involving serious abuses) and styles of life, though it is a method that tends to check rather than release the imagination, so that all too frequently – except in his masterpiece of 1861, *The Cloister and the Hearth* – his plotting is stagey and too many of his characters suggest melodrama.

Victoria's Heyday

(left) Charles Reade, by R. Lehman

(right) Laura Seymour (née Allison)

But Charles Reade, both as a writer and a man, was a bewildering bundle of contradictions. He was an Oxford scholar, a permanent Fellow of Magdalen and at one time its Vice-President, who, suddenly 'stage-struck', preferred to do more or less hack dramatic jobs in London, where he became the 'intimate friend' of a not very distinguished actress, Mrs Laura Seymour. He could toil like a muck-raking journalist accumulating information and evidence of abuses, yet was capable of creating scenes of imaginative brilliance. He was genuinely compassionate and open-handed, yet was always quarrelling with somebody and had an expensive passion for litigation. He was constantly behaving, out of wounded vanity and suspicion, like a fool, yet he was almost a great writer – and indeed at certain moments he *is* a great writer. One abuse, far from the prisons, lunatic asylums and his other targets, was the customary piracy of original work, from which so many authors suffered, and he was a vigorous advocate of international copyright that would put an end to this familiar thieving. And certainly he himself had some splendid copyrights to protect. Apart from his senseless litigation, his greatest weakness was his frequent return to the theatre when he was so much stronger in fiction. Nor can this be attributed to the influence of Laura Seymour, for in fact it was she who persuaded him to turn his comedy *Masks and Faces* into a novel (*Peg Woffington*), and without her there might never have been *It is Never Too Late to Mend* in 1856.

In June this year there were seventeen candidates for the Mendelssohn Scholarship at the Royal Academy of Music. It was won by the youngest competitor, a curly-headed, dark-eyed lad of fourteen who was a chorister at the Chapel Royal. He was the son of a military bandmaster, and his name was Arthur Seymour Sullivan. After two years the Royal Academy of Music would send him to the renowned Conservatorium of Leipzig, and four years after that a performance at the Crystal Palace of his *Tempest* music would bring him fame in a single night. In this same summer of 1856 a large young man called William Schwenk Gilbert, who was at King's College, London, began reading for an army examination that never in fact took place, no more officers being needed. There is something Gilbertian about this; but then Gilbert at the age of two had been kidnapped by the Neapolitan brigands and had had to be ransomed for £25, just as if he had begun living one of his subsequent plots. It would be nearly twenty years before he and Arthur Sullivan would sit down together and bring out, as they undoubtedly did, the best in each other. Oddly enough – and much to my regret – all the glorious nonsense for which the Victorians are famous, notably the *Alice* stories, Lear's mad verses, Gilbert's *Bab Ballads*, came later than the 1850s, which cannot show us one first-class specimen of crazy humour. Perhaps the age had to be opened out and heated up a little before the wilder drolls could be inspired.

We cannot leave 1856 without pointing out that it is notable for its births – a vintage year for twentieth-century intellectuals and historians. Among its babies were Sigmund Freud, J. J. Thomson, George Bernard Shaw and Oscar Wilde, and Woodrow Wilson.

1857

THIS WAS THE YEAR of the Indian Mutiny. It is true that 1858 saw some of its more important engagements, and that its last smouldering remains were not stamped out until 1859. But it was 1857 that felt the huge shock of the Mutiny. It was in 1857 that the Mutiny made its greatest impact on British opinion and feeling. In the history books of my schooldays the Indian Mutiny was overshadowed by the Crimean War. This was quite wrong, for really the Mutiny was more important and had far more important consequences. It was after the Mutiny that the control and powers exercised by the East India Company were transferred to the Crown, which then made India the largest and brightest gem in its imperial diadem. Later of course the artful Disraeli delighted Victoria by suggesting she should proclaim herself Empress of India. Imperialism in the grand manner, dominating the later decades of the century, would not have been achieved if the East India Company had not vanished after the Mutiny. Again, we were told that this ferocious conflict, spread over 1,000 miles, would never have come flaming out if native troops had not been compelled to use greased cartridges. But while these cartridges have their place in the story, they were no more than the sparks that ignited a great mass of highly combustible material. The Bengal Army, as distinct from the two smaller armies further south that remained loyal, was already feeling mutinous – cartridges or no cartridges. Not all its units mutinied. On the other hand, those who did were soon joined by the servants and hangers-on of rebellious princes, some religious fanatics, Kali thugs, highway robbers, and riffraff of various sorts from the towns and their bazaars. Yet the Mutiny was never a general uprising against British rule. The peasants in their villages took no part in it, and indeed at considerable risk often gave food and shelter to British soldiers and civilians who, wounded or exhausted, had to be hidden from the nearest bloodthirsty mob.

Though steamships brought the reinforcements that put an end to the Mutiny, it was also steamships, taking the place of the leisurely old sailing vessels, the East Indiamen, that indirectly helped to bring it about. They carried to India an increasing number of women and children – and missionaries. The presence of their women and children, who had to be protected at all costs, complicated the problems of the British once they were facing a mutiny; and the sight of so many missionaries fed the suspicions of the Indian troops, the sepoys, that they

Detail of 'The Relief of Lucknow and Triumphant Meeting of Sir Henry Havelock, Sir James Outram and Sir Colin Campbell', 1859, by T. Jones Barker

might soon be forcibly converted into Christians. Then the policy of the East India Company, to which the Indian Army still belonged, had not been wise. Cheeseparing, it had reduced or abolished some of the allowances of the sepoys, who naturally felt discontented. Moreover, promotion in the Company was strictly in terms of seniority, which meant that it was largely represented by men who had grown old, indolent and complacent, believing that the sepoy regiments, commanded by British officers but with their own liaison officers on a lower level, would be completely loyal in all circumstances.

But the circumstances were changing fast. Some old semi-religious customs disliked by the British – for example, *suttee*, the sacrifice exacted from widows – had been recently abolished. Many of the sepoys were Brahmins, who felt that all their caste privileges were now being ignored. Moreover, the Company had adopted a policy towards native states that was deeply resented, and not only by the princes themselves. If the line of succession was broken, the Company took over the state. It moved in too when any state was being flagrantly misruled. Before he retired in 1856 Lord Dalhousie, a progressive and energetic governor-general, annexed the large Muslim kingdom of Oudh, notorious for its bad government. Its own armies were disbanded; its rich landlords, losing money and prestige, were furiously resentful; and too many of the sepoys serving with the British actually came from Oudh. This was not a good time to take over such a kingdom. The Crimea and expeditions to China and Persia had dangerously reduced the British section of the Company's Indian Army. By 1857 there were probably about six sepoys to every British soldier.

Though the sepoys were not the born fighting men their northern neighbours – the Sikhs and Gurkhas – were, once they were well-trained and led by British officers who knew them all, they could do, and had done, great service both as infantry and cavalry. They took a pride in themselves as the Company's soldiers. But two things were disturbing that pride. A disastrous defeat in Afghanistan and then rumours rather than news of what had been happening in the Crimea had tarnished the old magical prestige of British arms. The other thing, more important, was that many of their best younger British officers, bored with regimental routine, had left their units to do more interesting work, being replaced by subalterns fresh from England who did not understand the sepoys or India. Moreover, this was happening at a time when discontent and suspicion were growing, with agents of the dispossessed princes busy with a whispering campaign, and from bazaar to bazaar there went the most fantastic reports of what the British and their Christian priests might do next.

It was in this darkening and ominous atmosphere that the notorious new cartridges arrived. (If they had never existed, something else might have soon set off the explosion.) Before the heavily greased cartridges of the Enfield rifle could be rammed home they had to be bitten to open

'Eastward Ho!', by Henry Nelson O'Neil, painted in 1857, at the time of the departure of troops for India to quell the Mutiny, and exhibited the following year. The companion painting is reproduced on page 225.

one end and free the powder. The word went round that this was a plot of the British against their Indian soldiers' religion and caste, forcing them to adopt Christianity. The grease, it was said, consisted of cow fat, an abomination blasphemous to Hindu believers, and pig fat, which any good Muslim regarded as filth. Yet even before the end of January 1857 the Indian Army had received orders not to issue these cartridges to sepoy regiments. They could use vegetable and not animal fats. Indeed it was no longer necessary to bite the cartridges – fingers could be used to open them. But the harm was done. There were more and more wild rumours. Even so, when the big Mutiny began, at Meerut in May, it was not so much the cartridges as shockingly bad leadership that was responsible for the outbreak.

Meerut was only about fifty miles from Delhi and was the one garrison town that had in it as many British troops as it had Indian, and the British were more heavily armed. It was the last place where serious trouble would have been expected; but harshness, obstinacy and folly did their work. We have a direct account of the circumstances in a letter written to his mother by one McNabb, a cavalry lieutenant only nineteen years old (quoted in the *History of the British Army*, edited by Young and Lawford). It was written on Sunday, 10 May 1857, Lt McNabb's last day on earth and the first day of the Indian Mutiny. He writes:

> Our Colonel, Smyth, most injudiciously ordered a parade of the skirmishers of the regiment (85 picked shots) to show them the new way of tearing the cartridge. I say injudiciously, because there was no necessity to have the parade at all. . . .

Against various protests, both from his officers and the sepoys, Col. Smyth insisted that the parade should take place, with the result that the eighty-five men refused to use the cartridges:

> They did not want to be the first regiment who had fired. But the real cause is that they hated Smyth, and if almost any other officer had gone down they would have fired them off. . . . A day or two afterwards these 85 mutineers were tried by Court-martial and sentenced to ten years on the road in chains! They could not have hit on a more severe punishment as it is much worse to them than death. . . . The sentence was carried out yesterday morning. We were paraded at 4 (a.m.) on foot and marched up the grand parade ground where all the troops in the station were paraded. It is lucky that this happened in Meerut where there are so many European troops for if it had been in a smaller station I would not have given much for the officers' lives. . . . When the irons were put on them, they were marched past the whole parade, and when they passed us, of course, they began to cry and curse the Colonel. It was very sad to see these fine men in such a condition. . . .

That night, in a sudden fury, all the Indian regiments mutinied, attacked the gaol and released its prisoners; they shot down many of their officers, including Lt McNabb, and before the British troops could be mustered to stop them most of the mutineers left Meerut for Delhi. At 8 a.m. on

'The Flight from Lucknow', 1858, by Abraham Solomon, brother of two other well-known painters, Rebecca and Simeon. Abraham Solomon had a knack of seizing upon public events and familiar situations in contemporary life and representing them in a vivid kind of artistic journalism. His 'Waiting for the Verdict' (see page 42) had a vast sale – even rivalling those of Frith's most popular pictures – when issued as a mezzotint engraving.

the 11th, some troopers of the native light cavalry were already entering the city, cutting down with their sabres any Europeans they met. So there began what was probably the greatest and most ferocious mutiny in all military history.

Some of the mutinous troops went to the Palace and hailed Bahadur Shah, eighty-two years old and a monarch merely in name, as their rightful king. Others were busy murdering all Europeans who could not escape, whatever their age and sex. The Indian garrison joined the mutineers. The only British troops in the city were a few Ordnance Corps officers and men, in charge of the immense arsenal, which they gallantly defended and then blew up so that the sepoys should not have it. So now, within two or three days, Delhi was in the hands of the mutineers, and the astounding news went flashing down to Calcutta, where the Governor-General, Lord Canning, was in residence, and up to Simla, where the Commander-in-Chief, General Anson, had gone to escape the heat of the summer. This appalling distance itself suggests a complacency and lack of foresight that should not have been there during this uneasy period. Again, the old General in command at Meerut should not have remained but ought to have pursued the mutineers, in order to save Delhi. The British were now about to pay a terrible price for this slackness. But so, very soon, were the mutinous regiments of sepoys and their followers. They were not carrying out any general plan. They had suddenly lost their heads, the victims of a wild hysteria, which sent them leaping in one bound from mere mutiny itself to senseless cruel massacre. (It is worth remembering that *after* the British left India in 1947 the quarrel between Hindus and Muslims flamed to such a height that the casualties completely dwarfed any known before. In the East it seems as if a long, long patience suddenly explodes into the most violent action.) Because this was not a national uprising, because it was not carrying out a plan, some sepoy regiments would remain loyal while others, apparently quiet enough, would instantly shoot down their officers and run amok through the cantonments. All this created an atmosphere of nervous anxiety, fear and ferocious resentment, both in the summer heat, rising to 110 degrees fahrenheit, and in the rains that followed it. Moreover, this was never an open war but one in which friends suddenly turned into foes, and there were innumerable spies and agents in disguise, secret messengers carrying anything from hard news to the wildest rumours.

Before General Anson could collect a sufficient force to march on Delhi he died. (There was a heavy mortality among elderly generals in the Mutiny.) Finally a scratch force from the North joined one emerging from Meerut, and together they defeated a larger army of mutineers trying to intercept their march on Delhi. But when they arrived outside the city they knew they were not strong enough to take it by storm, so they remained on the famous Ridge overlooking the city. John Lawrence was firmly in command in the Punjab and was able at last to send a

Mosque at the Khynabee Gate, Delhi, taken by Félice Beato in 1857

column of good fighting men, under the leadership of a superb fighting man, John Nicholson. On 11 September, after a heavy bombardment, the irrepressible Nicholson led a grand assault on Delhi, even though it had four defenders for every man who was attacking it. Only a quarter of the city could be occupied at first; the casualties had been heavy; and Nicholson himself – a great loss – was mortally wounded. However, by 20 September the mutineers had either escaped or surrendered, and Delhi was under British control again. Though there was to be a good deal of fighting, over a large area, during the months that followed, the capture of Delhi marked a turning-point in the history of the Mutiny.

Even so, much had happened elsewhere between May and September. The scene was set in Oudh, the home of so many of the mutinous sepoys. Two of its cities, not far from each other, now entered history – Cawnpore and Lucknow. Cawnpore had a garrison of an Indian Infantry Brigade, but early in June it mutinied and vanished. Sir Hugh Wheeler, in charge of the station, had no British regiments, only some military odds and ends of men and European volunteers, fewer than 250 in all. On the other hand, he had at least 400 women and children to protect. An army of mutineers, commanded by a native princeling, Nana Sahib, arrived to take Cawnpore, and for eighteen days Wheeler's tiny force, behind some improvised defences, kept this army at bay. But this could not last, so when Nana Sahib offered the garrison and the women and children a safe passage in boats down to Allahabad, the British agreed. On 27 June they all got into the boats, only to find that Nana Sahib had no intention of keeping his word. The men were fired on in the boats or taken out and executed. The women and children were taken back to

(right) General John Nicholson

(far right) The Prince of Oudh. Oudh was annexed from the native rulers and was the stronghold of the Mutiny.

Cawnpore, suffocatingly herded together for some days, and then systematically and coldly butchered (it was said that actual butchers were brought in to do the work), their bodies, not all lifeless, being thrown down a well. The murders in Delhi and elsewhere had immediately brought a certain ferocity, but after this massacre of the innocents at Cawnpore a howl for vengeance went up from the British, not only from the men actually fighting but also from the people at home. It is doubtful if the English have ever been so bloodthirsty as they were in 1857. A kind of berserk fury took possession of all ranks in the field, and it may account for the extraordinary feats of marching and fighting achieved by these men. There can be no question that any men who looked like mutinous sepoys were shot or hanged out of hand. Nevertheless, it is not true, as it has often been stated, that one method of execution, tying men to the mouth of a gun and then blowing them to pieces, was evidence of an almost insanely murderous mood. It was in fact the method of execution that the sepoys themselves preferred, as against being shot or hanged.

Now we must leave Cawnpore for the neighbouring and grander city of Lucknow. The second Lawrence brother, Sir Henry, was in charge of Oudh, which swarmed with mutineers, and now he began to fortify and provision his Residency in Lucknow. Unfortunately an attack on a large force of mutineers failed, with the result that Lawrence had to retreat into the Residency and await a siege, while an immense number of mutineers and other rebels joined the besiegers. His garrison consisted of about 700 loyal native troops, 150 civilian volunteers, and 600-odd British officers and men. Women and children and non-combatants amounted to nearly 1,300. Lawrence himself, severely wounded by a shell, died on 4 July. There now began one of the most famous sieges of the age. Constant shelling and exhaustion, followed by cholera, smallpox and dysentery, steadily reduced the garrison and ravaged the women and children it was defending. A determined attempt by the besiegers to storm the Residence, in spite of its stockades and entrenchments and detached blockhouses, must have succeeded, but only limited attacks were made.

There was published fairly recently a *Journal of the Siege of Lucknow* by Maria Germon. Mrs Germon's husband, Charlie, was an officer of a Native Infantry regiment, constantly on duty to repel the besiegers, and fortunate enough to come out of the siege alive, if somewhat damaged. His wife was not an imaginative woman, attempts no fine writing, but remains clear-headed and practical and is obviously quite truthful. There is space here only for two extracts, typical, not specially chosen:

Sunday, August 9th. Mrs Barwell taken ill during the night, at 8 a.m. a fine boy made his appearance. I thought of poor Mrs Darby who we were told was confined in the open in the rear of a gun – she and her child were both massacred afterwards. Mr Study and Mrs Kendall's baby died today. Mrs Halford very angry at being turned out of her room to give place to the new baby. Mrs Dashwood, who is expecting her confinement, had a fainting fit – a nice commotion in addition to a sharp attack with heavy firing from some of the guns close to us. A nine-pounder shot came into Mrs Clarke's room and just as we were talking of coming up to sleep again in the dining room two bullets came in quite hot, which settled the matter. . . .

And now, two-and-a-half months later, when there was very little food left:

Sunday, October 18th. Charlie came at 3 p.m. to service and was amused to hear we were going to have a sparrow curry for dinner. Dr Fayrer had shot 150 sparrows for it – most pronounced it very delicious but I could not be induced to taste it. I agreed with Charlie to pay Mrs Brien a visit as I had not seen her since the Major's death, so I went with Dr Partridge to the Brigade Mess and Charlie met me there. The ladies in the Brigade Mess are all living in dirty little rooms round a large square. Mrs Pitt's had only one opening serving as entrance, door, window and all. They say the rats are horrible and I should think centipedes and scorpions also. Mrs P. told me her husband sent her all his dirty linen to wash and she had to do it without soap. I think he might manage that for himself. Charlie always washes his own. . . .

Supplies were running short. General Havelock, who had taken Cawnpore, fought his way through the ring of besiegers, but, not having sufficient men to raise the siege, he and his troops had to take refuge in the Residency, which now had plenty of good fighting men but was sadly in want of fresh supplies.

Lucknow was not relieved until 16 November. Sir Colin Campbell, a great soldier, had been appointed Commander-in-Chief, with the responsibility of suppressing the mutiny. He arrived in Calcutta in August, and was busy for some time with administrative work and the organization of transport and supplies. He had also to wait for British troops diverted from China and elsewhere. He left Calcutta towards the end of October, and on 14 November he was within sight of Lucknow. He had about 4,500 men while the besieging army, occupying strong positions all round the city, now numbered about 60,000. Campbell could not hope to defeat such a force, but he was determined to bring the women and children, the wounded and the non-combatants, out of the Residency, so he cut his way through, to greet Outram and Havelock (who died a week later), and a skilful night operation took Mrs Germon and her Charlie, no longer fit for duty, and a thousand others to safety. Mrs Germon's account of this 'moonlight flit' is too long to be quoted here, but it is amusing as well as dramatic because, having been forbidden to take any baggage, she wore all the clothes she had left, making it hard either to get on or get off the pony she had been lent. This was the famous Relief of Lucknow. But the besieging army was not defeated until March 1858, by which time Campbell had been strongly reinforced and had been joined by 10,000 Gurkhas from Nepal.

Victoria's Heyday

Then Lucknow was again in British hands; but Oudh itself was not finally pacified for some time.

Delhi, Cawnpore and Lucknow were the names everybody in England knew, and the general public paid far less attention to what was undoubtedly the most brilliant campaign of the whole Indian Mutiny. This took place in Central India in the first five months of 1858. Here the rebels not only had the most strongly fortified places but also had, what was lacking elsewhere, two determined leaders – Tantia Topi, a genuinely capable soldier, and an extraordinary and most formidable woman, the Rani of Jhansi, the central strongpoint of the Mutiny in this region. Fortunately, the British forces were commanded by a man who combined fearlessness and astonishing tactical audacity, Sir Hugh Rose, who moved swiftly, never hesitated to attack forces far greater than his own, and led men who fought and won battles in temperatures that went up to 110 in the shade. By the end of June 1858 any real threat from Central India had gone, and indeed, though there was still work for the army to do for many months, both there and in the north the Indian Mutiny was over.

The point must be made again that the Indian Mutiny was very far from being a general uprising against British rule, which could never have survived such a challenge. It began with the mutiny of various

'Jessie's Dream of the Relief of Lucknow', by Frederick Goodall. Jessie Brown was the wife of a corporal in the 78th Highlanders who at the height of the siege had a dream that Lucknow would be relieved.

(left) 'Sikhs on horseback', by Lundgren. It is thought that Lundgren, a Swede, was the only European artist to have recorded the Indian Mutiny on the spot.

(right) Cross-examining a spy, by Egron Lundgren

sepoy regiments in the Bengal Army, which were then joined by the followers of dispossessed princes and other rulers and by all manner of riffraff that welcomed disorder. Some native regiments remained loyal and fought stoutly alongside British units. It may seem extraordinary that these were able, time after time, to defeat and scatter forces ten times the size of their own, but for the most part the mutineers were badly led and their numbers were always swollen by untrained mobs who could not face disciplined troops. Even so, what these troops achieved, especially during the appalling heat of the two early summers, must be counted among the most astonishing feats in British or any other military history. It is in the Indian Mutiny rather than the Crimea that the fighting men of the 1850s were blazingly triumphant, astonishing in their fortitude, determination and valour. These mid-Victorians were men indeed! Moreover, the civilian servants of the East India Company – these magistrates, engineers, doctors, schoolmasters – were often as remarkable as the soldiers, as anyone may discover in the chapter on the Mutiny that concludes the first volume of Philip Woodruff's *The Men Who Ruled India*. Certainly the Company had allowed itself to be represented in important posts by too many drowsy and complacent old hands, yet it had selected and sent to India a number of younger men of extraordinary quality, better men than could be found in comparable positions in England.

The Victorian English saw themselves as easy-going kind people, more inclined to tolerance and mercy than others, though in fact in their ordinary life at home – in their treatment of prisoners, in the savage discipline in the services – this could be proved to be an illusion. And as Mr Woodruff truly declares, the Indian Mutiny aroused in them a 'relentless fury for which there is no parallel in their long history.' The wretched mutineering sepoys, too often blamed for atrocities they did not commit, paid a terrible price for that massacre of women and children at Cawnpore. Officers in command who were normally decent

kindly men would give orders for villages to be destroyed – 'slaughter all the men; take no prisoners' – and troops after storming cities held by the rebels would go berserk. There was altogether too much indiscriminate execution. People safe at home, not marching and fighting in the intolerable heat, people thousands of miles from the sight of murdered Europeans, were if anything even louder and more ferocious in their demands for implacable vengeance. The England of 1857 shouted itself hoarse for bloody revenge, forgetting it was supposed to be a Christian country.

Yet if we read the letters and memoirs of the English in India, the people involved in the Mutiny, we discover over and over again the great strength of their religious belief, of one sort and another, which largely explains the common fortitude of both sexes. With the women, perhaps under siege, it would be a rather sentimental New Testament

'An incident during the Indian Mutiny', c. 1858, by Edward Hopley

kind of belief. So in a letter written in Cawnpore, not long before the massacre:

> I write this my dearest Henrietta in the belief that our time of departure is come [*i.e. to die*]. The whole of the troops rose here & we took refuge in a barrack. We are so hemmed in by overpowering numbers that there seems no hope of escape. . . . The walls are going. This is an awful hour, my darling Henrietta, Jessie Emily & Georgie cling to us. . . . It is sad & painful to reflect on that our lives are to be sacrificed in such a condition. Give my love to my sweet girls – tell them to seek searching that faith true & steadfast an anchor of the soul – Conny darling your Mama has longed to see & know you, seek your God and Saviour in *spirit*. Alice my sweet child serve & follow Him & always hate whatever is sinful – dearest Henrietta we leave them all in the hands of God & your tender watching. My dying love to all my dear friends. . . . We hope to meet where all imperfections are washed away. . . .

The men serving in the field – certainly most of the senior officers – looked to the stern Old Testament God of wrath and battles. They were serving Him in righteousness. The sword they bore was His. The terrible vengeance, which they pledged themselves to exact, would be His. His Word had gone forth against any natural tenderness, any weak pleas for mercy. In this grim faith, they drove their men on through dust and heat or torrential rains, to attack the heathen in their mindless masses, to storm the cities of the infidels. And where do we catch a last echo of this Old Testament style of the Mutiny, a taste of it lingering after many years? Surely in the works of that famous Anglo-Indian – Rudyard Kipling?

Maximilian of Mexico and his wife the Empress Charlotte shortly after their marriage

From Osborne, on 27 July 1857, we find Queen Victoria coming out of the shadow of the Indian Mutiny to write a letter, all excitement, to Leopold, King of the Belgians:

> MY DEAREST UNCLE, – At *this* very *moment* the marriage is going on – the *Knot* is being tied which binds your lovely sweet child to a thoroughly worthy husband – and I am sure you will be much moved. May every blessing attend her! I wish I could be present – but my dearest *Half* being there makes me feel as if I were there myself. I try to picture to myself how *all* will be. . . . We do all we can to fête in our very *quiet* way this dear day. We are all out of mourning; the younger children are to have a half-holiday, Alice is to *dine* for the first time in the evening with us; we shall drink *the Archduke and Archduchess's* healths; and I have ordered *wine* for the servants, and *grog* for our sailors to do the same. . . .

Alas! – the marriage on 'this dear day' was the one between the Archduke Ferdinand Maximilian of Austria and Princess Charlotte of Belgium. Ten years later, as Emperor of Mexico, after refusing to leave the country, he was court-martialled by the republicans and shot. The

Victoria's Heyday

Empress Charlotte had returned to Europe the year before and had worn herself out trying in vain to enlist support for her husband. She went out of her mind and was never quite sane again until she died, near Brussels, in 1927, thus outliving, in her own strange dream world, Victoria herself by over a quarter of a century and her husband by sixty years. It is like a sombre fairy tale.

Science and technology were – if the term be allowed – ripening this year. Clausius was explaining his theory of electrolysis, Julie his kinetic theory of gases, Clerk Maxwell disposing of Saturn's Rings; the transatlantic cable – or at least some of it – was being laid; and most important of all, in view of his future contributions to public health, the modest Louis Pasteur was announcing that fermentation was the result of minute organisms. In America, one E. G. Otis had contrived the first safety elevator, which meant that sooner or later skyscrapers would be built. Henry Thomas Buckle now published *The History of Civilization in England*, the first volume of a vast opus he never lived to finish. He was yet another mid-Victorian eccentric: well-off and invalidish, largely self-educated, able to read about nineteen languages, one of the best chess-players of his time, he had a prodigious memory and worked unceasingly. He held that travel provided man with the finest education, apparently never having met seasoned travellers who could be quite stupid. I have included him in this paragraph because he tried hard to turn history into a kind of science, and his *Civilization* became extremely popular with readers who were not acquainted with other and less sweeping historians.

Anthony Trollope

Science was moving in all directions. So we should not be surprised to learn that the National Association for the Promotion of Social Science was founded in 1857. Its President was Lord Brougham, who liked to have a finger in most pies, and its Secretary was G. W. Hastings, a great hand, as we shall see, at rhetorical questions. (I take what follows from *A Hundred Years of Sociology* by Professor Duncan Mitchell):

> And is social knowledge, the science of promoting the prosperity, happiness, and welfare of the human race, stamped less with the character of unity? Are the moral laws of the universe promulgated by the same Divine Legislator, less uniform, less simple, and less sure? Are not the whole family of men bound together, not merely by the inheritance of a common lot, but by the tie of a mutual influence? And do not we find that each one of the social problems we have been in any way at pains to unravel strikes its roots into the substance of the nation, ramifying through a hundred secret crevices into classes apparently the most removed from its influence?

Secretary Hastings wants us to cry *Yes* immediately and enthusiastically, but some of us – and I am one – are always tempted to meet this approach

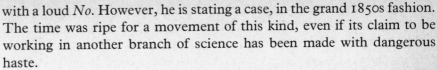

with a loud *No*. However, he is stating a case, in the grand 1850s fashion. The time was ripe for a movement of this kind, even if its claim to be working in another branch of science has been made with dangerous haste.

There was Karl Marx, who has not been mentioned before because he was in fact far more prominent in the 1840s and the 1860s than he was in these 1850s. There was John Stuart Mill, ready to consider Marx very carefully, and even more sympathetic, though with some reservations, to the work and outlook of Auguste Comte, the leading French positive social philosopher. Mill, liberal-minded and generous, had in fact been giving Comte a pension. Comte had had no difficulty proving that world history has passed through three stages – first the theological, then the metaphysical, then the positivist and scientific – and elaborating lists of great men and annual rational festivals; but he was rather unworldly about the number of francs coming in and going out. However, for the past twenty years or so his ideas had travelled far from France, reaching most parts of Europe and even having some influence among the more Utopian Americans, inspired originally by Fourier and Robert Owen. And now, in 1857, Comte had died, just when the National Association for the Promotion of Social Science was being formed.

Its members came from the more thoughtful section of that solid middle class of the 1850s. They were not, for the most part, men given to philosophical enquiry and speculation; they might be best described as cool-headed reformers, chiefly concerned with problems of administration and education. (There is, however, something to be said for hot-headed reformers, furious at suffering and waste of life and ready to burst some barriers.) The Association made it plain that 'its object was to elicit truth, not to propound dogmas', that it wanted help from 'all those interested in social improvement, without reference to classes and opinions': *fair enough!* – as we like to say. What it achieved would take us well beyond the boundary of the 1850s. But here, a cloud no larger than a man's hand, was sociology, now in our time, even though some good work has been done, almost a sort of smog extending from Southern California to our new universities, into which such enormous sums of money now vanish and out of which altogether too much unrewarding jargon has emerged.

The modern movement in literature may be said to have stirred in the womb this year, for Paris saw the publication of Baudelaire's *Les Fleurs du Mal* and Flaubert's *Madame Bovary*. In England there was nothing for the modern movement to look back upon with awe, but 1857 brought us, among other things, George Borrow's *Romany Rye* and Trollope's *Barchester Towers*. Borrow's *Romany Rye* was a sequel to his *Lavengro* published in 1851. His *Bible in Spain* went back to 1843 and had made him immensely popular, especially with Victorian boys who were allowed to enjoy Borrow's picaresque adventures on

Victoria's Heyday

Sundays, because their parents assumed that *The Bible in Spain* must be a suitable religious work. We are told that after *Lavengro* he was no longer generally admired, being now dismissed as a vulgar writer. But teenage lads stayed with him, right up to the time of my own youth, when 'The wind on the heath, Brother' and the gipsy style were in fashion. In spite of his philology and his imposing if rather confusing scholarship, there is a lot of the boy in Borrow: he might be described as a Superboy. He takes us on to the open road, to strange encounters in ale-houses, to loud arguments and fist fights. How much is truth, how much is fiction, we shall never know. He is one of those tremendous fellows, ready to stand up to anybody, whose occasional lies we like to believe. He is also one of the oddest fishes in that tank of odd fish, the mid-Victorian literary scene.

Trollope had published the first of his Barsetshire novels, *The Warden*, in 1855. It was comparatively slight and attracted little attention. *Barchester Towers*, though it did not bring Trollope much money (we know all about that if we have read his *Autobiography*), was altogether ampler and more entertaining, and it beckoned us all into Barsetshire. Desperately anxious to be published, Trollope ran into a lot of trouble from Longman's reader and literary adviser, who was astonishingly prudish even for the 1850s. If he had had his way we would never have made the acquaintance of Bishop and Mrs Proudie and the Signora Neroni, and the whole novel would have been severely cut. But Trollope stoutly held out for the novel's main design and cast of characters. He did, however, give way to idiotic demands for more prudish language, to our loss – so *fat stomach* became *deep chest*, which is not the same thing at all. In his *Autobiography* Trollope writes:

> Perhaps I may be assuming more to myself than I have a right to do in saying now that *Barchester Towers* has become one of those novels which do not quite die at once, which live and are read for perhaps a quarter of a century; but if that be so, its life has been so far prolonged by the vitality of some of its younger brothers. *Barchester Towers* would hardly be so well known as it is had there been no *Framley Parsonage* and no *Last Chronicle of Barset*.

He also tells us that in the writing of *Barchester Towers* he 'took great delight', and that he did most of it in railway trains, travelling on Post Office business. Now Trollope's is one of the best autobiographies of the nineteenth century, but it cannot be altogether trusted. Not that facts are suppressed; the facts are there and thrown at our head; it is Trollope's attitude of mind that comes under suspicion. He wrote his life when he was beginning to feel neglected and undervalued, so he was defiant, saying in effect, 'You think I'm no artist, just a plain man, so now I'll show you I'm even plainer than you think.' This knocked him out for at least two generations, but now most of us have found our way back into Barsetshire, even if fat stomachs there have been turned into deep chests. *Barchester Towers* is certainly one of the most entertaining

'Home Again', 1858, by Henry Nelson O'Neil, a companion picture to that reproduced on page 211

(overleaf) 'A Summer's Day in Hyde Park', 1858, by John Ritchie

JULLIEN'S
AMERICAN POLKA
COMPOSED ON POPULAR AMERICAN MELODIES & DEDICATED TO
Mr THOMPSON of GLASGOW.

novels of this decade, and at the end of the series, *The Last Chronicle*, we have one of the major novels of the whole Victorian age. Though he wrote his share of rubbish, Trollope at his best was an artist pretending to be just a hunting-man earning enough to keep four horses. But secretly he was hunting for fame, not foxes, and now he has it.

This summer there were aesthetic high jinks in Oxford. (For a full account of them see *The Pre-Raphaelite Tragedy* by William Gaunt, who in this and similar works ably combines good art criticism with lively and sensitive biography.) In 1856 William Morris and Edward Burne-Jones, lately Oxford undergraduates, had met Dante Gabriel Rossetti and had fallen at once under his curious spell. Though Rossetti was now an established figure, he was still under thirty, and he took to these two Oxford young men immediately, calling Morris 'Topsy' and Burne-Jones 'Ned'. He would talk to them seriously about painting and poetry, the Middle Ages and the Arthurian legends, then he would take them at night into Bohemian London and go rollicking round the town. He approached the arts and the life of the imagination with deep seriousness, but when among friends, solemnity and the day's work over, he would jump to the other extreme, talking nonsense and clowning. Serious painters he knew, like Holman Hunt and Ford Madox Brown, would have none of it, but with younger men, almost hypnotized by him, his high spirits were impossible to resist.

Benjamin Woodward, an architect from Ireland, was one of Ruskin's admirers and indeed, like Rossetti himself, one of Ruskin's protégés. No doubt largely through Ruskin's influence, Woodward had been commissioned to build the Oxford Museum, which he did 'in thirteenth-century Gothic style, strongly influenced by Venetian architecture' – hardly a perfect choice for an important Oxford building. He had a further commission, to create a large debating hall for the Oxford Union. This building was almost completed in 1857, and, paying it a visit then, Rossetti and Morris decided that the ample wall spaces, in the bays above the gallery, were crying out to be filled with murals. Woodward, out of sympathy with the Pre-Raphaelite movement, agreed that Rossetti and his friends should design and paint these murals. They asked for no fees, only the cost of their materials and board and lodging while they were engaged in the work – but these expenses turned out to be rather formidable. Out of the seven who were to supply the murals, only two, Rossetti and the minor Pre-Raphaelite, Arthur Hughes, were professional artists, and of the other five, four were artistic but untrained and high-spirited youths. One of them, Val Prinsep, said afterwards, 'What fun we had at that Union! What jokes! What roars of laughter!'

Rossetti was of course the ringleader. He went marching round the

John Brandard's lithograph music cover for an 'American Polka' composed by Louis Antoine Jullien 'on Popular American Melodies' after his visit to America in 1854

High and the Broad in a plum-coloured frock coat, giving a solemn burlesque of an Oxford character, keeping an eye for 'stunners' – that is, beautiful girls. But if it looked as if some notorious bore would be demanding their company for the evening, Rossetti would order a cab for himself and one or two of his young men, and take the first train to London, and stay at the Euston Hotel, returning to Oxford and work the next morning. He was all the freer because his mistress, later his wife, Lizzie Siddal, was ill at Matlock. At work their themes were Arthurian – the guilty love of Guinevere and Lancelot, the quest of the Holy Grail, fascinating in themselves but not quite right for a debating hall. But then the whole enterprise began to seem farcical.

Let William Gaunt take up the tale:

> The cream of the jest, which had also something of nightmare, was what happened to the paintings. The distemper, as everyone knows, flew off the thinly whitewashed brick surface like smoke. The vision of an age that never was disappeared almost at once. This was artistically consistent with the rest of the episode. The spectacle of the Fellow of a college and four untrained youths (Pollen, Prinsep, Stanhope, Jones and Morris) with two professional artists (Rossetti and Hughes), one of the latter having an outrageous indifference to the material he worked in: laughing like madmen; varying the representation of the Belle Iseult with that of an Australian badger, and putting in the dark angles of the roof little figures

An engraving of 1860 of the University Museum, Oxford, 1855–59, designed by the architects Sir Thomas Deane and Benjamin Woodward. This building was intended to be 'to a large extent a memorial to Ruskin'.

of Morris with his legs straddling out like the portraits of Henry VIII; painting on a wall too dark to allow of anything's being seen with touches that faded as soon as they were applied: has a strong likeness to the clowning of the Marx Brothers.

The murals vanished from the sight of the nineteenth century, but during the more ingenious twentieth century, using special photographic plates and reflected light and then, later, modern methods of restoration, the paintings were more or less brought back. What had really gone were the jokes, the high spirits.

But something else happened, during this Oxford spree, really more important than the evanescent murals. One night Morris and Rossetti, Burne-Jones and Hughes went to the local theatre and there discovered an astounding 'stunner'. She had exactly the kind of looks – known to us all now from their pictures – that the Pre-Raphaelites needed for their haughty queens and remote princesses. Her name was Jane Burden, and her father kept a livery stable in Oxford. Very soon they were using her as a model. Deeply in love, Morris married her, two years later, and later still, when Jane Morris was queen of Kelmscott and William was away, busy with his furniture and wallpapers, Rossetti, a widower now and beginning to feel weary and melancholy, would stay at Kelmscott, more than half in love with the face and figure he had painted so often. His Proserpine – and many another dark beauty – is the livery stableman's daughter they first saw at the theatre, during that uproarious summer of 1857.

(above) The interior of the University Museum, Oxford, as it is today

(below right) Detail of 'The Tune of the Seven Towers', 1857, by Dante Gabriel Rossetti

(opposite left) Dante Gabriel Rossetti

(opposite right) 'Queen Guinevere', 1858, by William Morris. The model for this picture was his wife Jane Burden.

A great orchestra was born this year. Carl Halle (b. 1819 in Westphalia) from his childhood successfully toured as a concert pianist. He lived in Paris for some years but the disturbing events of 1848 drove him to England, where, however, he settled not in London but in Manchester, which now had its own colony of substantial German merchants, mostly devoted to music. As Charles Hallé he dominated the musical life of the city. At the Manchester Exhibition of 1857 he conducted an orchestra that pleased him so much that he decided to make it permanent – as 'Hallé's Orchestra'. And as the Hallé it became the pride and joy of the North, and of course survives, not without some ups and downs, to this day. Though Hallé himself was more notable as a pianist than as a conductor, for some years after its creation his orchestra was the best in the country. Even so, the credit for first raising the standard of orchestral playing in England cannot be given to him. It belongs to Michael Costa, a Neapolitan who first arrived in England as a not very accomplished singer and throughout his life was a prolific but hardly distinguished composer. Where he really succeeded, well deserving the reputation he acquired, was in training and conducting orchestras both in operatic and symphonic music. London had plenty of fine instrumentalists but they were bad orchestral players, refusing to turn themselves into a fully disciplined and conscientious band of musicians. It was Costa, a really severe disciplinarian, who was responsible for this transformation.

If the Neapolitan Costa earned the respect of London musicians and critics, it was a Frenchman, Louis Antoine Jullien, who attracted the largest crowds and was given the widest publicity. He brought showmanship to concerts. Serious musicians considered him a charlatan, and some leading soloists like Joachim refused to appear with him. Promenade concerts were no novelty in London, but under Jullien they were almost a three-ring circus. He insisted upon enormous orchestras to which he added strange monstrous instruments – an 'octobass' from Paris that was a double bass nearly 15 feet high, the largest drum ever seen, a giant bass saxophone, and various bombardons. He almost always included in his programmes a 'monster quadrille' presented with special effects: if military, then army bands would arrive, cannon would be fired, and so forth; and if it was his *Fireman's Quadrille*, then the ceiling would apparently be in flames and fire brigades would come charging in, while women fainted and the orchestra continued its performance. But then Jullien's conducting was an exciting performance in itself. His whiskers, waistcoats, cravats, were famous. A crimson and gold platform would be erected in the centre of the huge orchestra, and on it was placed a large gold and white armchair, into which he could sink exhausted from time to time. But somewhere among all this showmanship and charlatanry was a musician. Once he could command regular large audiences, Jullien began to introduce Haydn, Mozart and Beethoven into his programmes. We are told that when he conducted

ECCE HOMO"

Caricature of Jullien, 1851, by
Edward Caldwell Rye

Beethoven he not only wore special white gloves but used a special
jewelled baton, brought to him by an attendant carrying it on a silver
salver. During the 1850s he repeated his London successes in America,
staying there nearly two years. However, after more triumphs in
London, by 1859 his luck was running out and his wits were beginning
to wander; he was arrested for debt in France, and died in a lunatic
asylum there in 1860. In spite of his antics, Jullien appears to have been
more than a competent conductor, and probably did more good than
harm.

This same summer, one of the most fascinating murder trials of the
nineteenth century took place in the High Court of Justiciary in
Edinburgh. Madeleine Smith was accused of murdering her lover,
Pierre Emile L'Angelier, by poisoning him with arsenic. She was only
21, the eldest daughter of a well-to-do Glasgow architect, a fine-looking
girl, at once bold and cool, quite a formidable character. L'Angelier
was ten years older, a Channel Islander who had spent some years in
Paris before working as a very humble clerk in Glasgow. He was a
smallish neat fellow, with rather pretty looks and probably plenty of
sexual experience, and a romantic figure to a middle-class girl who had
not long been back from an expensive boarding school in England. He

began a fervent courtship in 1855, and very soon she became his mistress, secretly admitting him into the house late at night. It is obvious from the many love letters she wrote that instead of submitting to sex she enjoyed it enormously and for a time doted upon her lover. (This proves, if proof were needed, that high-spirited mid-Victorian girls, living in a household of intense respectability, preferred practice to any theory of their sexuality advanced by Dr Acton or anybody else.) But L'Angelier, a rather commonplace and dictatorial little fellow once the bloom of romance had gone, began to bore her.

The marriage he insisted upon would have meant disgrace and poverty, with too much Pierre Emile day and night. Meanwhile, a neighbour and a friend of Papa's, William Minnoch, considerably older than Madeleine, but no worse for that, if only because he was devoted to her, and comfortably off, and Papa's choice, began to court her until she became engaged to him. Now L'Angelier, his eye on the main chance, turned ugly, threatening to expose their affair unless she agreed to marry him. Madeleine was caught in a trap and was determined to free herself. She bought arsenic, saying at the time that she needed it to kill rats but afterwards declaring she took it in small doses to improve her complexion, a common practice in those days. She sent L'Angelier some letters that apparently returned to the earlier impassioned style. Had she suffered a change of heart? Or was she determined that he should come to her late at night again, and be given cups of chocolate, cocoa or coffee?

In February 1857 L'Angelier, no invalid, suddenly went down with violent stomach pains and vomiting. This happened again in March, and then later in the month he had a still more violent attack, and on the 23rd he died. A post-mortem revealed the cause – arsenical poisoning. Letters from Madeleine were found in his room, and she was arrested and charged with his murder. The trial brought together Scotland's best legal talent, and throughout its nine days it seems to have been conducted with unusually scrupulous fairness. Throughout Britain people eagerly followed the trial, arguing about Madeleine's guilt. The prosecution had a strong case. She wanted to get rid of her former lover and she had the means to do it. Her last letters were written to entice him to visit her late at night again, so that she could give him arsenic in a hot drink. But the case for the defence was equally strong. Somebody else could have given L'Angelier arsenic; he might even have poisoned himself. Madeleine might have behaved foolishly with the man, but why should she want to murder him? His death from arsenic, which would have to be investigated, would reveal the whole scandal.

Finally, the defence defied the prosecution to produce any proof whatever that L'Angelier had visited Madeleine on the nights before his violent attacks of pain and vomiting. Moreover, her youngest sister, still a child, with whom she shared a bedroom, testified that Madeleine was with her when she went to sleep and there when she awoke in the morning. This child was the only other member of the family who made an appearance at the trial. The other Smiths contemplated the ruin of their respectability in their country house. On the other hand, Madeleine kept a bold bright face in court. The trial took a dramatic turn when a little diary of L'Angelier's was discovered. Entries in it proved that he had been taken ill twice after visiting Madeleine in February, but the

Madeleine Smith in court, from a contemporary sketch

attacks stopped about the middle of March, before he had the fatal dose. This diary would have been very damaging if it could be admitted as evidence. But defence argued that random jottings in a diary were inadmissible, and two out of the three judges, all law lords, agreed with the argument.

After some brilliant performances on each side and an elaborate and very careful summing-up by the Lord Justice-Clerk, the jury, of fifteen, returned with a verdict of not proven. (Only two of them voted her guilty, though it was said afterwards that many, perhaps most, of the others felt very dubious.) The verdict, which set free the imperturbable Madeleine, was greeted with cheers in court. It is hard to decide what would have happened if the trial had taken place in England, where there is no convenient 'not proven' verdict, where Madeleine would have been declared to be innocent or told she would shortly be hanged. My own belief, for what it is worth, is that once L'Angelier had tried to blackmail her into marriage and saw her as a meal ticket, she developed an intense hatred of him and coolly decided to destroy him. Unless my reading has been at fault, her later history is very vague. We know she left Glasgow for London, where a few years later she married a young artist and took an interest in political and social problems. It is generally agreed that some time after that she went to America, where she spent the rest of a long life. There is a story that in her old age she admitted that she had poisoned L'Angelier, and that in the same circumstances she *would do it again*. Not a very nice woman, we must admit, but one with formidable qualities. Had she been born fifty years later, she might have behaved differently from first to last, and might have been a more useful – and less murderous – member of society.

(overleaf) The marriage of the Princess Royal with Prince Frederick William of Prussia at the Chapel Royal, St James's, 25 January 1858 by G. Philip

1858

LTHOUGH, AS WE HAVE SEEN, the Indian Mutiny as a large-scale operation did not end until the middle of 1858, there was no longer the intense public interest and concern that had dominated 1857. Events at home began to seem more important. The chief ceremonial event of the New Year was the marriage in January, at the Chapel Royal, St James's, of the Princess Royal, the Queen's eldest daughter, to Prince Frederick William of Prussia, afterwards the Emperor Frederick. It served as a good excuse, after so much melancholy news, for much pomp and pageantry and what is always referred to, rather vaguely, as 'general national rejoicing'. But if Germany had come nearer, France had moved further away and might be said to be abusing Britain at the top of her voice. Though not altogether unreasonable, she was so vehement, and even threatening, that she roused British public opinion against her, and this in turn brought down the government, though Palmerston was at the head of it.

The whole weighty affair, which involved wide questions of political principle, turned on one Orsini and some fellow members of the revolutionary Carbonari Society. They had been plotting for some time the assassination of Napoleon III, and in January 1858 Orsini and his companion, Pierri, threw grenades under the imperial carriage. Napoleon himself was only slightly hurt, but as so often on these insane occasions some bystanders were killed and a great many more were wounded. The plot had been conceived and the grenades actually manufactured, not in France but in England, where Orsini, like so many political refugees at that time, had been living. Mid-Victorian Britain did not follow the example of most European states, which refused to admit revolutionaries denounced as criminals in their own countries. So long as they did not break the law, such people were freely admitted into England and were granted the right of asylum, with the result that London became the Mecca of political exiles. The Orsini affair enraged French public opinion; the *militaires* especially took a high angry line; and the Foreign Minister demanded some action from the British Government. Oddly enough, the high-handed Palmerston for once yielded to this pressure. He introduced a Bill to make conspiracy to murder a felony instead of a misdemeanour. Perhaps because he realized that he was defying English popular opinion, his defence of the Bill was weak and halting and he could not carry the House with him. He was finally defeated; his government had to resign; and Lord Derby became Prime Minister, to the great content of Queen Victoria.

This summer she proved that at certain times she could be wiser than some of her ministers and advisers. Though the British Government had for many years exercised some control over the East India Company, now, following the Mutiny, it insisted upon relieving the Company of all power in India, which was to be administered by a secretary of state and a council. This meant that officially the Queen would rule India. She took the deepest interest in the Proclamation that would have to be made. She wrote to Lord Derby in August:

> The Queen has asked Lord Malmesbury to explain in detail to Lord Derby her objections to the draft of Proclamation for India. The Queen would be glad if Lord Derby would write it himself in his excellent language, bearing in mind that it is a female Sovereign who speaks to more than 100,000,000 of Eastern people on assuming the direct Government over them after a bloody civil war, giving them pledges which her future reign is to redeem, and explaining the principles of her Government. Such a document should breathe feelings of generosity, benevolence, and religious feeling, pointing out the privileges which the Indians will receive in being placed on an equality with the subjects of the British Crown, and the prosperity following in the train of civilization.

She felt strongly the lack of any sympathetic references to Indian religions and customs, and approved with equal warmth the final draft of the Proclamation, which contained the following passage:

> Firmly relying ourselves on the truth of Christianity, and acknowledging with gratitude the solace of religion, we disclaim alike the right and the desire to impose our convictions on any of our subjects. We declare it to be our royal will and pleasure that none be in any wise favoured, none molested or disquieted by reason of their religious faith or observances, but that all shall alike enjoy the equal and impartial protection of the law; and we do strictly charge and enjoin all those who may be in authority under us that they abstain from all interference with the religious belief or worship of any of our subjects on pain of our highest displeasure. . . .

More easily said than done, of course; but it was not bad for 1858.

However, as usual in international affairs, folly was busier than wisdom. We can enjoy, if we have the stomach for it, the grim irony of history when we remember what was happening in the Far East at this time. All that China and Japan asked was to be let alone. They were satisfied with their own civilizations and styles of life, and had no wish to impose them on the West. The vast Celestial Empire of the Chinese was a world in itself, but the 'foreign devils', never satisfied themselves, restless and aggressive, would not allow it to slumber in peace. So this year, Lord Elgin compelled China to accept the Treaty of Tientsin, which meant that it had to establish diplomatic relations with the West, grant freedom to missionaries, and open its ports to Western commerce.

The fascination of the faërie world, so wonderfully expressed in George MacDonald's story, *Phantastes*, inspired a strange and tragic artist, Richard Dadd, to paint this extraordinary picture, 'The Fairy Feller's Master-stroke'. Dadd, who was born in 1819 and died in 1887, suffered some kind of brain disorder, and in 1843 murdered his father at Cobham, in Surrey, and fled to France. He was soon apprehended, and spent the rest of his life in Bedlam, where 'The Fairy Feller's Master-stroke' was begun in 1855, and at Broadmoor. The picture, whose subject matter defies rational analysis, combines a child-like vision with an almost surrealist sophistication of style.

If Britain pressed hardest on China, so the United States, almost at the cannon's mouth, compelled Japan to step outside its picturesque medievalism, leaving its tea ceremonies to sign treaties for unrestricted trade with the West, opening Yokohama and Nagasaki to traders whose great-grandchildren must have often regretted this blind move.

Meanwhile, during these summer and autumn months, something was happening in the Middle West of these United States that would have seemed almost as strange to London as it would to Tokyo. The states were in fact anything but united, and what divided them was slavery. The immediate issue, however, was not abolition but the determination of the South, where the slave-holding planters needed more territory, to introduce slavery into the new states now coming into existence in the West. Illinois was a key state, and here, competing for election to the Senate, were two remarkable men: Stephen Douglas, a Democrat, called 'The Little Giant' because he was a tiny man with a great head and wide shoulders, astute as a politician and a notable debater; and Abraham Lincoln, the Republican, tall and gaunt, with a wealth of folksy humour covering a deep seriousness – 'A house divided against itself cannot stand'. They decided to debate in public throughout the prairie towns of Illinois. And I have borrowed what follows from S. E. Ayling's excellent *Nineteenth-Century Gallery*:

> Widely reported, it developed into the most celebrated debate in the nation's history, and although it was conducted with high seriousness, and usually with good temper, it also became something of a gladiatorial contest. Something too of a travelling carnival: the 'Little Giant', with his immaculate suit and wide-brimmed white hat, would be delivered to the day's meeting-place in the personal Douglas train, which signalled its arrival by firing a timely salute from its own twelve-pounder. Brass bands played the hero to the speaking-platform; banners proclaimed slogans; flags and bunting festooned the streets; and the open-air crowds were there in their thousands, having driven in their buggies or come by special train. Lincoln's processions arrived accompanied by fireworks, singers, cavalcades of horsemen, bevies of pretty girls. The leonine Douglas strode purposefully to the platform, spoke masterfully, gestured powerfully; Lincoln by contrast would unwind his long limbs from the special wagon, shamble on to the stand, and take time to warm up his tones and his melancholy features. He spoke more shrilly as his theme began to excite him, his movements vigorous but awkward; he would bend at the knees a good deal as he spoke, and then shoot up on his toes to bring a point home. And the central point, the issue on which the argument hinged, was essentially a moral one; was slavery *wrong*? If it was, as Lincoln held, then America must at least forbid its extension.

Lincoln lost this election, but two years later he was President of the United States and took his long shambling figure, taller than ever with its tall hat, into world history. I feel that this debating tour is worth the space I have given it because in spite of the ballyhoo, which after all did

This life-size electioneering poster, 'The Railsplitter', depicting the folksy Abraham Lincoln on his father's farm with the Mississippi river in the background and the White House in the distance, was issued in 1858, when Lincoln was conducting his 'debates' with Stephen Douglas, the 'Little Giant'.

nobody any harm, it does represent genuine democracy-in-action, really taking the issues to the people while at the same time giving them a jolly day out. We might bear it in mind.

One man who ought not to have been four or five thousand miles away from those Illinois crowds, because he might have captured one of them in paint, is William Powell Frith (who was born in 1819 and died, surprisingly enough, as recently as 1909). His famous or notorious (take your choice) panoramic 'Derby Day' was first exhibited in 1858. Two points are worth making about Frith. He was not always busy with these elaborate realistic panoramas; in fact he painted only three, 'Ramsgate Sands', 1851–53, 'The Derby Day', 1856–58, and 'The Railway Station', 1862; most of the rest of his work, though not all, consisted of scenes from well-known novels and plays, pictures of no special merit. The second point about Frith is that after being vastly admired by mid-Victorian England, he was then denounced as a typical philistine of the period, but after half a century of derision or neglect our own art critics have recently begun to praise him, recognizing his limitations but granting him virtues of his own. There is of course something absurd about the way in which he tries to crowd a chapter or so of Dickens or Thackeray all within one frame. However, his sharp observation, clever composition, mastery of detail, cannot be denied. But what I for one am prepared to deny is the realism so often associated with his name. His 'Derby Day' never suggests to me a real afternoon at Epsom: it is like a huge dream tableau, a giant Still Life, and not our life.

(below left) Photograph taken by Howlett in 1857 for William Powell Frith when painting his picture 'The Derby Day'

(below right) A posed race-course scene by the London Stereoscopic Company, thought to have been used by Frith when painting 'The Derby Day'

Curiously enough, a very different kind of picture exhibited this year – 'Val d'Aosta', a wide landscape by John Brett, still in his twenties – creates the same sort of effect. Under Pre-Raphaelite influence, Brett painted so much close detail with so much fidelity that instead of taking us into reality, he moves us away into dreamland. Everything is there, but not really in this world. Dickens's invalidish but amiable friend, Augustus Egg, tried his hand in 1858 at pictorial story-telling in a triptych, the 'Fate of a Faithless Wife', in which the pure painter in him is at war with the narrative moralist, neither of them clearly winning. The brilliant and prolific Millais, now married to Ruskin's former wife (that marriage was annulled), exhibited nothing in 1858, an unusual year for him. He had now moved away from Pre-Raphaelitism, working more fluently but on inferior story-telling subjects, like magazine illustrations on the highest possible level. He took enormous pains both with his settings and his models in the studio, but in spite of his splendid technique, his knights, wounded officers, anxious ladies and the rest, still look like models posed in a studio who do not exist in the setting he has so carefully given them – at least, to my eye they do. I can never *believe* in these Victorian story pictures. However, forgetting Millais, who became too successful for what follows, I will venture a tip to modest collectors of fine drawings and watercolour sketches. Many early-Victorian and mid-Victorian artists might be responsible for ambitious Royal Academy pictures that leave us cold, but their preliminary sketches and the quick watercolours done for their own amusement are often quite superb and well repay a careful search.

Our literature was travelling much further than our art in these years. To prove it, here is part of a lively letter from Jane Carlyle to her

'The Derby Day', 1856–58, by William Powell Frith

famous husband, who was away in Scotland. It is dated Sunday night, 11 July 1858:

. . . Botkin (what a name!), your Russian translator, has called. Luckily Charlotte had been forewarned to admit him if he came again. He is quite a different type from Tourgueneff, though a tall man this one too. I should say he must be a Cossack – not that I ever saw a Cossack or heard one described, *instinct* is all I have for it. He has flattened high-boned cheeks – a nose flattened towards the point – small, very black, deep-set eyes, with thin semi-circular eyebrows – a wide thin mouth – a complexion whity-grey, and the skin of his face looked thick enough to make a saddle! He does not possess himself like Tourgueneff, but bends and gesticulates like a Frenchman.

He burst into the room with wild expressions of his 'admiration for Mr Carlyle'. I begged him to be seated, and he declared 'Mr Carlyle was the man for Russia'. I tried again and again to 'enchain' a rational conversation, but nothing could I get out of him but rhapsodies about you in the frightfullest English that I ever heard out of a human head! It is to be hoped that (as he told me) he *reads* English much better than he speaks it, else he must have produced an inconceivable translation of 'Hero Worship'. Such as it is, anyhow, 'a large deputation of the Students of St Petersburg' waited on him (Botkin), to thank him in the strongest terms for having translated for them 'Hero Worship', and made known to them Carlyle. And even the young Russian ladies now read 'Hero Worship', and 'unnerstants it thor-lie'. He was all in a perspiration when he went away, and so was I!

This was the time when Carlyle's monumental *Frederick the Great* made its first appearance, but I prefer to notice a more modest work that crept out in its shadow. This was *Phantastes : A Faërie Romance*, by George MacDonald, a Highlander, born in 1824, who was a Congregationalist minister for some years before retiring to devote himself entirely to writing and lecturing. He was a poet and novelist but best remembered as a teller of fairy tales. *Phantastes*, a fairy tale for adults, was his first prose work – and on the whole his most successful. (It has been enthusiastically praised by critics as wide apart as George Saintsbury and C. S. Lewis.) Many people could never fall under its spell, but there will be some readers here, not as yet acquainted with *Phantastes*, who will thank me for bringing it to their notice. It has its faults: as a narrative it is occasionally clumsy; there are moments, especially in the beginning, when it is too arch and winsome for our taste; and now and again its deeply imaginative symbolism shrinks and hardens into obvious allegory. MacDonald owed something to the German Romanticists, the *Märchen* specialists; but he owes a great deal more to the breadth and depth of his own imagination, with a wonderful sense of atmosphere and the ability to create eerie effects. It is now over sixty years since I wandered with his Anodos through the enchanted forest, loitered with him in the Fairy Palace with its dancers who immediately turned into statues, and arrived at that remote strange cottage, with its eternal

Victoria's Heyday

Mother figure and the four doors through which you could plunge into a different life altogether. Re-reading it (not for the first time) to discuss it here, I find the magic not as potent as it was so long ago, but some of it still remains. Faults or no faults, it is a curiously haunting tale, with more depth in it, more of it dredged from the unconscious, than the conscious allegory of the self and selflessness. Mid-Victorian England is always capable of surprising us – and one of its surprises is *Phantastes*.

Though George MacDonald could count Tennyson, Carlyle and Browning among his friends, it is unlikely that many fashionable women were reading *Phantastes* in 1858. Yet a few of the young ladies growing misty-eyed over it must have been wearing crinolines. They were now *in*. The men might be growling at France and the French, but this did not prevent English ladies from following the example of the Empress Eugénie. We are told she deliberately created the fashion to encourage the trade in expensive stuffs, yards and yards of them being necessary for each crinoline. One of the ladies of her court said later, 'The fashionable ladies of today, who like to make themselves as slim as possible, would be horrified if they had to appear enveloped in such a mass of material, which being further held out by a steel framework reached such a circumference, that it was almost impossible for three ladies to sit together in one small room.' She added that wearing a crinoline it was necessary to watch every movement carefully and to walk with a gliding step. Sitting down was tricky, and moving around

'Dressing for the Ball in 1857', by John Leech

could be disastrous in a room full of small fancy tables. But it humbled the haughty male, who was always to be seen dodging about uneasily in the background. Ironically enough, just when the crinoline was being worn by all the fashionable women in Europe, as early as 1859 the Empress Eugénie coolly banished it from her court.

But in 1858 it was making the staff of *Punch* happy, as I have discovered after going through (no light work) this year's volume of it. Here there are jokes about special luggage trains being necessary to carry the enormous trunks that crinolines demanded, and about fashionable young ladies, visiting the Agricultural Show, being unable to use the ordinary entrances and so being compelled to go through the same gateway as the fat cattle. Though *Punch* was still a radical journal – there is in this volume a fierce protest against street music and street cries being forbidden in Mayfair – it was not devised for a bohemian readership and had to be fairly sedate. Even so, it appreciated what we should now call the 'sexy' aspect of the crinoline, as well it might; and it is clear from some of its drawings that both in the London and at the seaside of 1858 Brown, Jones and Robinson had an eye for a leg, and the saucier Amelias, Angelas, Henriettas, swaying in their crinolines, were well aware of this interest. However, there had now arrived a type – and there was to be great deal more of him in the 1860s – who was socially high above Brown, Jones and Robinson. This was the 'heavy swell' already sporting a full beard, because the officers returning from the Crimea

'Heavy swells'

had worn them, or opulent side-whiskers. He spoke in a very languid drawl, to indicate his social superiority, made a lot of *aw-aw* noises, and to prove he need not take any trouble with his speech turned all his r's into w's – all 'weally wather dweadful'. If *Punch* is a sure guide – and I think it is – this cweature awwived round about 1858 and lasted, finally clean-shaved, monocled, with hair parted in the middle, well into this century. Indeed, if we went to the right parties, we might find a few specimens surviving to this day.

One man who was beginning to turn a sharp bright eye on fashionable young ladies and heavy swells was of course Charles Dickens. Though in fact he published no new novel in 1858, it was in many respects the most important year in his later life, which we cannot fully understand if we ignore it. What happened during and after the various moves he made this year direct a searching light on him, his work, and the character of the age. But to understand the events of 1858 we must leave it for a while and go back many months, to what we might label portentously the 'Maria Beadnell Fiasco' and the 'Ellen Ternan Discovery'. As a very young man, before he married Catherine Hogarth, he had fallen violently in love with Maria Beadnell, a very pretty girl but capricious, teasing, alternately encouraging and discouraging until in despair he put an end to his unhappy courtship. But he never forgot her and there are memories of her in David Copperfield's first wife, Dora. Now, over twenty years later, in his restless and dissatisfied middle age, there came an entirely unexpected letter from her, his Maria, but now a matronly Mrs Winter. At once it re-animated the youth in him. (Dickens sexually never seemed to grow out of his youth. Even his fairly numerous though innocent flirtation-friendships were with girls, not mature women.) His letters to Maria were at once eager and intimate, as if he saw himself addressing the bewitching if capricious girl of his youth. When they actually met again, he returned to reality with a bump. What a fool he had been to imagine he could fall in love with this fat, affected, foolish woman! He began to dodge all further encounters, but what he could not ignore was the emptiness of his heart – that 'something wanting' he had mentioned more than once to his friend, John Forster. So he felt more restless and dissatisfied than ever. As for this silly middle-aged Maria, he turned her, not without a touch of cruelty, into Flora Finching, one of the funniest characters in *Little Dorrit*, immensely successful while appearing in monthly numbers, and finally coming out in volume form in 1857.

Anything but the briefest notice of *Little Dorrit* would keep us away from 1858 too long. We know – or should know – that it is an important novel, but it has a curious effect upon us, partly because it is dominated by prisons, not only the Marshalsea but also the prisons people built to sentence themselves. So we return to *Little Dorrit* reluctantly, as if we had to visit some grey dusty place. Then we discover all over again how brilliant it is in patches – the character and acid comedy of Dorrit

W. Telbin. Evans. Shirley Brooks. Mark Lemon jun. W. Jones. E. Evans. Marcus Stone. H. Berger. Mark Lemon. A. Egg.
Albert Smith. Stanfield. Miss Evans. E. Pigott. Jane Francis. Luard.
Keith C. Dickens jun Kate Dickens. Miss Hogarth. Mary Dickens. Wilkie Collins. Helen Hogarth.
Charles Dickens.

The Dickens Dramatic Company in 1854

himself, the glorious satire in the Circumlocution Office and its Barnacles, Flora Finching and Mr F's Aunt and other drolls and eccentrics – but then once more we see the last of Arthur Clenham and Little Dorrit rather hurriedly and thankfully, as if taking a quick train out of that same grey dusty place. Much of it was written in Paris, where Dickens was sumptuously fêted by the new millionaires of the Second Empire. This influenced the novel itself, especially the Merdle chapters (notice the name) and had an even stronger influence on the restless and now unhappy Dickens. Though he disliked the Second Empire, he could not help comparing unfavourably London respectability and sexual cant and humbug with French frankness and the greater liberty (in sex, not politics) the writers in Paris enjoyed. He returned finally to Tavistock House more impatient than ever with English society, and brought with him an empty hungry heart.

He needed only one fairly good excuse – this time to raise a fund for Douglas Jerrold's family – to plunge into amateur theatricals. The closest of his new younger friends, Wilkie Collins, wrote, with some help from Dickens, a melodrama of Arctic exploration, *The Frozen*

Victoria's Heyday

Deep. It was produced by Dickens, who also played the self-sacrificing hero: it was to play this part convincingly that he grew the beard he wore for the rest of his life. For the first performance the schoolroom at Tavistock House was turned into a theatre: 'Already', he wrote, 'the schoolroom is in the hands of carpenters; men from underground habitations in theatres, who look as if they lived entirely upon smoke and gas, meet at unheard of hours. Mr Stanfield [the R. A. who was responsible for the scenery] is perpetually measuring the boards with a chalked piece of string and an umbrella. . . .' The play, with a tremendous performance by Dickens, whose death-scene made everybody cry, was produced later, in the Gallery of Illustration, at the special request of the Queen. Later still, the company was invited to visit Manchester, where it would perform in the Free Trade Hall. This meant making some changes because the amateur actresses would never be heard in such a large auditorium. So three professionals, from an experienced theatrical family, were engaged: Mrs Ternan and her two daughters. The younger daughter, Ellen, fair-haired, demure, delicious, was still in her 'teens and she played only a very minor part in *The Frozen Deep*. But she played a starring role in another drama, that of the unfrozen Dickens, for she tripped into an empty space waiting for somebody like her. Already in his middle forties, more than twice Ellen's age, Dickens fell shatteringly in love.

Although this brings us close to the curious events of 1858, we must delay them to say something about Ellen Ternan, whose relationship with Dickens, of immense importance in his later life and work, was one of the best-kept secrets of the nineteenth century. After some years she

Scene from *The Frozen Deep*

Ellen Ternan

became his mistress, and he provided her with a modest establishment of her own at Peckham. She may or may not have had a child there: the debate will probably still continue. Though we must depend upon circumstantial evidence and guesswork when considering her relationship with Dickens, we know now a great deal more about her later life than even his later biographers did. We know that later she was happily married to an invalidish anaemic schoolmaster, gave him two children, taught elocution and deportment, and long outlived him, her death occurring as late as April 1914. How much she could have told us! And how significant it is that she preferred to keep silent (except for the widely quoted remark that she found the long liaison detestable).

Certainly her situation as a secret kept mistress was one any conventional Victorian woman would resent. And all the evidence suggests she was conventional, not particularly intelligent, and that while she could not resist the passion, the blazing infatuation, of this masterful man, at no time was she really in love with him. We can risk a further guess to suppose that while Ellen remained the image of his heart's desire, Dickens did not find much happiness, nor even much content, in this relationship, which probably provided his last heroines with their petulance and wilfulness. Married to him or openly living with him, she might have been a decorative smiling helpmate. But she must have bitterly resented the secrecy, and he in his turn found himself deeper and deeper in despair, finally driving himself to the limit of endurance – to earn the money he needed, to seek excitement and applause, to forget one disillusionment after another.

Some of his acquaintances said Dickens behaved so absurdly in 1858 because the rapturous reception of his acting and public reading had turned his head. (There seems to be no doubt about the range, force, and almost hypnotic power of his performances.) But it was not his audiences but the pretty looks and blushes of young Ellen Ternan that had begun to turn his head. No doubt his marriage had been unsatisfactory for some years. His wife was fat, lazy, absent-minded, comically or infuriatingly accident-prone, and the house and family were run not by her but by her younger and far more capable sister, Georgina, who was devoted to Dickens though there were not, as gossip soon suggested there were, any sexual relations between them. But now Dickens was telling John Forster that the marriage was unendurable, that there would have to be an official separation. And of course chance took a hand in the sad game: Catherine discovered that a bracelet delivered to the house was not intended for her but for Ellen Ternan. A decent but not wildly generous settlement was drawn up for an official separation: Mrs Dickens was to live in London with her eldest son, Charley, and the younger children would remain at Gad's Hill, now Dickens's home, with their father and Aunt Georgina. Certainly this was not a good move. True, his wife had disappointed him, and he had come to detest her family, the Hogarths, except Georgina. But either he should have had his separation long before she had borne him ten children – incidentally he appeared always to blame her for the later pregnancies, as if childbirth was an odd hobby of hers – or, Ellen Ternan or no Ellen Ternan, he should have let his marriage alone and not smashed it in public.

Inevitably London was buzzing with gossip, some of it vaguely involving 'a little actress' but most of it directed unfairly against Georgina Hogarth. By this time Dickens was half out of his mind. Against all sensible advice he decided to publish a solemn and fatuous statement about his domestic affairs. This he forced into *Household Words* in June 1858, and he sent copies of it to various newspapers and periodicals. By mistake, a much longer and even more fatuous statement found its way to the *New York Tribune* and after a few weeks was reported in the English press, bringing Dickens some sharp criticism of his behaviour. Meanwhile, he had been busy quarrelling with any editor or publisher who refused to print his original statement. Mark Lemon, though a friend, rightly declared it quite unsuitable for *Punch*. So Dickens in a fury decided to have done with Bradbury and Evans, who published *Punch* as well as *Household Words*, and took his magazine, as well as his future novels, away from them, going over to Chapman and Hall. This is why *Household Words* vanished and there arrived *All The Year Round*, a weekly in exactly the same style, edited to the end of his life by Charles Dickens. He had not behaved sensibly; he had been intolerant and to some extent, driven by his reckless will, rather cruel. Clearly this was no way for the novelist of cosy domesticity to behave. So he was attacked in the press, sneered at by shrugging and winking acquaintances, sadly reproached by some close friends. Yet the total effect, both private and public, was remarkably small. His admirers were still his admirers. His public readings were soon greater triumphs than ever. The longest and strongest effect was on Dickens himself, shaping in secret his despairing image of society – and perhaps too of himself.

This summer brought another quarrel, which attracted much publicity, created two ill-tempered factions, and destroyed any friendship there had been between Dickens and Thackeray. However, this time Dickens did not start the row. Edmund Yates was a rather brash young man who had a job in the Post Office but was busy with a career as journalist. Dickens had befriended him because he was the son of two favourite players. It happened that Yates, compelled to write something in a hurry for a gossipy weekly, dashed off an impudent and unpleasant piece about Thackeray, who resented it very strongly. (He forgot, as Yates pointed out, that he himself in earlier days had written satirical pieces just as personal and even nastier.) Thackeray sent Yates a very severe letter, accusing him of eavesdropping at the Garrick Club, of which he and Yates – and Dickens – were members. If the matter had ended there, no harm would have been done. But Thackeray, still smarting, took his complaint to the committee of the club. As Yates's

Thackeray and Dickens at the time of their quarrel

friend and confidant, Dickens vigorously objected to this move, for, after all, the Garrick Club had not been mentioned in Yates's article. But Yates was told by the committee he must resign from the club, a decision he refused to accept, and now there was talk, which went on for many weeks, of a legal action. The situation was described by Dickens: 'Frightful mess, muddle, complication, and botheration ensue. Which witch's broth is now in full boil.' Thackeray had made matters worse because in a new number of *The Virginians*, following a familiar and inartistic practice of his, he had pointedly referred to Yates as 'Young Grubstreet, who corresponds with three penny papers and describes the persons and conversation of gentlemen whom he meets at his clubs.' Hardly Thackeray at his best.

Dickens wrote a conciliatory letter to Thackeray but received a very stiff reply, ending 'Yours, &c.' This made John Forster, after reading the reply, explode with, 'He be damned with his *Yours, &c*!' And now Thackeray confessed to a friend he was no longer quarrelling with Yates but was 'hitting the man behind him.' In the end there was no legal action. Yates did not resign from the Garrick, and was officially expelled. But the supposed rivalry between Dickens and Thackeray did appear to come out now into the open. Their quarrel had been taken over by their immediate circles of friends and admirers. These circles were quite different from one another. Thackeray's might be said to be 'gentlemanly' and Dickens's 'bohemian'; they represented two different strata of London society. But the two novelists were not really moved to oppose each other by rivalry, which existed in other men's minds rather than in theirs. Even when there had been some friendship between them, there was no deep sympathy. To Thackeray, huge and shy, socially very self-conscious, not free from the snobbery he had pilloried, Dickens must have always seemed something of a bounder, an exhibitionist, a caterer to the big stupid public. On his part Dickens considered himself to be a conscientious servant of the public. He took his profession and its responsibilities very seriously indeed. What he disliked in Thackeray was his air of gentlemanly amateurishness, his suggestion of accepting the money he was anxious to make with a kind of cynical shrug, as if he felt that writing was a weary game he had to play, some sort of compensation for the other games that had cost him his patrimony in his youth. There was a touch of Thackeray in Henry Gowan of *Little Dorrit*, a novel that Thackeray, talking to a friend, dismissed as 'damned stupid'. So their quarrel and estrangement, which lasted for five years, was not altogether childish: it had fairly deep roots. In spite of that, there had been a kind of struggling affection between them, at work on them through their children. They were genuinely glad in the end to shake hands, in the hearty Victorian style, and forget their quarrel. This was in 1863 and only a few days before Thackeray's death. As for Dickens, he had then not quite seven more years to live.

1859

WHAT WAS THE GREATEST EVENT of 1859? It was not the defeat of Lord Derby's government (on a Reform Bill introduced by Disraeli) nor the subsequent arrival of a Liberal government, headed by Lord Palmerston. It was not the routing of the Austrian armies by the French at Magenta and Solferino, nor the growing suspicion of Napoleon III in England that encouraged the formation of volunteer rifle corps. It was not the failure of John Brown and his tiny group of abolitionist followers to seize and hold the arsenal at Harper's Ferry, Virginia, and the capture and execution of Brown. It was not the first appearance of Wagner's *Tristan and Isolde* and Gounod's *Faust* or of some excellent English poetry and fiction, to which we shall come later. No, it was the modest publication (1,250 copies) of a book by a modest scientist: *The Origin of Species*. There was no public fuss at the time, but within a few years it began to look as if Darwin had published a gigantic earthquake.

Born in 1809, Charles Darwin was the son of a successful doctor, an enormous man and an extremely autocratic father, who for many years – and the point is important – was consciously revered by Charles and unconsciously resented. His grandfather was Erasmus Darwin, the versifying naturalist. His mother was the daughter of Josiah Wedgwood, who, like Erasmus, was a Fellow of the Royal Society. (It is worth noting that both the Darwins and the Wedgwoods, down to the present time, have produced generation after generation of men and women of unusual ability.) It looked at first as if Charles would not be a credit to his family. He did not do well at school and did no better at Edinburgh University, where he spent two years, at his father's command, reading medicine. But as it was clear that he did not want to be a doctor, his father packed him off to Cambridge, where he was expected to find his way – it was a familiar last resort – into the Church. There he had the good fortune to attract the attention and then the friendship of Henslow, Professor of Botany, and Adam Sedgwick, Professor of Geology. Both of them frequently took him on botanical or geological excursions, and welcomed him at home. Recalling these valuable friendships, Darwin said later: 'Looking back, I infer there must have been something in me a little superior to the common run of youth, otherwise the above-mentioned men, so much older than me and higher in academic position, would never have allowed me to associate with them.'

Charles Darwin

Victoria's Heyday

Here we might pause, bearing in mind Darwin's vast fame later, to ask if our boasted progress in education has been entirely in the right direction. To begin with, if entrance to a university had been by competitive examination in those days, Darwin would never have gone to Edinburgh or Cambridge. And indeed in our time a youth who wasted two years on a medical course he did not want, then arrived in Cambridge to fit himself for Holy Orders he did not want either, would be told to go away and find some suitable employment. Moreover, our professors of botany and geology would have far too many students, would be altogether too busy with lectures, seminars and reports, to spend much time with one vaguely promising youth. Indeed, under modern conditions his whole career would have been impossible. Nowadays, a young man of twenty-two, with no obvious qualifications, would not be invited to sail the world in an official survey ship, as Darwin did in the *Beagle*. Thanks to some private means, a small government grant, and the low cost of living, though always invalidish he was able to marry his cousin, Emma Wedgwood, settle in a comfortable country house, bring up a family of ten, and continue his immensely detailed researches through decade after decade. But as things are now, all this would have been impossible.

The Voyage of the Beagle is now a classic of sharply detailed travel, so there is no need for me to do anything except recommend it. It is worth noting, however, that a study on the voyage of Lyell's famous *Principles of Geology* opened his eyes and mind, made him fall in love with the subject, and brought him later the close and valuable friendship of Lyell himself. If there was a story of natural evolution in the rocks, there might be a similar story in the widening field of biology. We noticed earlier that the idea of evolution was in the air, and had been since the time of Lamarck. Ironically enough, while Lamarck's main theories – the response of a new organ in a creature to a new want of it, and the inheritance of acquired characteristics – were temporarily defeated by Darwin's 'natural selection', a later rebellion against Darwinism has been partly inspired by a return to Lamarck. There was Lyell's evidence from geology. There was, as we saw, the great popularity of *Vestiges of Creation*. There are evolutionary guesses and hints in Tennyson's *In Memoriam* and *Maud*, banishing any sentimental view of Nature.

> The Mayfly is torn by the swallow, the sparrow spear'd by the shrike,
> And the whole little wood where I sit is a world of plunder and prey....

Scientists who knew their field and yet were deeply committed to Genesis had to face a dilemma. The best instance of a desperate way out of the dilemma can be found in Edmund Gosse's *Father and Son*, without doubt his best book. His father, Philip Gosse, was a well-known geologist but at the same time a rigid Plymouth Brother, incapable of defying the biblical account of the world's creation. What

258

Edmund Gosse and his father Philip Gosse

(left) Sir Charles Lyell

was he to do? He could not deny the fossils; he could not deny the Book of Genesis. How was he to reconcile them? Edmund Gosse explains:

> My Father, after long reflection, prepared a theory of his own, which, he fondly hoped, would take the wind out of Lyell's sails, and justify geology to godly readers of 'Genesis'. It was, very briefly, that there had been no gradual modifications of the surface of the earth, or slow development of organic forms, but that when the catastrophic act of creation took place, the world presented, instantly, the structural appearance of a planet on which life had long existed.
>
> The theory, coarsely enough, and to my Father's great indignation, was defined by a hasty press as being this – that God hid the fossils in the rocks in order to tempt geologists into infidelity. . . .

Philip Gosse's book, presenting this ingenious but absurd theory, was published in 1857. Apart perhaps from the Plymouth Brethren, it was not appreciated. Charles Kingsley, for example, wrote to Gosse that he could not 'give up the painful and slow conclusions of five and twenty years' study of geology, and believe that God has written on the rocks one enormous and superfluous lie'. Quite so; but so many charges and counter-charges, so much mutual abuse and agonizing, might have been saved, if more people had understood that the biblical account of Creation is not history but symbolical mythology.

But we must return to Charles Darwin, settled in his country house, something of an invalid but busy accumulating evidence for his theory of evolution yet still not ready to publish it – after twenty-two years. Something must be said about his invalidism. Was he, as some experts tell us, the victim of an infection picked up in South America during his *Beagle* years? Or, as other experts believe, was he suffering from a neurosis produced by his relations with his father and a convenient desire to shield himself from social occasions and any interruptions to his work? We do not know. But we do know that his was a happy marriage and that he was an affectionate, indulgent father. Neurotic or not, Darwin is to my mind an attractive human being.

One thing certainly made him very cautious about publication. As early as 1839 he had published a theory to account for some strange 'parallel roads' in Scotland, and it had been proved to be quite wrong. So he continued year after year assembling evidence for a monumental work on natural selection. But then in 1858 something happened that seemed at first to be disastrous but soon turned out to be a gift of fortune. He received a letter from a fellow biologist, Alfred Russel Wallace, who was at work in the East Indies, and with this letter was a brief but clear account of evolution by natural selection that exactly matched Darwin's own theory. This seemed disastrous because Darwin had been working longer and more laboriously than Wallace, and now it looked as if his neurotic reluctance to publish his conclusions would leave him behind. He consulted his friends Lyell and Hooker, the botanist, and a decent compromise was reached. On 1 July 1858, at a meeting of the Linnean Society, Wallace's short statement and an equally short summary of Darwin's work were presented together, and later they appeared together in the Society's *Journal*. And of course they attracted little or no public attention.

Wallace's letter proved to be a gift of fortune for various good reasons. It cut through Darwin's reluctance to publish his conclusions. It compelled him to ignore the monumental work and to write a comparatively short book, which he called a mere 'abstract': something the ordinary educated reader could tackle. It came out at exactly the right time, with the result that the original edition of 1,250 copies was soon sold out, and then the book was reprinted over and over again and found its way all over the world. A final stroke of luck was that in T. H. Huxley, the zoologist, who was enthusiastic, combative and eloquent, Darwin, shy and withdrawn, found the perfect propagandist and defender. Right or wrong, *The Origin of Species* changed the whole direction of nineteenth-century thought. But almost immediately many hard aggressive conclusions – of the 'survival of the fittest' and 'might is right' variety – were drawn from it that had no place in Darwin's thought. He had not written the book to challenge religious belief, and he was entirely sincere when he wrote: 'I see no good reason why the views given in this volume should shock the religious feelings of any one.' But they did, with the result that *The Origin of Species* received some extremely hostile reviews and was denounced and derided for years. Certainly Darwin implied that *Homo sapiens* was a species that must take its place in the evolutionary scheme, but the resulting 'Man and Monkey' fuss was none of his making.

Alfred Russel Wallace

In point of fact, something else happened at this very time, of considerable importance in the history of Man, that was largely overlooked, at least by the general public and by Darwin's opponents. Joseph Prestwich and a young archaeologist, John Evans (father of the Evans of Cretan fame), went to Amiens and Abbeville in April 1859 to examine the findings in the Somme gravel. At the end of May, Prestwich read a paper to the Royal Society formidably entitled: *On the Occurrence of Flint Instruments, associated with the Remains of Animals of Extinct Species in beds of late Geological Period at Amiens and Abbeville and in England at Hoxne.* Among his audience were Lyell, Huxley and Faraday. In June, John Evans lectured on the flint instruments to the Society of Antiquaries. Later, Lyell told the British Association he was fully prepared to corroborate Prestwich's conclusions. The evidence was clear: men capable of shaping and using flint instruments had already existed in an astonishingly remote age. Most English scientists now accepted this evidence, but their French colleagues were sceptical, until, a few years later, one of them digging in the Dordogne found the portrait of a mammoth engraved by a palaeolithic artist on a mammoth tusk. So in the last year of this decade, by what may or may not have been an odd coincidence (what do we really know about coincidences?), the geologists and archaeologists, the biologists and zoologists, found themselves moving forward together on a broad front, and the old fortress of fundamentalism, or any literal interpretation of biblical history, began to shake and send out signals of distress.

Though not so momentous a publication as *The Origin of Species*, John Stuart Mill's essay *On Liberty*, first drafted in 1854 but not published until 1859, must be given the next highest place. It was his masterpiece, and the most widely and deeply influential of all his works. It was still admired even when his general philosophy came under constant attack, partly because his philosophy was thought by the neo-Hegelians to be too superficial, partly because, trying to modify his early Utilitarianism, he was held to be too indefinite. His personal history is important. He was born in 1806, was soon found to be an unusually precocious child, and was systematically educated by his father, James Mill, the grim Utilitarian philosopher, who crammed knowledge into him as geese are stuffed in Strasbourg. This ought to have ruined him for life, but there was an inherent sweetness of character in John Stuart Mill that saved him, and indeed enabled him to extend the range and deepen the nature of his thought. But he had to struggle against his Utilitarian upbringing, with its shallow 'happiness of the greatest number' principle, throughout his later life. Like Charles Lamb, Peacock and several exceptional men, he was fortunate enough to be employed by the easy-going East India Company, to which we are all indebted for its short office-hours, six at the most, and even then with a chance of doing some private writing. In 1830 he met a Mrs Taylor, two years younger than he was, and undoubtedly this was the most important event of his life.

Here I quote Leslie Stephen's dry account in D.N.B. of Mill's relationship with Mrs Taylor, because I could not hope to improve upon it:

Her husband was a 'drysalter and wholesale druggist' in Mark Lane; and his grandfather had been a neighbour and friend of James Mill at Newington Green. Mill rapidly formed an intimacy with Mrs Taylor, who profoundly affected the rest of his life. She was an invalid, and obliged to live in the country apart from her husband. Mill visited her regularly in the country, dined with her twice a week in London, and occasionally travelled with her alone. Her husband accepted the situation with singular generosity, and dined out when Mill dined at his house. He was, according to Mill, a man of most honourable character, and regarded with steady affection by his wife, although he could not be her intellectual companion. The relationship between Mill and Mrs Taylor was, as he intimates (*Autobiography* p. 229), purely one of friendship. It was, however, inevitable that it should cause some scandal, and it led to difficulties with his family. His father strongly disapproved, and his marriage to her (in 1851) led to a complete estrangement from his mother and sisters. He never spoke of her to his friends or in his family, and the connection was probably the main cause of his complete withdrawal from society in later years. . . .

John Stuart Mill

Victoria's Heyday

They married in 1851 because Mrs Taylor was by that time a widow. In 1858 Mill retired, when the East India Company was taken over by a government department, and he and his wife decided to spend the winter in the South of France. She died at Avignon, and for the rest of his life Mill spent half the year in a house he had acquired in Avignon, just to be near his wife's grave. His dedication of *Liberty*, beginning 'To the beloved and deplored memory of her who was the inspirer, and in part the author, of all that is best in my writings', and ending with a reference to 'her all but unrivalled wisdom', must be one of the most fervent in literary history. To call this 'friendship' is nonsense. They must have fallen in love with each other almost at once. But it was certainly a platonic relationship: she was an invalid, and Mill was a delicate and fastidious man, under no sexual pressure. It is possible, as his friends mostly believed, that it was the adoring lover in him who acknowledged and praised her invaluable co-operation, her 'inestimable' ability to revise his work, 'her all but unrivalled wisdom'. Nevertheless, her influence was strong and all to the good. There can be little doubt, I feel, that it broadened and deepened his thought, made him more sensitive and perceptive than his father and his Utilitarian friends.

Though Mill's *Liberty* has been accepted as a classic for over a century, like most classics it is not as widely read today as it was in Victorian times, so for readers who do not know it I am going to quote its famous concluding statement:

> The worth of a State, in the long run, is the worth of the individuals composing it; and a State which postpones the interests of *their* mental expansion and elevation to a little more of administrative skill, or of that semblance of it which practice gives, in the details of business; a State which dwarfs its men, in order that they may be more docile instruments in its hands even for beneficial purposes – will find that with small men no great thing can really be accomplished; and that the perfection of machinery to which it has sacrificed everything will in the end avail it nothing, for want of the vital power which, in order that the machine might work more smoothly, it has preferred to banish.

It provides us with an essential clue to the whole essay, which is far from being a plea for ruthless and greedy 'rugged individualism'. Mill wholeheartedly believed that the civilizing process was largely the work of exceptional individuals, original characters, minds touched with genius. (He carried this belief into his personal life, being a generous friend to men whose whole outlook was different from his own – Carlyle, for example.) Unless such men could freely develop, civilization would be doomed. If they did not directly harm other people, society had a duty to protect them from interference. So long as a man does not make himself a nuisance to other people, he has a right to hold any opinion he prefers to hold. So – to quote a famous passage:

> If all mankind minus one, were of one opinion, and only one person were of the contrary opinion, mankind would be no more justified in silencing

that one person, than he, if he had the power, would be justified in silencing mankind. . . .

or again:

We can never be sure that the opinion we are endeavouring to stifle is a false opinion; and if we were sure, stifling it would be an evil still. . . .

Mill concentrates his and our attention on the two powerful enemies of his Liberty, of that diversity of opinion and outlook which sustain a living society, of that free flowering of individual original minds and temperaments. ('All good things which exist', he wrote, 'are the fruits of originality.') One of these enemies is of course bureaucracy. Where there were mere brigades of bureaucrats in the 1850s, now we have armies of them, but already Mill was keeping a sharp eye on them; and we must not forget that by 1859 Dickens's Circumlocution Office and its Barnacles had been introduced to the public. After the disastrous confusion of the Crimean War, a suspicion of bureaucracy was in the air. But the second menace to Mill's Liberty is less obvious and more interesting. He discovers it in the prejudice and constant pressure of public opinion, at once very strong and very stupid in mid-Victorian England: he must have been influenced here to some extent by his relationship with Mrs Taylor. Character, orginality, 'individual spontaneity', he felt, were now threatened by the intolerant and unthinking mass mind, envious or suspicious of anything above mediocrity. And here for once Mill is – at least to us, looking back – surprisingly pessimistic. He shares de Tocqueville's mistrust of social and cultural democracy, and is curiously unfair to his own age, which certainly did not lack remarkable men and women. He writes as if character, in his large sense, was already vanishing – far too gloomy a conclusion, though I for one would add that the first half of the Victorian Age does show us more strikingly original creative characters than the second half of it does.

But I must also add that on re-reading *On Liberty* after many years I was much impressed by its final chapter, 'Applications'. Here he moves away from generalities and scrupulously examines various borderline cases – such as Prohibition, Sabbatarianism, Fornication, Gambling – in terms of State interference and personal liberty. These are issues that are alive today, and Mill's analysis of them, which must have influenced several generations of British legislators, still cannot be dismissed as so much radical philosophizing. His whole eloquent essay is still alive too. Such weaknesses as it has come from his rather too high-minded, anything-but-earthy outlook and temperament; but even so, there is courage, there is generosity, there is valuable insight, in and behind his eloquence.

Mill on Liberty was – and ought still to be – one of the main props, one of the enduring inspirations, of a broad liberal philosophy of life.

Victoria's Heyday

Now, of course, this is out of fashion. In the East it is denounced as 'revisionism'. In the West it has been derided and dismissed as being ineffectual, too soft, too vaguely idealistic. (In America, 'liberal' seems to be a term of abuse.) Very well, it will not do. But has anything better turned up? All that we have been shown so far has been a great deal worse. At a time when the young jeer and throw stones in the streets, when the old demand more heavily armed police, a course of John Stuart Mill, defining and praising Liberty in 1859, might help to bring our society out of its sickness.

The kind of character Mill had in mind, the original and creative type, could well have been represented by Isambard Kingdom Brunel. The son of a distinguished civil engineer, Sir Marc Isambard Brunel, of French descent, I. K. Brunel worked with his father for some years, tunnelling under the Thames and designing and building bridges. Then he went from docks to railways, not only in England but abroad. To everything he brought originality, exact control of detail, and enormous energy. Though a friendly and generous man, 'he exhibited an almost excessive indifference to public opinion', which Mill would certainly have applauded. His last and greatest work was with ships, and he constructed the largest and strongest iron steamships of his time. He also made experiments with screw propulsion, to which he finally converted the Admiralty. The best ship he built, the *Great Britain*, had a propeller, and for some years after 1845 was the largest and fastest ship in the Liverpool – New York service. But then, like many another overworked man full of ideas, he over-reached himself and began to run out of luck. He decided to build what seemed to people then a gigantic ship. Because she was intended not for the North Atlantic trade but for Australia via Colombo, she was called the *Great Eastern*.

A few figures will give us some idea of her size and of Brunel's audacity. The ship to compare her with is the *Adriatic*, built in New York just before the *Great Eastern*, and when launched the largest ship afloat:

	ADRIATIC	GREAT EASTERN
Length	355 ft	680·0 ft
Breadth	50 ft	82·8 ft
Depth	35 ft	48·2 ft
Displacement	7,564 tons	32,160 tons
Gross Tonnage	3,670	18,915
Propulsion	Paddles	Sails, screw and paddles
Indicated horse power	4,000	11,000

There was to be no larger ship than the *Great Eastern* until 1901, when the White Star launched the *Celtic*. Her sheer size produced a crop of jokes and gibes, brand-new in June 1857 (appearing in *Punch* then) though familiar enough in our century:

. . . . As there are to be six hundred first class passengers, other captains will be appointed to administer to the domestic wants of the floating colony. There will be a Dining Captain, with great carving powers, and a miraculous flow of after-dinner oratory; and there will be a Flirtation Captain, whose business it will be to render the brief voyage still briefer to the ladies. . . . A very handsome church is being built on the after-deck, and four chapels, for Methodists, Catholics, Baptists, and Independents, are being erected forward. . . . Weather permitting, races will take place at stated periods, and the *Great Eastern* Derby will be a feature in the voyage. Once round the vessel being a third of a mile, the heats will be easily arranged. A movable Grand Stand is being constructed. . . .

And so it goes on. Meanwhile, there was the great ship – 'frightening people', *Punch* declared – in Millwall yard, where work had begun on her in 1853. She was strongly built, as her later history proved, Brunel, with his usual bold originality, having given her the double skin that Cunard designers built into their ships fifty years afterwards.

But even Brunel could not solve all the problems that a ship this size posed. Experience was needed. So, for example, the *Great Eastern* was seriously underpowered. The launch itself, in 1858, brought immediate disaster. Brunel decided she must be launched sideways, but then she ran aground, and by the time, months afterwards, she was afloat, the company that commissioned her went bankrupt. She had been intended

(below) Isambard Kingdom Brunel

(right) The *Great Eastern* in dock

from the first for the Colombo-Australian trade, but now she was pressed into the North Atlantic run, where she soon went groaning into trouble. Finally, in the middle 1860s she was chartered as a cable-laying ship, to complete the telegraph service between London and New York. Brunel had had many other things on his mind – he made some improvements in large guns, designed a floating gun carriage and hospital buildings for the Crimea – but it was the *Great Eastern* that wore him out, and in September 1859, after an attack of paralysis, he died, still only in his early fifties. He was conspicuously one of those very remarkable individuals, scorning routine methods and any pressure of public opinion, who flourished during the early and mid-Victorian age, who lent force to John Stuart Mill's plea for Liberty and the flowering of exceptional original personalities.

This year saw the publication of two first novels that cannot be ignored, George Eliot's *Adam Bede* and George Meredith's *Ordeal of Richard Feverel*. Both writers had been published before. As we have seen, George Eliot had brought out, not without success, the three stories in her *Scenes from Clerical Life*. Meredith had published some early poems back in 1851 and had followed them with his tale, a brilliant *Arabian Nights* pastiche, *The Shaving of Shagpat*. But *Adam Bede* and *The Ordeal of Richard Feverel* were their first *novels*, and both of them, though not to be despised, would be succeeded by much better work. Oddly enough, the innocent excitement of first love plays a notable part in both these novels, which also provide their lovers with rustic settings. In all other respects the novels and their authors are very different indeed, almost at opposite poles. It shows the breadth and range of mid-Victorian fiction when *Adam Bede* and *Feverel* could arrive in the same year. However, their reception and subsequent history were as sharply different as their two authors. Poor Meredith, just into his thirties, was almost penniless and had to scratch around for a bare living. His wife, Thomas Love Peacock's daughter, had left him. His novel had received a few favourable reviews, but a notice in the *Spectator*, shaking a head over its 'low ethical tone', had frightened circulating libraries like Mudie's, and it was nineteen years before a second edition of *Feverel* was printed. On the other hand, *Adam Bede* was a triumph, being enthusiastically received and selling briskly from the first. Blackwood, who had paid George Eliot £800 in advance, was soon paying her another £800, and much more later. And in any event, she was now comfortably situated.

However, she was not without troubles of her own. She had been living as unofficial wife with George Henry Lewes for the last five years; they made a devoted and happy pair; the personal relationship gave her no trouble at all. But though Lewes was no fool, he often behaved

Fashion plate:
Day Dress for 1858

Laure Noël

like one; both his judgment and his taste could be uncertain. So, in a letter to John Chapman of the *Westminster Review*, a letter he need not have written, he ends with a thumping great lie, saying that 'Mrs Lewes' – as he preferred to call her – 'authorizes me to state, as distinctly as language can do so, that she is not the author of *Adam Bede*.' They were still hard at it keeping up the pretence, which since the novel's success had to be carried to a tiresome length, that Mary Ann Evans, the reviewer, translator and essayist, and George Eliot, the novelist, were two quite different persons. The elaborate deceit was pointless, especially now that literary London was beginning to guess the truth. Meanwhile – and they ought to have anticipated this – an obscure Warwickshire character called Liggins announced that *he* was really George Eliot and was letting Blackwood, the publisher, have all the profits from the book. This was amusing for a few days, but then embarrassing, and a letter had to be sent to *The Times* denouncing Liggins. But not everybody believed this denial, and 'a Mr Quirk of Attleborough', surely well-named, came out as a defender of Liggins. What was worse still, an unscrupulous publisher, taking advantage of the confusion, announced that he was bringing out a sequel, *Adam Bede Junior*. Dickens, who had suffered from similar publishers in the past, promised an article that would throw light on these old tricks. And now, sensible at last, George Eliot and Lewes allowed the secret to leak out. There were to be no more Ligginses and Quirks and *Adam Bede Juniors*.

Yet there is a sense in which the rationalizing and moralizing Mary Ann Evans and the warmly creative George Eliot *were* two different persons. Most of *Adam Bede* – the story of Hetty Sorrel and Donnithorne, the glorious Mrs Poyser and the rest – belongs to George Eliot, realistic, humorous, deeply sympathetic; but moralizing Mary Ann keeps intervening, both as a commentator and as part-creator of Adam Bede himself and the stiffishly spiritual Dinah Morris. Though George Eliot remembered hearing what was more or less the Hetty Sorrel story from an aunt, it follows a pattern so familiar to mid-Victorian novel-readers – the pretty foolish girl not able to resist temptation, with pregnancy, shame, crime to follow – that it is astonishing they were not tired of it. (We realize now that the villain here, no matter how much of a blackguard the seducer might be, was brutally intolerant, cold-hearted public opinion.) But unlike a hundred other novelists of doubtful talent, and for that matter unlike even Dickens himself, George Eliot took the familiar story and *rooted it*, setting it among what seem to us real people in a real place, bringing to life early Victorian rural England. She was to do still better very soon, but she strode forward a long way even in *Adam Bede*, and marched out of the 1850s a major novelist.

This the younger George Meredith certainly did not do. By the time he had written *The Egoist* – his masterpiece, even though its prelude is an example of his later teasing mannerism, obscurity through forced wit – he was recognized as a major novelist. This did not bring

'Too Late', by William Lindsay Windus, was exhibited at the Royal Academy in 1859 with a quotation from Tennyson's poem 'Come not when I am dead':

. . . if it were thine error or thy crime
I care no longer, being all unblest;
Wed whom thou wilt, but I am sick of
*   time:*
And I desire to rest.

Tennyson's poem gives little clue to the meaning of the picture, for which many different explanations have been advanced. Ruskin, who had praised Windus's earlier work, wrote: 'Something wrong here; either the painter has been ill . . . or he has sickened his temper by reading melancholy ballads . . . A stout arm, a merry heart, and a bright eye are essential to a great painter'. Windus's self-confidence was so shattered by this attack, and by the death of his wife three years later, that he abandoned painting.

him popularity; he never became a popular novelist. In an interview towards the end of his life he said, 'My name is celebrated, but no one reads my books.' After his death (1909) his novels fell out of favour, even among the younger intellectuals. But there are signs now of a long-delayed resurrection. *The Ordeal of Richard Feverel* might be regarded as a preliminary tasting sample of the later and stronger Meredith. The reader who dislikes it will not enjoy the rest of Meredith. Hostile criticism is all too easy. This story and these characters are not rooted as George Eliot's are. They seem to exist in some kind of mid-air. We cannot find a time and place for them. Moreover, unlike most of Meredith's later novels, this one ends badly, because a huddled last chapter rushes us into tragedy, with the unexpected death of its heroine, Lucy, a victim of that standby of mid-Victorian novelists – brain-fever. But then this is a youngish man's first novel, into which he wants to pack everything, all he feels capable of: in this instance, intellectual comedy, the lyrical romance of young love, action and drama, an unnecessary and unprepared-for tragic ending.

Appreciation of Meredith demands close attention and a keen sensibility. He has unique qualities, there from the first, though not fully developed, in *Feverel*. He is a poetic novelist – moving swiftly, cutting out the dead wood of conventional fiction – with a very sharp sense of intellectual comedy. (E. M. Forster, much admired by critics who ignore Meredith, would never have written as he did if Meredith had not led the way, half a century earlier. And Meredith is a far more richly creative novelist.) He may seem to be outside any definite time and place, but he can create characters and with them memorable scenes, ranging from high comedy to landscapes of stunning beauty. He is the novelist of splendid heroines. On the very first page of *Feverel*, its readers will remember, there occurs the famous aphorism, 'I expect that Woman will be the last thing civilized by Man', but this, coming from a conceited stiff-necked man, is double-edged, deeply ironical. For Meredith from first to last upheld the feminine principle. It is always his men that he craftily stalks and then brings down. But unlike most novelists who keep close to their female characters and would rather take tea with them than join the men over their wine, there was nothing effeminate about him, in or out of his work: he is the essentially virile male sufficiently sensitive and perceptive to understand and appreciate Woman. Now we see him moving out of our 1850s, disappointed and wondering how to earn a living. But then he was no mid-Victorian. Probably he was not even a later Victorian – not even an Edwardian or Georgian. Perhaps his right time has still to come.

However, we cannot ignore Queen Victoria during this last year of her happiest decade. It began splendidly because on 27 January 1859 her daughter, the Princess Royal, gave birth to a son in Berlin, so at thirty-nine Victoria became a grandmother, a role she was to play later on a formidable scale. She was, we might say, a born grandmother, one

George Meredith

of the great matriarchs of royal history. Time transformed this grand-child into Emperor William II, the Kaiser Bill whose ferocious moustache and Wagnerian helmets were to become meat and drink to so many cartoonists. He was always terrified of Victoria, and if she had lived into her nineties, keeping her impressive faculties, the Great War might never have happened: she would probably have told him not to make a fool of himself but keep his army out of Belgium.

The Infant Prince William in the cradle presented by Queen Victoria to her daughter Victoria, the Princess Royal

The year's political events turned tiresome and even distressing. Lord Derby's Tory government, nice and cosy, was turned out. Victoria tried hard to bring in two pleasant men, Granville as Prime Minister and Clarendon as Foreign Secretary, but this was impossible and she had to accept 'those two dreadful old men' – Palmerston as Prime Minister again and Lord John Russell as Foreign Secretary. Both of them, like all British Liberals, looked forward to Italian independence and the end of the Austrian occupation of Northern Italy, which, as Palmerston wrote, 'makes her odious to all liberal and enlightened men throughout the world'. In this matter, Victoria and the Prince Consort were not liberal and enlightened. What they had at heart was the security of German and Austrian governments: after all, so many dear relatives were involved. Napoleon III, still sending charming messages but now suspiciously belligerent, had allied himself with Sardinia and Piedmont, and was now busy defeating the Austrians with what was beginning to look like a menacingly efficient French Army. However, in June the incalculable Napoleon went no further in trying to free the Italian people, concluding a compromise peace with Austria at Villafranca. The Italians now had Lombardy, but they had to cede Savoy and Nice to France.

This cynical grab had several important consequences. One of them was that Lord John Russell, even more enthusiastic about Italian liberty than Palmerston, was able to halt the drift towards a European war and clear a space in which the heroic Garibaldi and his small but indomitable group of followers began their astonishing invasion of Italy. A further consequence was that Napoleon was now the villain of the piece again, moving in the green limelight. This brought the Queen, her two chief minsters, and the general public, more or less into line: they must stand together against France. Fortifications of a sort were hastily constructed along the Channel coast. A royal command officially created a volunteer force, to repel any attempt to land a French army. Watched by admiring wives, sisters, sweethearts – and artists working for *Punch* – sedentary men left their desks and office stools to be drilled and taught how to use a rifle. (It must have been rifles, because Tennyson thundered his 'Form, Riflemen, Form'.) Not everybody took this volunteering seriously, but one person did – and that was Queen Victoria. She also enjoyed it all – special levees for volunteer officers, reviews of the men in Hyde Park. The plump little queen did not lack military ardour. Later, in the summer of 1860, when the National Rifle Association had been formed, she fired the first shot at its opening meeting on Wimbledon Common. But the height of felicity must have been reached when from her beloved Balmoral she was able to review the Scottish Volunteers. What with all this pleasing fuss and exchanges of visits with German relatives, 1859 ended happily for her.

Edward FitzGerald

I will do now what I would have gladly done before, on more than one occasion, if I could have found the space: I will quote a passage from one of Edward FitzGerald's letters. It is a long way from being one of his best – he was a wonderful correspondent, being fond of his friends (Tennyson, Thackeray, Carlyle among them) though determined to live like a recluse in remote corners of East Anglia – but my reason for quoting it here will soon emerge. He is writing to his friend, Professor Cowell, an authority on Persian literature, on 27 April 1859:

> . . . I sent you poor old Omar who has *his* kind of Consolation for all these Things. I doubt you will regret you ever introduced him to me. And yet you would have me print the original, with many worse things than I have translated. . . . I hardly know why I print any of these things, which nobody buys; and I scarce now see the few I give them to. But when one has done one's best, and is sure that that best is better than so many will take pains to do, though far from the best that *might be done*, one likes to make an end of the matter by Print. I suppose very few People have ever taken such Pains in translation as I have: though certainly not to be literal. But at all Cost, a Thing must *live*: with a transfusion of one's own worst Life if one can't retain the Original's better. Better a live Sparrow than a Stuffed Eagle. . . .

But what FitzGerald gave us in 1859 has wider wings than any sparrow: it was his *Rubáiyát of Omar Khayyám*. Its best-known lines, though not necessarily its finest, must be quoted somewhere at least fifty times every day. Whatever it may owe to 'poor old Omar', we might as well consider it an original English poem, and it is a poem with a curious history. A magazine editor had had it in his office for two years and had ignored it. When it was published in 1859 it attracted so little attention that it could be bought for a few pence in secondhand bookshops. But then some people who knew about poetry, Swinburne among them, discovered it. This was the end of Phase One. Gradually new editions came out until towards the end of Phase Two, as I well remember from my youth, fancy editions of *Omar Khayyám* bound in buckram, limp leather, velvet, were customary Christmas and birthday presents; and there can hardly have been any middle-class house without a copy. (And tenors were for ever singing 'Ah, Moon of my Delight!') Phase Three, bringing complete neglect of it *as a poem*, was now inevitable: it was just one of the silly old presents Great-aunt Clara had. But if we try to forget its hackneyed lines and the shallow philosophy they appear to express, if we try to read it freshly as if it were a poem we had just noticed, FitzGerald's *Omar* will astonish us. Chesterton, who could be a very perceptive literary critic when he chose to be, indicates its singular quality in his *Victorian Age in Literature*:

> . . . In the technical sense of literature it is one of the most remarkable achievements of that age; as poetical as Swinburne and far more perfect. In this verbal sense its most arresting quality is a combination of something haunting and harmonious that flows by like a river or a song, with something else that is compact and pregnant like a pithy saying picked out in rock by the chisel of some pagan philosopher. It is at once a tune that escapes and an inscription that remains. . . .

This is well said. We have here in FitzGerald's *Omar* a completely original performance. In one quatrain he will make full Miltonic use of names, in the true high style: as for example:

> They say the Lion and the Lizard keep
> The Courts where Jamshýd gloried and drank deep;
>   And Bahrám, that great Hunter – the Wild Ass
> Stamps o'er his Head, and he lies fast asleep.

And in some other quatrain, where he wants to make a sardonic point, he will be deliberately spare and bare:

> Myself when young did eagerly frequent
> Doctor and Saint, and heard great Argument
>   About it and about; but evermore
> Came out by the same Door as in I went.

The 'About it and about' is a stroke of genius: it reveals in four words the weariness and futility of so many debates, conferences, committee meetings. There was more in those limp-leather Christmas presents of my youth than most of the givers or receivers ever understood – to say nothing of some recent historians of 'Eng. Lit.'.

Victoria's Heyday

It was one thing to be Edward FitzGerald, hard to find in remote East Anglia and equally hard to sell; it was quite another thing to be Alfred Tennyson, Poet Laureate. He had now published his first four – and best – *Idylls of the King*, beginning with four sharply and cunningly contrasted women: Enid, the staunch wife; Vivien, the treacherous mistress; Guinevere, the guilty wife; and Elaine, the love-sick doomed maid. This time there was to be no bitter disappointment as there had been after *Maud*. Though he said he was ready 'to be thick-skinned' about hostile criticism, he ordered 40,000 copies to be printed for the first edition. He had been composing the poems, off and on, for the last four years. He had read them aloud to many of his friends. He was in fact fairly confident they would succeed. There was some head-shaking among more pious reviewers about the 'morality' of the scenes between Vivien and Merlin, but the press as a whole was enthusiastic, and such pillars of the Establishment as Gladstone and Macaulay echoed its praise. Tennyson cannot really have been surprised: that order of 40,000 copies tells its own tale. The poems themselves also tell their own tales. Tennyson took great care to avoid the mistakes he made in *Maud*. Every story is properly told, in highly ornamented but very flexible blank verse contrived with enormous skill. Unlike *Maud*, it is Poet Laureate work, so there are moments in the *Idylls* when we feel that King Arthur might turn into the Prince Consort. The tastes and prejudices of the middle class have quietly invaded that study at Farringford. Tennyson's incredible skill is as much concerned with what must be left out as what can go in. Yet when we consider the verse itself, it is what went in, not simply to tell the story but as a great poet's bonus, that we remember best.

Thus, with Merlin, still silently wondering:

> So dark a forethought roll'd about his brain,
> As on a dull day in an Ocean cave
> The blind wave feeling round his long sea-hall
> In silence. . . .

Or with Elaine, screaming her despair at dawn:

> As when we dwell upon a word we know,
> Repeating, till the word we know so well
> Becomes a wonder, and we know not why,
> So dwelt the father on her face, and thought
> 'Is this Elaine?'

Or that image of Modred's sense of injury:

> But, ever after, the small violence done
> Rankled in him and ruffled all his heart,
> As the sharp wind that ruffles all day long
> A little bitter pool about a stone
> On the bare coast. . . .

Illustration by Daniel Maclise to *Idylls of the King*, by Tennyson

Certainly there is prudery, there is priggishness, there is a kind of bland complacency that occasionally jerks us out of dark forests and enchanted castles into a place at a Victorian tea-table ('O selfless man and stainless gentleman', cries Merlin of Arthur, as if recommending him to the head of a college); yet these very limitations at least enabled us who are old now to read these tales in school and gather a little harvest of poetry as we went along, so enriching our memory.

Although both Matthew Arnold and William Morris had published Arthurian poems before the *Idylls* appeared, Tennyson owed nothing to them or to any growing taste for these particular legends. In his *Poems* of 1842 there had been memorable Arthurian fragments, and for years he had been deep in Malory, Geoffrey of Monmouth, the

Mabinogion and the rest. He cannot be accused of following a fashion; he came nearer to creating it. Rossetti and his younger friends venerated the earlier Arthurian fragments in the *Poems* of 1842. By 1859 and the arrival of the first four *Idylls*, the dreamland of Camelot and the Round Table was floating in the air. Writing from Oxford in 1854, Edward Burne-Jones, then a very young undergraduate, wrote 'in a delirium of joy' after a brief medieval pilgrimage describing what he had seen in his mind's eye – 'the abbey and long processions of the faithful, banners of the cross, copes and croziers, gay knights and ladies by the river bank – and all the pageantry of the golden age – it made me so wild and mad I had to throw stones into the water to break the dream.' But in fact he never broke it. However, we must make a distinction here between a genuine strong interest in what the Middle Ages had actually created, from the great cathedrals down to their smallest pieces of decoration, and the fascination of the Arthurian dreamland, the mythology of Malory. Here it is worth noting that Tennyson in his *Idylls*, bent on telling dramatic tales, tended always to move away from the curiously empty, almost uninhabited world of myth and legend, folklore and fairy tale, by at least sketching in busy and almost crowded backgrounds, suggesting all manner of people at work and play. This shrank and thinned out the mythological and symbolic content of the legends. But even so, we have only to spend an hour with Chaucer to discover that Tennyson was not making any real attempt to return us to the medieval world. He might be said to be keeping one foot in dreamland and the other in Queen Victoria's England.

From the poets and painters of these 1850s there came a kind of Arthurian coloured mist, soon hovering over one grim industrial city after another. It was said that drink was the shortest way out of Manchester, and so it remained for a great many people, overworked and underpaid; but for the masters of industry, their ladies, and the wistful educated young, there was more to be said for taking, at one bound, the magic road to Camelot. After entertaining Mr Gradgrind and Mr Bounderby in Coketown, many a weary hostess tried to catch sight again of Prince Geraint and Sir Lancelot or imagined herself Enid the Fair or Queen Guinevere. There might be even more violence in these legends than in the dark drunken streets behind the mills, but it was a dream violence, in which no real blood flowed, no guts spilled out. There was sex but it was as delicate as that of flowers, without any straining of sweaty bodies, fishy or goat smells, pregnancies and miscarriages. Everything happened in an entrancing landscape of fields rich with blossom or harvest, shining white towns, dusky forests between magicians' towers and huge castles, milky lakes darkening with enchantment, a land from which all the railways, black factories, pit-heads, and cholera-stricken hovels, had vanished. Tournaments, quests, adventures in love took the place of economics, trade returns, dividends, invoices and bills-of-lading. The Arthurian dream world was everything that Victorian industrial England was not. It was no accident that Tennyson's *Idylls of the King* finally found their way into all the libraries, private or public, and that the best-known painters' representations of this dream world can be discovered to this day in places like Manchester, Liverpool, Birmingham. Only a few persons, eccentrics like Ruskin and Morris, though they loved poems and pictures, felt that these were not enough, that somehow or other Coketown should not be left on the ground and Camelot left in the air, that the real world and the dream world should be brought much closer together. And after all, that longing, that challenge, that hope, these were Victorian too.

Macaulay died just before the year and this decade ended, on 28 December 1859. There was an obvious heart weakness, though he had not been told yet to stay in bed. In the morning he had gone into his library as usual, but he had only just sufficient strength to dictate and sign one letter: it was to a poor curate, enclosing twenty-five pounds, and this was the last time he ever wrote his name. In the evening, as his nephew tells us:

> As we drove up to the porch of my uncle's house, the maids ran crying out into the darkness to meet us, and we knew that all was over. We found him in the library, seated in his easy chair, and dressed as usual; with his book on the table beside him, still open at the same page. He had told his butler that he should go to bed early, as he was very tired. The man proposed his lying on the sofa. He rose as if to move, sat down again, and ceased to breathe. He died as he had always wished to die; – without pain; without any formal farewell; preceding to the grave all whom he loved; and leaving behind him a great and honourable name, and the memory of a life every action of which was as clear and transparent as one of his own sentences. . . .

With a service and ceremony 'in the highest degree solemn and impressive', he was buried in Westminster Abbey, not far from Johnson and Handel, Goldsmith and Gay, and closer still to Addison. Though Palmerston and Russell were still in office, we might say that a whole rationalistic and optimistic Whig age was buried with Macaulay. Though critical at times, he accepted the 1850s cheerfully; I think he would have hated the 1860s. This next decade might still be mid-Victorian, but it was rapidly leaving behind the world Thomas Babington Macaulay had known and loved and had interpreted so clearly and eloquently. He slipped quietly away from an England he would soon have failed to understand.

It is not an England, this of the 1860s, that I have to understand, because now that we have come to the end of 1859 my formal task is done. But as I spent so much time, trying to explain where we were, on the *Arrival* platform, it would be impolite, even impudent, to hustle and bustle everybody off immediately. We ought to have a few minutes together, though possibly breathless, on the *Departure* platform.

Departure

MANY OF THE WOMEN are wearing something white – a bonnet, a shawl, or a whole gown. Dickens's friend, Wilkie Collins, has done this. Now in 1860 his eerie mystery story, *The Woman in White*, is what everybody is reading, from the Prince Consort and Mr Gladstone downwards. So, to give themselves an air of mystery and to prove they know what is in fashion, the ladies are wearing white. Crinolines are half in, half out: there are some quite reasonable skirts to be seen. A few more dashing girls, defying the growing prejudice against the Emperor Napoleon and the French, are sporting the tight Zouave jackets, fetching even if unpatriotic.

Their more sedate gentlemen are still in black and still insist upon cramming on their heads the flat-brimmed but very tall stove-pipe hats. A few younger men, however, have taken to very low-crowned bowlers that look too small for them. Then there are some bohemian fellows – artists perhaps, journalists, authors – who prefer rather loud tweed suits or capes with slouch hats or 'wide-awakes', and keep pipes in their mouths. (There is a lot of smoking now, and the duty on imported tobacco, though still very modest, is amounting to over $5\frac{1}{4}$ million pounds sterling.) There are even some men, not all young but some well into middle-age, who are wearing uniforms, with rather flattened *képi*-style headgear, each with a small cockade in front; and clearly they are not regular soldiers. They are all Volunteers, learning a 'Goose Step' among other things, and busy supplying *Punch* now with half its comic drawings and jokes. There are at least 200,000 of them altogether, ready if necessary to man some of the fortifications being built along the South Coast.

There seem to be more 'heavy swells' about, with full beards (as if they were still returning from the Crimean War, which set this fashion) or those absurdly long side-whiskers; and they are all still drawling and *aw-awing* away and turning r's into w's in a wather weawisome style. One or two probably know 'Skittles' and Cora Pearl and other famous courtesans, for whom these 1860s will be the triumphant era, both in London and Paris.

Lord Palmerston is still Prime Minister and will continue to be until his death in 1865. But though all the cartoons present the same confident, wide-grinning Old Pam, he is now beginning to show his age, with eighty not so far away. He has taken to wearing a green eyeshade, and

'Sweethearts and Wives', 1860, by John J. Lee. The place is Liverpool.

has been described as looking 'like a retired old croupier'. He will still keep a bold front, but the impudent bluff of twenty years ago will no longer work, and he no longer quite understands this newer game of power politics, overshadowed by a Bismarck and a Prussia beyond his comprehension. It is all very well fighting a war in China, but the armies of Europe are growing fast, as well as being more and more heavily armed. Bismarck's world is not the one in which the threat of a few battleships settled everything. Palmerston, though still wearing the old grin, would now be out of touch.

Again, Lincoln has now been elected President and South Carolina has taken alarm at once. So there will be the American Civil War, which will divide the English classes almost as sharply as it will the States – the upper classes favouring the South, the lower classes the North, with the British Government contriving to disappoint and displease both sides and so creating a lingering hostility. (But their prizefighter, Jack Heenan, licked our man, Tom Sayers.) However, the English have a new popular hero in Garibaldi, whose red-shirted volunteers, some English among them, are sweeping aside whole armies. Then the Prince Consort, already showing signs of a certain debility, will die at the end of 1861, and Queen Victoria will vanish into her huge dark widowhood.

History, of course, does not give a sudden jerk when one decade ends and another begins: the 1850s glide into the 1860s without any obvious change at all; but even so, there will be changes soon, taking place in a different atmosphere. The political scene will open out, with more and more workmen combining in their unions, and more and more demands for an extension of the franchise that these 1860s will have to satisfy. Long before then, Lancashire, deprived of its American cotton by the Federal blockade of Southern ports, will be threatened by starvation; there will be more talk of Birmingham and less of Manchester; and London, well supplied with financial jugglers, will begin to boom. The whole social scene will be opening out too, running to further extremes than it did in the 1850s, which had a certain sedate cosiness – the atmosphere that sustained and soothed Macaulay – that was fretted away. If not unreasonably we take Trollope as a kind of social barometer, we can ask ourselves what happened between, let us say, *Dr Thorne* in the later 1850s and *The Eustace Diamonds* and *The Way We Live Now* in the earlier 1870s; then the answer – the 1860s – will have a deeper significance than that of mere dates. What we must not imagine is that it is all a mid-Victorian much of a muchness. There were changes, always changes, almost in the taste of the air.

This will be a time of mistaken Great Expectations, and, to keep with Dickens, there will soon be his Veneerings – 'bran-new people in a bran-new quarter of London' – with everything about them so new that 'if they had set up a great-grandfather, he would have come home in matting from the Pantechnicon, without a scratch upon him, French polished to the crown of his head.' All their things 'were in a state of

Two sheets from the juvenile drama *The Rifle Volunteers*, published by W. Webb, founded on the play of the same name at the Adelphi Theatre, 1859

(overleaf) 'The Opening of Brunel's Royal Albert Bridge at Saltash by the Prince Consort on 2 May 1859'. Painting by Thomas Valentine Robins. Brunel's master work, carrying the main railway line from Plymouth into Cornwall, is here seen from the Devon bank of the River Tamar. The Prince Consort can be seen on the deck of the Royal Yacht, raising his hat to acknowledge the salute. Brunel, a dying man, was too ill to attend, and was only able to inspect his completed handiwork lying on his back on a flat truck that was drawn across the bridge by a locomotive.

'The Railway Station' (detail), by William Powell Frith was begun in 1860 though not completed until 1862. It was commissioned by the dealer L. F. Flatour for £4,500. The scene is Paddington Station, which was designed by Brunel. In the complete picture there are some eighty figures. The detail reproduced is a section from the right-hand side of the painting which includes a wedding group and two top-hatted detectives – portraits of the famed Haydon and Brett – about to arrest a fleeing miscreant.

high varnish and polish', with the Veneerings themselves smelling a little too much of the workshop and 'a trifle sticky'. Dickens is describing, with profound distaste behind the humorous exaggeration, this opening out of the 1860s from the 1850s, whose solidly respectable middle class would not have sprouted into the Veneerings. No doubt all the seeds were there even in 1850 itself, but more room and a more heated atmosphere were needed to produce such curious blossoms.

I think that England was substantially Victorian until about the middle 1880s, but I also think we are entitled to say that it was during the 1850s that England was *most* Victorian, closer than at any other time to our idea of what it meant *to be* Victorian. It was then, and only then, that the Queen herself, still a youngish happy wife, still an eager little woman, was ready to go here and go there and be excited and delighted. This decade may not have been England's heyday, though before we dismiss it we might remember a few things and then ask ourselves a searching question or two. Perhaps the Great Exhibition itself was rather a joke, but we are in no position to sneer at the fury of energy and will that erected its vast glass palace in seven months. We might do well to recall the sheer creative force the 1850s possessed and employed, whether in poetry and fiction or in working its iron into bridges and ships. It will do us no harm to remember a certain strength and fortitude – the infantrymen who captured the heights of the Alma *twice* in a day, the women who never lost hope during the months they were besieged in the Lucknow Residency, or Rose's men who fought and won battles against huge odds when the temperature was 110 in the shade. One of England's heydays? There is perhaps a case to be answered here.

But one thing is certain – and now I can end as I began – this was Victoria's heyday.

Medal of Queen Victoria by J. S. & A. B. Wyon

Select Bibliography

The following short list chiefly covers titles that are mentioned or quoted from in the text or have been consulted in connection with the illustrations. It does not attempt to include all the large number of books and periodicals the author consulted in writing the book.

Acton, Dr William, *The Functions and Disorders of the Re-productive Organs in Youth, in Adult Age, and in Advanced Life,* 1857

Ayling, S. E., *Nineteenth-Century Gallery: Portraits of Power and Rebellion,* 1970

Benson, A. C. and Esher, Viscount, ed., *The Letters of Queen Victoria, 1837–61,* 1907–8

Bliss, Trudy, ed., *Jane Welsh Carlyle: A New Selection of her letters,* 1949

'By Two', *Home life with Herbert Spencer,* 1906

Cecil, Lord David, *Early Victorian Novelists,* 1934

Chesterton, G. K., *The Victorian Age in Literature,* 1913

Cooper, T., *The Life of Thomas Cooper: Written by Himself* 1872

Duberly, Frances Isabella, *Journal kept during the Russian War,* 1855

Gaunt, William, *The Pre-Raphaelite Tragedy,* 1942

Germon, Maria Vincent, *Journal of the Siege of Lucknow,* ed. M. Edwardes, 1958

Gosse, Sir Edmund, *Father and Son,* 1907

Gowing, T., *A Voice from the Ranks: A Personal Narrative of the Crimean Campaign,* ed. K. Fenwick, 1954

Guedalla, Philip, *The Duke,* 1931

Huxley, L., ed., *Elizabeth Barrett Browning: Letters to her Sister, 1846–59,* 1929

Ironside, R. and Gere, J., *Pre-Raphaelite Painters,* 1948

Johnson, Edgar, *Charles Dickens,* 1953

Kinglake, A. W., *Invasion of the Crimea,* 1863–87

Klingender, F. D., *Art and the Industrial Revolution,* ed. and revised by Sir Arthur Elton, 1968

Longford, Lady Elizabeth, *Victoria R. I.,* 1964

Maas, J., *Victorian Painters,* 1969

Maison, Margaret M., *Search Your Soul, Eustace,* 1961

Marcus, S., *The Other Victorians,* 1967

Martin, Kingsley, *The Triumph of Lord Palmerston,* 1963

Mayhew, Henry, *London Labour and the London Poor,* 1851

Mitchell, G. Duncan, *A Hundred Years of Sociology,* 1968

Mitford, Nancy, ed., *The Stanleys of Alderley: Letters 1851–65,* 1968

Ray, G. N., *Thackeray,* 1958

Redesdale, Lord, *Memories,* 1915

Reid, Sir T. W., ed., *Memoirs and Correspondence of Lyon Playfair,* 1899

Reynolds, G., *Victorian Painting,* 1966

Rolt, L. T. C., *Victorian Engineering,* 1970

Russell, William Howard, *Despatches from the Crimea, 1854–56,* ed. N. Bentley, 1967

Spencer, Herbert, *An Autobiography,* 1904

Strachey, Lytton, *Eminent Victorians,* 1918

Taylor, G. Rattray, *The Angel-Makers,* 1958

Tennyson, Sir Charles B. L., *Alfred Tennyson,* 1949

Trevelyan, Sir G. O., *The Life and Letters of Lord Macaulay,* 1889

Trollope, Anthony, *An Autobiography,* ed. H. M. Trollope 1883

'Walter', *My Secret Life,* ed. E and P. Kronhausen, 1967

Wey, Francis, *A Frenchman sees the English in the 'Fifties,* adapted by Valerie Pirie, 1935

Wilson, P. W., ed., *The Greville Diary,* 1927

Woodham-Smith, C., *Florence Nightingale,* 1964

Woodham-Smith, C., *The Reason Why,* 1953

Woodruff, Philip, *The Men Who Ruled India,* 1953–54

Wyndham, the Hon. Mrs Hugh, ed., *Correspondence of Sarah Spencer, Lady Lyttelton, 1787–1870,* 1912

Yates, Edmund, *Recollections and Experiences,* 1884

Young, G. M. *Victorian England: Portrait of an Age,* 1936

Young, Brigadier P. and Lawford, Lt Col. J. P., ed., *History of the British Army,* 1970

Illustrations: Acknowledgments and Photographic Credits

(reverse of frontispiece) Obverse of a Council Medal of the Great Exhibition designed by W. Wyon, and struck by the Royal Mint. Victoria and Albert Museum, London (By courtesy of Mrs Dutnall of Cheam, descendant and also Trustee for the Cole family of Sir Henry Cole's manuscripts, etc. in whom the copyright is vested.) (Photo S. Eost and P. Macdonald)

(frontispiece) 'The Soldier's Farewell', 1853, by John Callcott Horsley. Thomas Agnew and Sons Limited, London

Page 10 One of the popular exhibits at the Great Exhibition in 1851. Victoria and Albert Museum, London (Photo S. Eost and P. Macdonald)

Page 12 (top left) Balmoral Castle, designed by William Smith in 1853. National Monuments Record of Scotland, Edinburgh

Page 12 (below left) Osborne House. Radio Times Hulton Picture Library, London

Page 14 Thomas Babington Macaulay. By courtesy of the London Library (Photo J. R. Freeman)

Page 15 (left) Lord John Russell. Radio Times Hulton Picture Library, London

Page 15 (right) Lord John Russell. Radio Times Hulton Picture Library, London

Page 15 (far right) William Ewart Gladstone. Radio Times Hulton Picture Library, London

Page 17 The Field Lane Refuge as depicted in the *Illustrated Times*. Collection Mr C. P. Norbury (Photo Don J. Adams, Worcester)

Page 19 'The Last of England', 1852–55, by Ford Madox Brown. Museum and Art Gallery, Birmingham (Photo Reilly and Constantine/Commercial)

Page 20 'The Tryst', c. 1852, by Frank Stone. Present whereabouts unknown (Photo Mr John Hadfield)

Page 22 'Answering the Emigrant's Letter', 1850, by James Collinson. City Art Gallery, Manchester

Page 23 (above) The title-page of Part 1 of Mrs Isabella Beeton's *Book of Household Management*, first published in 1859–60. British Museum, London (Photo J. R. Freeman)

Page 23 (below) 'The Harvest Cradle', 1859, by John Linnell. City Art Gallery, York

Page 24 (above) 'South-east view of Sheffield', 1854, by William Ibbitt. City of Sheffield Museum, Weston Park, Sheffield

Page 24 (below) 'The Forge', 1849–59, by James Sharples. Museum and Art Gallery, Blackburn

Page 27 Six photographic portraits by Camille de Silvy. Mander and Mitchenson Theatre Collection, London

Page 28 'Finish of a race at Hoylake', 1851, by John Dalby. Walker Art Gallery, Liverpool

Page 29 'Nameless and Friendless', 1857, by Emily Mary Osborn. Collection Sir David Scott (Photo Rainbird Picture Library, London

Page 31 (above) 'Only a Lock of Hair', 1859, by Sir John Everett Millais. City Art Gallery, Manchester

Page 31 (right) 'Mary Ann, wife of Leonard Collman', c. 1854, by Alfred Stevens. Tate Gallery, London

Page 32 A lacquered bedstead, c. 1850. Victoria and Albert Museum, London (Photo S. Eost and P. Macdonald)

Page 33 A sideboard of 1857, designed and executed by G. Robinson. Victoria and Albert Museum, London (Photo S. Eost and P. Macdonald)

Page 33 A stove with painted earthenware Minton panels, designed and modelled by Alfred Stevens. Victoria and Albert Museum, London (Photo S. Eost and P. Macdonald)

Page 35 (above) 'Ophelia', 1851–52, by Sir John Everett Millais. Tate Gallery, London

Page 35 (below) 'Chatterton', 1856, by Henry Wallis. Tate Gallery, London

Page 36 'Kit's Writing Lesson', 1852, by Robert Braithwaite Martineau. Tate Gallery, London

Page 38 Evans's Song and Supper Room, 1859, from *Twice Round the Clock*, by G. A. Sala. Mander and Mitchenson Theatre Collection, London

Page 40 'The Outcast', 1851, by Richard Redgrave. Royal Academy of Arts, London

Page 41 'Adopting a Child', 1857, by F. B. Barwell. M. Newman Limited, London (By courtesy of J. S. Maas and Co. Limited, London)

Page 42 'Waiting for the Verdict', c. 1857, by Abraham Solomon. Museum and Art Gallery, Tunbridge Wells, Kent

Page 43 (below left) A parian-ware statue of Queen Victoria, c. 1850. County Museum, Hartlebury Castle, Worcestershire (Photo Don J. Adams, Worcester)

Page 43 (bottom) A medallion of Prince Albert modelled by Louis Megret and executed in Paris by J. Gille. Collection Mr and Mrs A. G. C. Sanders

Page 43 (below right) 'Paolo and Francesca', 1852, by Alexander Munro. Museum and Art Gallery, Birmingham

Page 45 'Past and Present, No. 1', 1858, by Augustus Egg. Tate Gallery, London (Photo Rainbird Picture Library, London)

Mr C. P. Norbury (Photo Don J. Adams, Worcester)

Page 167 (right) Initial letter to Chapter XV, 'The Old Ladies', of *The Newcomes*, Vol I, by William Thackeray, 1854–55, by Richard Doyle. Collection Mr C. P. Norbury (Photo Don J. Adams, Worcester)

Page 169 A Staffordshire earthenware figure depicting the Queen and her Allies, 1854. Thomas Balston Collection of Staffordshire Portrait Figures, Stapleford Park, near Melton Mowbray, Leicestershire, by kind permission of Lord Gretton and the National Trust (Photo Iona Cruikshank)

Pages 170 & 171 'Florence Nightingale receiving the wounded at Scutari, 1856', *c.* 1856, by Jerry Barrett. National Portrait Gallery, London

Page 172 'The Cavalry Charge at Balaklava, October 25, 1854', by Ed. Morin, lithographed by Day & Son, and published by Paul and Dominic Colnaghi, 28 November 1854; from *Russian War Series of Views*, 1854–55. British Museum, London (Photo J. R. Freeman)

Page 174 General Simpson. Radio Times Hulton Picture Library, London

Page 175 General Pélissier. Radio Times Hulton Picture Library, London

Page 176 'Entry of Queen Victoria into Paris, August 18, 1855', by E. Guérard; from *Souvenir Album*, IV. Royal Collection, Windsor. Reproduced by Gracious Permission of Her Majesty The Queen

Page 177 'Their Majesties at the Opera, August 21, 1855', by Eugène Lami; from *Souvenir Album*, IV. Royal Collection, Windsor. Reproduced by Gracious Permission of Her Majesty The Queen

Page 178 Charlotte Brontë. Radio Times Hulton Picture Library, London

Page 179 John Ruskin, 1854, by Sir John Everett Millais. Collection Sir William Acland

Page 180 'Study of gneiss rock', 1853, by John Ruskin. Ashmolean Museum, Oxford

Page 183 'A Chelsea Interior' – Mr and Mrs Thomas Carlyle at home, 1858, by Robert Tait. Collection the Marquess of Northampton

Page 185 Thomas Carlyle and Frederick Denison Maurice, a detail from 'Work', 1852–65, by Ford Madox Brown. City Art Gallery, Manchester

Page 186 'April Love', 1856, by Arthur Hughes. Tate Gallery, London (Photo Derrick Witty, London)

Page 189 Daniel Dunglas Home. Radio Times Hulton Picture Library, London

Page 190 'Visit of the Emperor and Empress of the French, Queen Victoria and Albert to the Crystal Palace, Sydenham'; from *The Illustrated London News*, 28 April 1855. Mander and Mitchenson Theatre Collection, London

Page 191 A popular song sheet connected with the visit of Napoleon III and Empress Eugénie in 1855. Mander and Mitchenson Theatre Collection, London

Page 192 'Emperor Napoleon III, Queen Victoria, Empress Eugénie and Prince Albert at . . . Covent Garden, 1855'. Radio Times Hulton Picture Library, London

Page 194 Illustration ' " The Kitchen", Fox-Court, Gray's-Inn-Lane', from Henry Mayhew's, *London Labour and the London Poor*, 1851. By courtesy of the London Library, London (Photo J. R. Freeman)

Page 198 'The Flight of the Masqueraders during the fire at Covent Garden'. Mander and Mitchenson Theatre Collection, London

Page 199 Covent Garden rebuilt. Mander and Mitchenson Theatre Collection, London

Page 200 Rhubarb and spice seller, from Henry Mayhew's, *London Labour and the London Poor*, 1851. By courtesy of the London Library, London (Photo J. R. Freeman)

Page 201 'Buckingham Street, off the Strand, London', 1854, by Edmund John Niemann. London Museum, London

Page 202 'Black Lion Wharf, Wapping', 1859, by James McNeill Whistler. Tate Gallery, London

Page 204 (left) Robert Browning, 1859, by R. Lehmann. Radio Times Hulton Picture Library, London

Page 204 (right) Elizabeth Barrett Browning, engraved by T. O. Barlow from a photograph by Macaire Havre, 1858. Radio Times Hulton Picture Library, London

Page 206 (left) Charles Reade, by R. Lehman. Mander and Mitchenson Theatre Collection, London

Page 206 (right) Laura Seymour (née Allison). Mander and Mitchenson Theatre Collection, London

Page 208 'The Relief of Lucknow and Triumphant Meeting of Sir Henry Havelock, Sir James Outram and Sir Colin Campbell', 1859, by T. Jones Barker, from sketches by Egron Lundgren. Formerly the Corporation Galleries, Glasgow (destroyed World War II) (Photo Radio Times Hulton Picture Library, London)

Page 211 'Eastward Ho!', 1857, by Henry Nelson O'Neil. Collection Major Sir Richard G. Proby (Photo Studio 2000, Northampton)

Page 212 'The Flight from Lucknow', 1858, by Abraham Solomon. Museum and Art Gallery, Leicester (Photo K. & S. Commercial Photos Limited)

Page 214 Mosque at the Khynabee Gate, Delhi, taken by F. Beato, 1857. Radio Times Hulton Picture Library, London

Page 215 (right) General John Nicholson. Radio Times Hulton Picture Library, London

Page 215 (far right) The Prince of Oudh. Radio Times Hulton Picture Library, London

Page 218 'Jessie's Dream of the Relief of Lucknow', by Frederick Goodall. Graves Art Gallery, Sheffield. By permission of the Sheffield Corporation

Page 219 (left) 'Sikhs on horseback', by Egron Lundgren. Nationalmuseum, Stockholm

Page 219 (right) 'Cross examining a spy', by Egron Lundgren. Nationalmuseum, Stockholm

Page 220 'An Incident during the Indian Mutiny', *c.* 1858, by Edward Hopley. Private Collection, India (By courtesy of J. S. Maas and Co. Limited, London) (Photo Rodney Todd-White and Son, Limited)

Index